# The English Reader;

Miss Rebecca's Creesshaw
Bath April 9th 1838

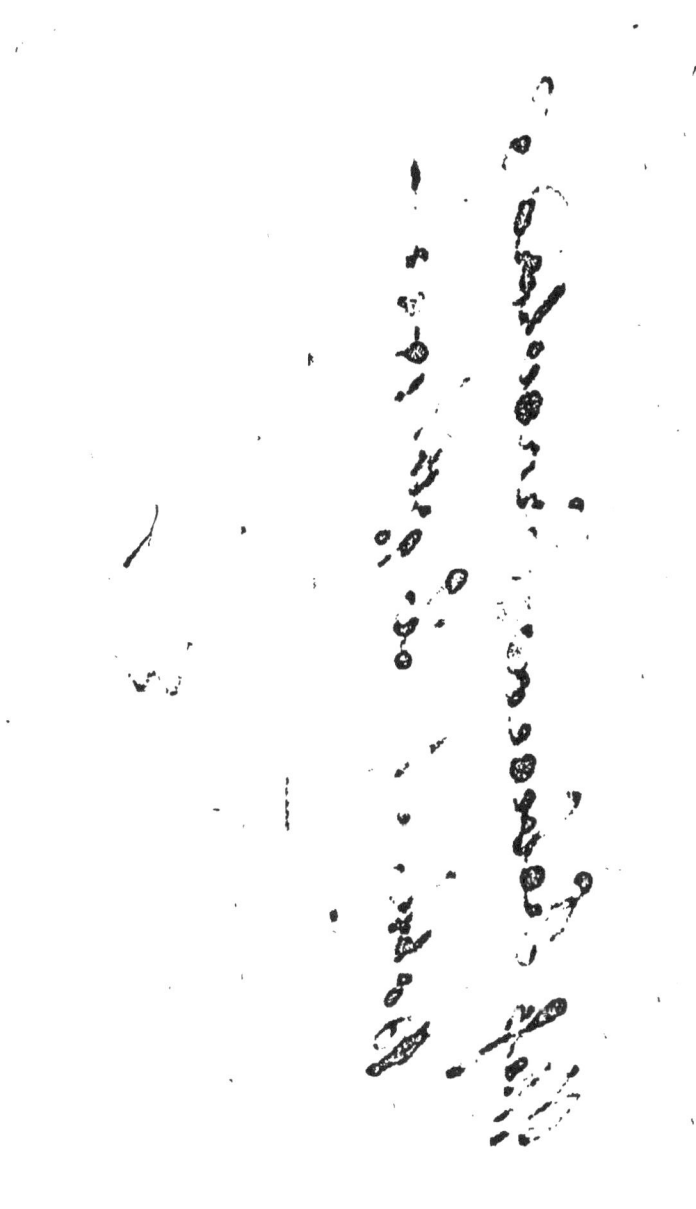

THE

# ENGLISH READER:

OR,

## PIECES IN PROSE AND POETRY,

SELECTED

FROM THE BEST WRITERS.

DESIGNED TO ASSIST YOUNG PERSONS TO READ WITH PROPRIETY AND EFFECT; TO IMPROVE THEIR LANGUAGE AND SENTIMENTS; AND TO INCULCATE SOME OF THE MOST IMPORTANT PRINCIPLES OF PIETY AND VIRTUE.

WITH A FEW PRELIMINARY OBSERVATIONS

ON THE PRINCIPLES OF GOOD READING.

BY LINDLEY MURRAY,
Author of an English Grammar, &c. &c.

New-York:
PUBLISHED AND SOLD BY DANIEL D. SMITH,
AT THE FRANKLIN JUVENILE BOOK AND STATIONARY STORE,
No. 190 Greenwich-street.

1826.

PE1120
.M83
1826

Gift
Rebekah Crawford
Jan 24, 1929

# PREFACE.

MANY selections of excellent matter have been made for the benefit of young persons. Performances of this kind are of so great utility, that fresh productions of them, and new attempts to improve the young mind, will scarcely be deemed superfluous, if the writer make his compilation instructive and interesting, and sufficiently distinct from others.

The present work, as the title expresses, aims at the attainment of three objects: to improve youth in the art of reading; to meliorate their language and sentiments; and to inculcate some of the most important principles of piety and virtue.

The pieces selected, not only give exercise to a great variety of emotions, and the correspondent tones and variations of voice, but contain sentences and members of sentences, which are diversified, proportioned, and pointed with accuracy. Exercises of this nature are, it is presumed, well calculated to teach youth to read with propriety and effect. A selection of sentences, in which variety and proportion, with exact punctuation, have been carefully observed, in all their parts as well as with respect to one another, will probably have a much greater effect, in properly teaching the art of reading, than is commonly imagined. In such constructions, every thing is accommodated to the understanding and the voice; and the common difficulties in learning to read well are obviated. When the learner has acquired a habit of reading such sentences, with justness and facility, he will readily apply that habit, and the improvements he has made, to sentences more complicated and irregular, and of a construction entirely different.

The language of the pieces chosen for this collection has been carefully regarded. Purity, propriety, perspicuity, and, in many instances, elegance of diction, distinguish them. They are extracted from the works of the most correct and elegant writers. From the sources whence the sentiments are drawn, the reader may expect to find them connected and regular, sufficiently important and impressive, and divested of every thing that is either trite or eccentric. The frequent perusal of such composition naturally tends to infuse a taste for this species of excellence; and to produce a habit of thinking, and of composing, with judgment and accuracy.*

That this collection may also serve the purpose of promoting piety and virtue, the Compiler has introduced many extracts, which place religion in the most amiable light; and which recommend a

---

\* The learner, in his progress through this volume and the Sequel to it, will meet with numerous instances of composition, in strict conformity to the rules for promoting perspicuous and elegant writing contained in the Appendix to the Author's English Grammar. By occasionally examining this conformity, he will be confirmed in the utility of those rules; and be enabled to apply them with ease and dexterity.

It is proper further to observe, that the Reader and the Sequel, besides teaching to read accurately, and inculcating many important sentiments, may be considered as auxiliaries to the Author's English Grammar: as practical illustrations of the principles and rules contained in that work.

## PREFACE.

great variety of moral duties, by the excellence of their nature, and the happy effects they produce. These subjects are exhibited in a style and manner which are calculated to arrest the attention of youth; and to make strong and durable impressions on their minds.\*

The Compiler has been careful to avoid every expression and sentiment, that might gratify a corrupt mind, or, in the least degree, offend the eye or ear of innocence. This he conceives to be peculiarly incumbent on every person who writes for the benefit of youth. It would, indeed, be a great and happy improvement in education, if no writings were allowed to come under their notice, but such as are perfectly innocent; and if, on all proper occasions, they were encouraged to peruse those which tend to inspire a due reverence for virtue, and an abhorrence of vice, as well as to animate them with sentiments of piety and goodness. Such impressions deeply engraven on their minds, and connected with all their attainments, could scarcely fail of attending them through life, and of producing a solidity of principle and character, that would be able to resist the danger arising from future intercourse with the world.

The Author has endeavoured to relieve the grave and serious parts of his collection, by the occasional admission of pieces which amuse as well as instruct. If, however, any of his readers should think it contains too great a proportion of the former, it may be some apology, to observe that, in the existing publications designed for the perusal of young persons, the preponderance is greatly on the side of gay and amusing productions. Too much attention may be paid to this medium of improvement. When the imagination, of youth especially, is much entertained, the sober dictates of the understanding are regarded with indifference; and the influence of good affections is either feeble, or transient. A temperate use of such entertainment seems therefore requisite, to afford proper scope for the operations of the understanding and the heart.

The reader will perceive, that the Compiler has been solicitous to recommend to young persons, the perusal of the sacred Scriptures, by interspersing through his work some of the most beautiful and interesting passages of those invaluable writings. To excite an early taste and veneration for this great rule of life, is a point of so high importance, as to warrant the attempt to promote it on every proper occasion.

To improve the young mind, and to afford some assistance to tutors, in the arduous and important work of education, were the motives which led to this production. If the Author should be so successful as to accomplish these ends, even in a small degree, he will think that his time and pains have been well employed, and will deem himself amply rewarded.

\* In some of the pieces, the Compiler has made a few alterations, chiefly verbal, to adapt them the better to the design of his work.

# INTRODUCTION.

## OBSERVATIONS ON THE PRINCIPLES OF GOOD READING.

TO read with propriety is a pleasing and important attainment; productive of improvement both to the understanding and the heart. It is essential to a complete reader, that he minutely perceive the ideas, and enter into the feelings of the author, whose sentiments he professes to repeat: for how is it possible to represent clearly to others, what we have but faint or inaccurate conceptions of ourselves? If there were no other benefits resulting from the art of reading well, than the necessity it lays us under, of precisely ascertaining the meaning of what we read; and the habit thence acquired, of doing this with facility, both when reading silently and aloud, they would constitute a sufficient compensation for all the labour we can bestow upon the subject. But the pleasure derived to ourselves and others, from a clear communication of ideas and feelings; and the strong and durable impressions made thereby on the minds of the reader and the audience, are considerations, which give additional importance to the study of this necessary and useful art. The perfect attainment of it doubtless requires great attention and practice, joined to extraordinary natural powers: but as there are many degrees of excellence in the art, the student whose aims fall short of perfection will find himself amply rewarded for every exertion he may think proper to make.

To give rules for the management of the voice in reading, by which the necessary pauses, emphasis, and tones, may be discovered and put in practice, is not possible. After all the directions that can be offered on these points, much will remain to be taught by the living instructer · much will be attainable by no other means, than the force of example influencing the imitative powers of the learner. Some rules and principles on these heads will, however, be found useful, to prevent erroneous and vicious modes of utterance; to give the young reader some taste of the subject; and to assist him in acquiring a just and accurate mode of delivery. The observations which we have to make, for these purposes, may be comprised under the following heads: LOUDNESS OF VOICE; DISTINCTNESS; SLOWNESS; PROPRIETY OF PRONUNCIATION; EMPHASIS; TONES; PAUSES; and MODE OF READING VERSE.

## SECTION I.
### Proper Loudness of Voice.

THE first attention of every person who reads to others, doubtless, must be, to make himself be heard by all those to whom he reads. He must endeavour to fill with his voice the space occupied by the company. This power of voice, it may be thought, is wholly a natural talent. It is, in a good measure, the gift of nature; but it may receive considerable assistance from art. Much depends, for this purpose, on the proper pitch and management of the voice. Every person has three pitches in his voice; the HIGH, the MIDDLE, and the LOW one. The high, is that which he uses in calling aloud to some person at a distance. The low is, when he approaches to a whisper. The middle is, that which he employs in common conversation, and which he should generally use in reading to others. For it is a great mistake, to imagine that one must take the highest pitch of his voice, in order to be well heard in a large company. This is confounding two things which are different, loudness or strength of sound, with the key or note on which we speak. There is a variety of sound within the compass of each key. A speaker may therefore render his voice louder, without altering the key: and we shall always be able to give most body, most persevering force of sound, to that pitch of voice, to which in conversation we are accustomed. Whereas by setting out

*NOTE.*

For many of the observations contained in this preliminary tract, the Author is indebted to the writings of Dr. Blair, and to the Encyclopedia Britannica.

on our highest pitch or key, we certainly allow ourselves less compass, and are likely to strain our voice before we have done. We shall fatigue ourselves, and read with pain; and whenever a person speaks with pain to himself, he is always heard with pain by his audience. Let us therefore give the voice full strength and swell of sound; but always pitch it on our ordinary speaking key. It should be a constant rule never to utter a greater quantity of voice than we can afford without pain to ourselves, and without any extraordinary effort. As long as we keep within these bounds, the other organs of speech will be at liberty to discharge their several offices with ease; and we shall always have our voice under command. But whenever we transgress these bounds, we give up the reins, and have no longer any management of it. It is a useful rule too, in order to be well heard, to cast our eye on some of the most distant persons in the company, and to consider ourselves as reading to them. We naturally and mechanically utter our words with such a degree of strength, as to make ourselves be heard by the person whom we address, provided he is within the reach of our voice. As this is the case in conversation, it will hold also in reading to others. But let us remember, that in reading, as well as in conversation, it is possible to offend by speaking too loud. This extreme hurts the ear, by making the voice come upon it in rumbling, indistinct masses.

By the habit of reading, when young, in a loud and vehement manner, the voice becomes fixed in a strained and unnatural key; and is rendered incapable of that variety of elevation and depression which constitutes the true harmony of utterance, and affords ease to the reader, and pleasure to the audience. This unnatural pitch of the voice, and disagreeable monotony, are most observable in persons who were taught to read in large rooms; who were accustomed to stand at too great a distance, when reading to their teachers; whose instructers were very imperfect in their hearing; or who were taught by persons, that considered loud expression as the chief requisite in forming a good reader. These are circumstances which demand the serious attention of every one to whom the education of youth is committed.

## SECTION II.
### Distinctness.

In the next place, to being well heard and clearly understood, distinctness of articulation contributes more than mere loudness of sound. The quantity of sound necessary to fill even a large space, is smaller than is commonly imagined; and, with distinct articulation, a person with a weak voice will make it reach farther, than the strongest voice can reach without it. To this, therefore, every reader ought to pay great attention. He must give every sound which he utters, its due proportion; and make every syllable, and even every letter in the word which he pronounces, be heard distinctly; without slurring, whispering, or suppressing any of the proper sounds.

An accurate knowledge of the simple, elementary sounds of the language, and a facility in expressing them, are so necessary to distinctness of expression, that if the learner's attainments are, in this respect, imperfect, (and many there are in this situation) it will be incumbent on his teacher, to carry him back to these primary articulations; and to suspend his progress, till he become perfectly master of them. It will be in vain to press him forward, with the hope of forming a good reader, if he cannot completely articulate every elementary sound of the language.

## SECTION III.
### Due Degree of Slowness.

In order to express ourselves distinctly, moderation is requisite with regard to the speed of pronouncing. Precipitancy of speech confounds all articulation, and all meaning. It is scarcely necessary to observe, that there may be also an extreme on the opposite side. It is obvious that a lifeless, drawling manner of reading, which allows the minds of the hearers to be always outrunning the speaker, must render every such performance insipid and fatiguing. But the extreme of reading too fast is much more common, and requires the more

INTRODUCTION.

be guarded against, because, when it has grown into a habit, few errors are more difficult to be corrected. To pronounce with a proper degree of slowness, and with full and clear articulation, is necessary to be studied by all, who wish to become good readers; and it cannot be too much recommended to them. Such a pronunciation gives weight and dignity to the subject. It is a great assistance to the voice, by the pauses and rests which it allows the reader more easily to make; and it enables the reader to swell all his sounds, both with more force and more harmony.

## SECTION IV.
### Propriety of Pronunciation.

AFTER the fundamental attentions to the pitch and management of the voice, to distinct articulation, and to a proper degree of slowness of speech what the young reader must, in the next place, study, is propriety of pronunciation; or, giving to every word which he utters, that sound which the best usage of the language appropriates to it; in opposition to broad, vulgar, or provincial pronunciation. This is requisite both for reading intelligibly, and for reading with correctness and ease. Instructions concerning this article may be best given by the living teacher. But there is one observation, which it may not be improper here to make. In the English language, every word which consists of more syllables than one, has one accented syllable. The accents rest sometimes on the vowel, sometimes on the consonant. The genius of the language requires the voice to mark that syllable by a stronger percussion, and to pass more slightly over the rest. Now, after we have learned the proper seats of these accents, it is an important rule, to give every word just the same accent in reading, as in common discourse. Many persons err in this respect. When they read to others, and with solemnity, they pronounce the syllables in a different manner from what they do at other times. They dwell upon them and protract them; they multiply accents on the same word; from a mistaken notion, that it gives gravity and importance to their subject, and adds to the energy of their delivery. Whereas this is one of the greatest faults that can be committed in pronunciation: it makes what is called a pompous or mouthing manner; and gives an artificial, affected air to reading, which detracts greatly both from its agreeableness and its impression.

Sheridan and Walker have published Dictionaries, for ascertaining the true and best pronunciation of the words of our language. By attentively consulting them, particularly "Walker's Pronouncing Dictionary," the young reader will be much assisted, in his endeavours to attain a correct pronunciation of the words belonging to the English language.

## SECTION V.
### Emphasis.

BY Emphasis is meant a stronger and fuller sound of voice, by which we distinguish some word or words, on which we design to lay particular stress, and to show how they affect the rest of the sentence. Sometimes the emphatic words must be distinguished by a particular tone of voice, as well as by a particular stress. On the right management of the emphasis depends the life of pronunciation. If no emphasis be placed on any words, not only is discourse rendered heavy and lifeless, but the meaning left often ambiguous. If the emphasis be placed wrong, we pervert and confound the meaning wholly.

Emphasis may be divided into the *Superior* and the *Inferior* emphasis. The superior emphasis determines the meaning of a sentence, with reference to something said before, presupposed by the author as general knowledge, or removes an ambiguity, where a passage may have more senses than one. The inferior emphasis *enforces, graces,* and *enlivens,* but does not *fix,* the meaning of any passage. The words to which this latter emphasis is given, are, in general, such as seem the most important in the sentence, or, on other accounts, to merit this distinction. The following passage will serve to exemplify the superior emphasis.

"Of man's first disobedience, and the fruit
"Of that forbidden tree, whose mortal taste

## INTRODUCTION.

"Brought death into the world, and all our wo," &c.
"Sing heavenly Muse!"

Supposing that originally other beings, besides men, had disobeyed the commands of the Almighty, and that the circumstance were well known to us, there would fall an emphasis upon the word *man's* in the first line; and hence it would read thus:

"Of *man's* first disobedience, and the fruit," &c.

But if it were a notorious truth, that mankind had transgressed in a peculiar manner more than once, the emphasis would fall on *first;* and the line be read,

"Of man's *first* disobedience," &c.

Again, admitting death (as was really the case) to have been an unheard of and dreadful punishment, brought upon man in consequence of his transgression; on that supposition the third line would be read,

"Brought *death* into the world," &c.

But if we were to suppose that mankind knew there was such an evil as death in other regions, though the place they inhabited had been free from it till their transgression, the line would run thus:

"Brought death into the *world*," &c.

The superior emphasis finds place in the following short sentence, which admits of four distinct meanings, each of which is ascertained by the emphasis only.

"Do you ride to town to-day?"

The following examples illustrate the nature and use of the inferior emphasis:

"Many persons mistake the *love* for the *practice* of virtue."

"Shall I reward his services with *falsehood?* Shall I forget *him* who cannot forget *me?*"

"If his principles are *false*, no apology from *himself* can make them *right*; if founded in *truth*, no censure from *others* can make them *wrong*."

"Though *deep,* yet *clear;* though *gentle,* yet not *dull;*
Strong without *rage;* without o'*erflowing, full.*"

"A *friend* exaggerates a man's *virtues;* an *enemy,* his *crimes*."

"The *wise man* is happy, when he gains his *own* approbation; the *fool,* when he gains that of *others.*"

The superior emphasis, in reading as in speaking, must be determined entirely by the *sense* of the passage, and always made *alike:* but as to the inferior emphasis, *taste* alone seems to have the right of fixing its situation and quantity.

Among the number of persons, who have had proper opportunities of learning to read, in the best manner it is now taught, very few could be selected, who, in a given instance, would use the inferior emphasis alike, either as to place or quantity. Some persons, indeed, use scarcely any degree of it; and others do not scruple to carry it far beyond any thing to be found in common discourse; and even sometimes throw it upon words so very trifling in themselves, that it is evidently done with no other view, than to give greater variety to the modulation.* Notwithstanding this diversity of practice, there are certainly proper boundaries, within which this emphasis must be restrained, in order to make it meet the approbation of sound judgment and correct taste. It will doubtless have different degrees of exertion, according to the greater or less degrees of importance of the words upon which it operates; and there may be very properly some variety in the use of it: but its application is not arbitrary, depending on the caprice of readers.

* By modulation is meant that pleasing variety of voice, which is perceived in uttering a sentence, and which, in its nature, is perfectly distinct from emphasis, and the tones of emotion and passion. The young reader should be careful to render his modulation correct and easy; and, for this purpose, should form it upon the mode of the most judicious and accurate speakers.

As emphasis often falls on words in different parts of the same sentence, so it is frequently required to be continued with a little variation, on two, and sometimes more words together. The following sentences exemplify both the parts of this position: "If you seek to make one *rich*, study not to *increase his stores*, but to *diminish his desires*." "The Mexican figures, or picture writing, represent *things*, not *words:* they exhibit *images to the eye*, not *ideas to the understanding*."

Some sentences are so full and comprehensive, that almost every word is emphatical: as, "Ye hills and dales, ye rivers, woods, and plains!" or, as that pathetic expostulation in the prophecy of Ezekiel, "Why will ye die!"

Emphasis, besides its other offices, is the great regulator of quantity. Though the quantity of our syllables is fixed, in words separately pronounced, yet it is mutable, when these words are arranged in sentences; the long being changed into short, the short into long, according to the importance of the word with regard to meaning. Emphasis also, in particular cases, alters the seat of the accent. This is demonstrable from the following examples. "He shall *increase*, but I shall *decrease*." "There is a difference between giving and *forgiving*." "In this species of composition, *plausi*bility is much more essential than *prob*ability." In these examples, the emphasis requires the accent to be placed on syllables, to which it does not commonly belong.

In order to acquire the proper management of the emphasis, the great rule to be given, is, that the reader study to attain a just conception of the force and spirit of the sentiments which he is to pronounce. For to lay the emphasis with exact propriety, is a constant exercise of good sense and attention. It is far from being an inconsiderable attainment. It is one of the most decisive trials of a true and just taste; and must arise from feeling delicately ourselves, and from judging accurately of what is fittest to strike the feelings of others.

There is one error, against which it is particularly proper to caution the learner; namely, that of multiplying emphatical words too much, and using the emphasis indiscriminately. It is only by a prudent reserve and distinction in the use of them, that we can give them any weight. If they recur too often; if a reader attempts to render every thing he expresses of high importance, by a multitude of strong emphases, we soon learn to pay little regard to them. To crowd every sentence with emphatical words, is like crowding all the pages of a book with Italic characters; which, as to the effect, is just the same as to use no such distinctions at all.

## SECTION VI.
### Tones.

TONES are different both from emphasis and pauses; consisting in the notes or variations of sound which we employ, in the expression of our sentiments. Emphasis affects particular words and phrases, with a degree of tone or inflexion of voice; but tones, peculiarly so called, affect sentences, paragraphs, and sometimes even the whole of a discourse.

To show the use and necessity of tones, we need only observe, that the mind, in communicating its ideas, is in a constant state of activity, emotion, or agitation, from the different effects which those ideas produce in the speaker. Now the end of such communication being, not merely to lay open the ideas, but also the different feelings which they excite in him who utters them, there must be other signs than words, to manifest those feelings; as words uttered in a monotonous manner can represent only a similar state of mind, perfectly free from all activity and emotion. As the communication of these internal feelings was of much more consequence in our social intercourse, than the mere conveyance of ideas, the Author of our being did not, as in that conveyance, leave the invention of the language of emotion to man; but impressed it himself upon our nature, in the same manner as he has done with regard to the rest of the animal world; all of which express their various feelings, by various tones. Ours, indeed, from the superior rank that we hold, are in a high degree more comprehensive; as there is not an act of the mind, an exertion of the fancy, or an emotion of the heart, which has not its peculiar tone, or note of the voice, by which it is to be expressed; and which is suited exactly to the degree of internal feeling. It is chiefly in the proper use of these tones, that the life, spirit, beauty, and harmony of delivery consist.

The limits of this Introduction do not admit of examples, to illustrate the variety of tones belonging to the different passions and emotions. We shall, however, select one, which is extracted from the beautiful lamentation of David over Saul and Jonathan, and which will, in some degree, elucidate what has been said on this subject. "The beauty of Israel is slain upon thy high places; how are the mighty fallen! Tell it not in Gath; publish it not in the streets of Askelon; lest the daughters of the Philistines rejoice; lest the daughters of the uncircumcised triumph. Ye mountains of Gilboa, let there be no dew nor rain upon you, nor fields of offerings; for there the shield of the mighty was vilely cast away; the shield of Saul, as though he had not been anointed with oil." The first of these divisions expresses sorrow and lamentation: therefore the note is low. The next contains a spirited command, and should be pronounced much higher. The other sentence, in which he makes a pathetic address to the mountains where his friends had been slain, must be expressed in a note quite different from the two former; not so low as the first, nor so high as the second, in a manly, firm, and yet plaintive tone.

The correct and natural language of the emotions is not so difficult to be attained, as most readers seem to imagine. If we enter into the spirit of the author's sentiments, as well as into the meaning of his words, we shall not fail to deliver the words in properly varied tones. For there are few people, who speak English without a provincial note, that have not an accurate use of tones, when they utter their sentiments in earnest discourse. And the reason that they have not the same use of them, in reading aloud the sentiments of others, may be traced to the very defective and erroneous method in which the art of reading is taught; whereby all the various, natural, expressive tones of speech, are suppressed; and a few artificial, unmeaning reading notes, are substituted for them.

But when we recommend to readers, an attention to the tone and language of emotions, we must be understood to do it with proper limitation. Moderation is necessary in this point, as it is in other things. For when reading becomes strictly imitative, it assumes a theatrical manner, and must be highly improper, as well as give offence to the hearers; because it is inconsistent with that delicacy and modesty, which are indispensable on such occasions. The speaker who delivers his own emotions must be supposed to be more vivid and animated, than would be proper in the person who relates them at second hand.

We shall conclude this section with the following rule, for the tones that indicate the passions and emotions. "In reading, let all your tones of expression be borrowed from those of common speech, but, in some degree, more faintly characterised. Let those tones which signify any disagreeable passion of the mind, be still more faint than those which indicate agreeable emotions; and, on all occasions, preserve yourselves from being so far affected with the subject, as to be able to proceed through it, with that easy and masterly manner, which has its good effects in this, as well as in every other art."

## SECTION VII.
### Pauses.

Pauses or rests, in speaking or reading, are a total cessation of the voice, during a perceptible, and in many cases, a measurable space of time. Pauses are equally necessary to the speaker, and the hearer. To the speaker, that he may take breath, without which he cannot proceed far in delivery; and that he may, by these temporary rests, relieve the organs of speech, which otherwise would be soon tired by continued action: to the hearer, that the ear also may be relieved from the fatigue, which it would otherwise endure from a continuity of sound; and that the understanding may have sufficient time to mark the distinction of sentences, and their several members.

There are two kinds of pauses: first, emphatical pauses; and next, such as

## INTRODUCTION.

mark the distinctions of sense. An emphatical pause is generally made *after* something has been said of peculiar moment, and on which we desire to fix the hearer's attention. Sometimes, *before* such a thing is said, we usher it in with a pause of this nature. Such pauses have the same effect as a strong emphasis; and are subject to the same rules; especially to the caution, of not repeating them too frequently. For as they excite uncommon attention, and of course raise expectation, if the importance of the matter be not fully answerable to such expectation, they occasion disappointment and disgust.

But the most frequent and the principal use of pauses, is to mark the divisions of the sense, and at the same time to allow the reader to draw his breath; and the proper and delicate adjustment of such pauses is one of the most nice and difficult articles of delivery. In all reading, the management of the breath requires a good deal of care, so as not to oblige us to divide words from one another, which have so intimate a connexion, that they ought to be pronounced with the same breath, and without the least separation. Many a sentence is miserably mangled, and the force of the emphasis totally lost, by divisions being made in the wrong place. To avoid this, every one, while he is reading, should be very careful to provide a full supply of breath for what he is to utter. It is a great mistake to imagine, that the breath must be drawn only at the end of a period, when the voice is allowed to fall. It may easily be gathered at the intervals of the period, when the voice is suspended only for a moment; and, by this management, one may always have a sufficient stock for carrying on the longest sentence, without improper interruptions.

Pauses in reading must generally be formed upon the manner in which we utter ourselves in ordinary, sensible conversation; and not upon the stiff artificial manner, which is acquired from reading books according to the common punctuation. It will by no means be sufficient to attend to the points used in printing; for these are far from marking all the pauses, which ought to be made in reading. A mechanical attention to these resting places, has perhaps been one cause of monotony, by leading the reader to a similar tone at every stop, and a uniform cadence at every period. The primary use of points, is to assist the reader in discerning the grammatical construction; and it is only as a secondary object, that they regulate his pronunciation. On this head, the following direction may be of use: "Though in reading great attention should be paid to the stops, yet a greater should be given to the sense; and their correspondent times occasionally lengthened beyond what is usual in common speech."

To render pauses pleasing and expressive, they must not only be made in the right place, but also accompanied with a proper tone of voice, by which the nature of these pauses is intimated; much more than by the length of them, which can seldom be exactly measured. Sometimes it is only a slight and simple suspension of voice that is proper; sometimes a degree of cadence in the voice is required; and sometimes that peculiar tone and cadence which denote the sentence to be finished. In all these cases, we are to regulate ourselves by attending to the manner in which nature teaches us to speak, when engaged in real and earnest discourse with others. The following sentence exemplifies the *suspending* and the *closing* pauses: "Hope, the balm of life, sooths us under every misfortune." The first and second pauses are accompanied by an inflection of voice, that gives the hearer an expectation of something further to complete the sense: the inflection attending the third pause signifies that the sense is completed.

The preceding example is an illustration of the suspending pause, in its simple state: the following instance exhibits that pause with a degree of cadence in the voice: "If content cannot remove the disquietudes of mankind, it will at least alleviate them."

The suspending pause is often, in the same sentence, attended with both the rising and the falling inflection of voice; as will be seen in this example: "Moderate exercise', and habitual temperance', strengthen the constitution."\*

\* The rising inflection is denoted by the acute; the falling, by the grave accent.

INTRODUCTION.

As the suspending pause may be thus attended with both the rising and the falling inflection, it is the same with regard to the closing pause: it admits of both. The falling inflection generally accompanies it; but it is not unfrequently connected with the rising inflection. Interrogative sentences, for instance, are often terminated in this manner: as, "Am I ungrateful'?" "Is he in earnest'?"

But where a sentence is begun by an interrogative pronoun or adverb, it is commonly terminated by the falling inflection: as, "What has he gained by his folly'?" "Who will assist him'?" "Where is the messenger'?" "When did he arrive'?"

When two questions are united in one sentence, and connected by the conjunction *or*, the first takes the rising, the second the falling inflection: as, "Does his conduct support discipline', or destroy it'?"

The rising and falling inflections must not be confounded with emphasis. Though they may often coincide, they are, in their nature, perfectly distinct. Emphasis sometimes controls those inflections.

The regular application of the rising and falling inflections, confers so much beauty on expression, and is so necessary to be studied by the young reader, that we shall insert a few more examples to induce him to pay greater attention to the subject. In these instances, all the inflections are not marked. Such only are distinguished, as are most striking, and will best serve to show the reader their utility and importance.

"Manufactures', trade', and agriculture', certainly employ more than nineteen parts in twenty of the human species."

"He who resigns the world has no temptation to envy', hatred', malice', anger'; but is in constant possession of a serene mind: he who follows the pleasures of it, which are in their very nature disappointing, is in constant search of care', solicitude', remorse', and confusion'."

"To advise the ignorant', relieve the needy', comfort the afflicted', are duties that fall in our way almost every day of our lives."

"Those evil spirits, who, by long custom, have contracted in the body habits of lust' and sensuality'; malice', and revenge'; an aversion to every thing that is good', just', and laudable', are naturally seasoned and prepared for pain and misery."

"I am persuaded, that neither death', nor life'; nor angels', nor principalities', nor powers'; nor things present', nor things to come'; nor height', nor depth'; nor any other creature', shall be able to separate us from the love of God.'"

The reader who would wish to see a minute and ingenious investigation of the nature of these inflections, and the rules by which they are governed, may consult Walker's Elements of Elocution.

## SECTION VIII.
### Manner of reading Verse.

WHEN we are reading verse, there is a peculiar difficulty in making the pauses justly. The difficulty arises from the melody of verse, which dictates to the ear pauses or rests of its own: and to adjust and compound these properly with the pauses of the sense, so as neither to hurt the ear, nor offend the understanding, is so very nice a matter, that it is no wonder we so seldom meet with good readers of poetry. There are two kinds of pauses that belong to the melody of verse: one is, the pause at the end of the line; and the other, the cæsural pause in or near the middle of it. With regard to the pause at the end of the line, which marks that strain or verse to be finished, rhyme renders this always sensible; and in some measure compels us to observe it in our pronunciation. In respect to blank verse, we ought also to read it so as to make every line sensible to the ear: for, what is the use of melody, or for what end has the poet composed in verse, if, in reading his lines, we suppress his numbers, by omitting the final pause; and degrade them, by our pronunciation, into mere prose? At the same time that we attend to this pause, every appearance of sing-song and tone must be carefully guarded against.

## INTRODUCTION.

The close of the line where it makes no pause in the meaning, ought not to be marked by such a tone as is used in finishing a sentence; but, without either fall or elevation of the voice, it should be denoted only by so slight a suspension of sound, as may distinguish the passage from one line to another, without injuring the meaning.

The other kind of melodious pause, is that which falls somewhere about the middle of the verse, and divides it into two hemistichs; a pause, not so great as that which belongs to the close of the line, but still sensible to an ordinary ear. This, which is called the cæsural pause, may fall, in English heroic verse, after the 4th, 5th, 6th, or 7th syllable in the line. Where the verse is so constructed, that this cæsural pause coincides with the slightest pause or division in the sense, the line can be read easily; as in the two first verses of Pope's Messiah:

"Ye nymphs of Solyma"! begin the song;
"To heav'nly themes", sublimer strains belong."

But if it should happen that words which have so strict and intimate a connexion, as not to bear even a momentary separation, are divided from one another by this cæsural pause, we then feel a sort of struggle between the sense and the sound, which renders it difficult to read such lines harmoniously The rule of proper pronunciation in such cases, is to regard only the pause which the sense forms; and to read the line accordingly. The neglect of the cæsural pause may make the line sound somewhat unharmoniously; but the effect would be much worse, if the sense were sacrificed to the sound. For instance, in the following lines of Milton,

———— "What in me is dark,
"Illumine; what is low, raise and support."

The sense clearly dictates the pause after *illumine*, at the end of the third syllable, which, in reading, ought to be made accordingly; though, if the melody only were to be regarded, *illumine* should be connected with what follows, and the pause not made till the fourth or sixth syllable. So in the following line of Pope's Epistle to Dr. Arbuthnot,

"I sit, with sad civility I read."

The ear plainly points out the cæsural pause as falling after *sad*, the fourth syllable. But it would be very bad reading to make any pause there, so as to separate *sad* and *civility*. The sense admits of no other pause than after the second syllable *sit*, which therefore must be the only pause made in reading this part of the sentence.

There is another mode of dividing some verses, by introducing what may be called demi-cæsuras, which require very slight pauses; and which the reader should manage with judgment, or he will be apt to fall into an affected sing-song mode of pronouncing verses of this kind. The following lines exemplify the demi-cæsura:

"Warms' in the sun", refreshes' in the breeze.
"Glows' in the stars", and blossoms' in the trees;
"Lives' through all life"; extends' through all extent,
"Spreads' undivided", operates' unspent."

Before the conclusion of this introduction, the Compiler takes the liberty to recommend to teachers, to exercise their pupils in discovering and explaining the emphatic words, and the proper tones and pauses, of every portion assigned them to read, previously to their being called out to the performance. These preparatory lessons, in which they should be regularly examined, will improve their judgment and taste; prevent the practice of reading without attention to the subject; and establish a habit of readily discovering the meaning, force, and beauty, of every sentence they peruse.

B

# CONTENTS.

## PART I.

*PIECES IN PROSE.*

### CHAPTER I.
*Select Sentences and Paragraphs.* . . . . . . . . . Page 17

### CHAPTER II.
*Narrative Pieces.*

Sect. 1. No rank or possessions can make the guilty mind happy . . . . 28
2. Change of external condition often adverse to virtue . . . . 29
3. Haman; or the misery of pride . . . . . . . . . 30
4. Lady Jane Grey . . . . . . . . . . . . . 31
5. Ortogrul; or the vanity of riches . . . . . . . . 33
6. The hill of science . . . . . . . . . . . . 35
7. The journey of a day; a picture of human life . . . . . 37

### CHAPTER III.
*Didactic Pieces.*

Sect. 1. The importance of a good education . . . . . . . . 40
2. On gratitude . . . . . . . . . . . . . . 41
3. On forgiveness . . . . . . . . . . . . . ib.
4. Motives to the practice of gentleness . . . . . . . . 42
5. A suspicious temper the source of misery to its possessor . . . 43
6. Comforts of religion . . . . . . . . . . . . 44
7. Diffidence of our abilities a mark of wisdom . . . . . . ib.
8. On the importance of order in the distribution of our time . . . 45
9. The dignity of virtue amidst corrupt examples . . . . . . 46
10. The mortifications of vice greater than those of virtue . . . . 47
11. On contentment . . . . . . . . . . . . . 48
12. Rank and riches afford no ground for envy . . . . . . 50
13. Patience under provocations our interest as well as duty . . . 51
14. Moderation in our wishes recommended . . . . . . . 52
15. Omniscience and omnipresence of the Deity, the source of consolation to good men . . . . . . . . . . . . 54

### CHAPTER IV.
*Argumentative Pieces.*

Sect. 1. Happiness is founded in rectitude of conduct . . . . . . 56
2. Virtue and piety man's highest interest . . . . . . . 57
3. The injustice of an uncharitable spirit . . . . . . . 58
4. The misfortunes of men mostly chargeable on themselves . . . ib.
5. On disinterested friendship . . . . . . . . . . 60
6. On the immortality of the soul . . . . . . . . . 62

### CHAPTER V.
*Descriptive Pieces.*

Sect. 1. The Seasons . . . . . . . . . . . . . . 64
2. The cataract of Niagara, in Canada, North America . . . . 65
3. The grotto of Antiparos . . . . . . . . . . . 66
4. The grotto of Antiparos, continued . . . . . . . . 67
5. Earthquake at Catanea . . . . . . . . . . . 68
6. Creation . . . . . . . . . . . . . . . ib.
7. Charity . . . . . . . . . . . . . . . 69
8. Prosperity is redoubled to a good man . . . . . . . ib.
9. On the beauties of the Psalms . . . . . . . . . 70
10. Character of Alfred, king of England . . . . . . . 71
11. Character of Queen Elizabeth . . . . . . . . . 72
12. The slavery of vice . . . . . . . . . . . . 73
13. The man of integrity . . . . . . . . . . . . 74
14. Gentleness . . . . . . . . . . . . . . ib.

### CHAPTER VI.
*Pathetic Pieces.*

Sect. 1. Trial and execution of the Earl of Strafford . . . . . . 76
2. An eminent instance of true fortitude of mind . . . . . . 77

## CONTENTS.

| | Page |
|---|---|
| Sect. 3. The good man's comfort in affliction | 78 |
| 4. The close of life | ib. |
| 5. Exalted society, and the renewal of virtuous connections, two sources of future felicity | 80 |
| 6. The clemency and amiable character of the patriarch Joseph | 81 |
| 7. Altamont | 82 |

### CHAPTER VII.
*Dialogues.*

| | |
|---|---|
| Sect. 1. Democritus and Heraclitus | 84 |
| 2. Dionysius, Pythias, and Damon | 86 |
| 3. Locke and Bayle | 87 |

### CHAPTER VIII.
*Public Speeches.*

| | |
|---|---|
| Sect. 1. Cicero against Verres | 91 |
| 2. Speech of Adherbal to the Roman Senate, imploring their protection against Jugurtha | 94 |
| 3. The Apostle Paul's noble defence before Festus and Agrippa | 96 |
| 4. Lord Mansfield's speech in the House of Lords, 1770, on the bill for preventing the delays of justice, by claiming the privilege of parliament | 97 |
| 5. An address to young persons | 100 |

### CHAPTER IX.
*Promiscuous Pieces.*

| | |
|---|---|
| Sect. 1. Earthquake at Calabria, in the year 1638 | 103 |
| 2. Letter from Pliny to Germinius | 105 |
| 3. Letter from Pliny to Marcellinus, on the death of an amiable young woman | 106 |
| 4. On Discretion | 107 |
| 5. On the government of our thoughts | 109 |
| 6. On the evils which flow from unrestrained passions | 110 |
| 7. On the proper state of our temper with respect to one another | 111 |
| 8. Excellence of the Holy Scriptures | 113 |
| 9. Reflections occasioned by a review of the blessings pronounced by Christ on his disciples, in his sermon on the mount | ib. |
| 10. Schemes of life often illusory | 114 |
| 11. The pleasures of virtuous sensibility | 116 |
| 12. On the true honour of man | 117 |
| 13. The influence of devotion on the happiness of life | 118 |
| 14. The planetary and terrestrial worlds comparatively considered | 119 |
| 15. On the power of custom, and the uses to which it may be applied | 121 |
| 16. The pleasures resulting from a proper use of our faculties | 122 |
| 17. Description of candour | 123 |
| 18. On the imperfection of that happiness which rests solely on worldly pleasures | 124 |
| 19. What are the real and solid enjoyments of human life | 126 |
| 20. Scale of beings | 127 |
| 21. Trust in the care of Providence recommended | 129 |
| 22. Piety and gratitude enliven prosperity | 130 |
| 23. Virtue, when deeply rooted, is not subject to the influence of fortune | 132 |
| 24. The speech of Fabricius, a Roman ambassador, to king Pyrrhus | 133 |
| 25. Character of James I. king of England | 134 |
| 26. Charles V. emperor of Germany, resigns his dominions, and retires from the world | ib. |
| 27. The same subject continued | 137 |

## PART II.

### *PIECES IN POETRY.*

### CHAPTER I.
*Select Sentences and Paragraphs.*

| | Page |
|---|---|
| Sect. 1. Short and easy sentences | 139 |
| 2. Verses in which the lines are of different length | 140 |
| 3. Verses containing exclamations, interrogations, and parentheses | 142 |
| 4. Verses in various forms | 143 |
| 5. Verses in which sound corresponds to signification | 145 |
| 6. Paragraphs of greater length | 146 |

## CONTENTS.

### CHAPTER II.
*Narrative Pieces.*

| | Page |
|---|---|
| Sect. 1. The bear and the bees | 148 |
| 2. The nightingale and the glow-worm | 149 |
| 3. The trials of virtue | ib. |
| 4. The youth and the philosopher | 151 |
| 5. Discourse between Adam and Eve, retiring to rest | 152 |
| 6. Religion and death | 154 |

### CHAPTER III.
*Didactic Pieces.*

| | |
|---|---|
| Sect. 1. The vanity of wealth | 156 |
| 2. Nothing formed in vain | ib. |
| 3. On pride | 157 |
| 4. Cruelty to brutes censured | ib. |
| 5. A paraphrase on the latter part of the 6th chapter of Matthew | 158 |
| 6. The death of a good man a strong incentive to virtue | 159 |
| 7. Reflections on a future state, from a review of winter | ib. |
| 8. Adam's advice to Eve, to avoid temptation | 160 |
| 9. On procrastination | 161 |
| 10. That philosophy, which stops at secondary causes, reproved | 162 |
| 11. Indignant sentiments on national prejudices and hatred; and on slavery | 163 |

### CHAPTER IV.
*Descriptive Pieces.*

| | |
|---|---|
| Sect. 1. The morning in summer | 164 |
| 2. Rural sounds, as well as rural sights, delightful | ib. |
| 3. The rose | 165 |
| 4. Care of birds for their young | ib. |
| 5. Liberty and slavery contrasted | 166 |
| 6. Charity. A paraphrase on the 13th chapter to the First Corinthians | 167 |
| 7. Picture of a good man | 168 |
| 8. The pleasures of retirement | 169 |
| 9. The pleasure and benefit of an improved and well-directed imagination | 170 |

### CHAPTER V.
*Pathetic Pieces.*

| | |
|---|---|
| Sect. 1. The hermit | 171 |
| 2. The beggar's petition | 172 |
| 3. Unhappy close of life | 173 |
| 4. Elegy to pity | 174 |
| 5. Verses supposed to be written by Alexander Selkirk, during his solitary abode in the Island of Juan Fernandez | ib. |
| 6. Gratitude | 175 |
| 7. A man perishing in the snow; from whence reflections are raised on the miseries of life | 177 |
| 8. A morning hymn | 178 |

### CHAPTER VI.
*Promiscuous Pieces.*

| | |
|---|---|
| Sect. 1. Ode to content | 179 |
| 2. The shepherd and the philosopher | 180 |
| 3. The road to happiness open to all men | 182 |
| 4. The goodness of Providence | 183 |
| 5. The Creator's works attest his greatness | ib. |
| 6. Address to the Deity | 184 |
| 7. The pursuit of happiness often ill directed | 185 |
| 8. The fire-side | 186 |
| 9. Providence vindicated in the present state of man | 187 |
| 10. Selfishness reproved | 188 |
| 11. Human frailty | 189 |
| 12. Ode to Peace | 190 |
| 13. Ode to Adversity | ib. |
| 14. The Creation required to praise its Author | 191 |
| 15. The universal prayer | 193 |
| 16. Conscience | 194 |
| 17. On an infant | ib. |
| 18. The cuckoo | 195 |
| 19. Day. A pastoral in three parts | ib. |
| 20. The order of Nature | 197 |
| 21. Confidence in Divine Protection | 199 |
| 22. Hymn, on a review of the seasons | ib. |
| 23. On solitude | 201 |

# THE ENGLISH READER.

## PART I.
*PIECES IN PROSE.*

### CHAPTER I.
SELECT SENTENCES AND PARAGRAPHS.

#### SECTION I.

1. DILIGENCE, industry, and proper improvement of time, are material duties of the young.
2. The acquisition of knowledge is one of the most honourable occupations of youth.
3. Whatever useful or engaging endowments we possess, virtue is requisite, in order to their shining with proper lustre.
4. Virtuous youth gradually brings forward accomplished and flourishing manhood.
5. Sincerity and truth form the basis of every virtue.
6. Disappointments and distress are often blessings in disguise.
7. Change and alteration form the very essence of the world.
8. True happiness is of a retired nature, and an enemy to pomp and noise.
9. In order to acquire a capacity for happiness, it must be our first study to rectify inward disorders.
10. Whatever purifies, fortifies also the heart.
11. From our eagerness to grasp, we strangle and destroy pleasure.
12. A temperate spirit, and moderate expectations, are excellent safeguards of the mind, in this uncertain and changing state.
13. There is nothing, except simplicity of intention, and purity of principle, that can stand the test of near approach and strict examination.
14. The value of any possession is to be chiefly estimated, by the relief which it can bring us in the time of our greatest need.
15. No person who has once yielded up the government of his mind, and given loose rein to his desires and passions, can tell how far they may carry him.
16. Tranquillity of mind is always most likely to be attained, when the business of the world is tempered with thoughtful and serious retreat.
17. He who would act like a wise man, and build his house on the rock, and not on the sand, should contemplate human life, not only in the sunshine, but in the shade.

*NOTE.*

In the first chapter, the compiler has exhibited sentences in a great variety of construction, and in all the diversity of punctuation. If well practised upon, he presumes they will fully prepare the young reader for the various pauses, inflections, and modulations of voice, which the succeeding pieces require. The Author's "English Exercises," under the head of Punctuation, will afford the learner additional scope for improving himself in reading sentences and paragraphs variously constructed.

18. Let usefulness and beneficence, not ostentation and vanity, direct the train of your pursuits.

19. To maintain a steady and unbroken mind, amidst all the shocks of the world, marks a great and noble spirit.

20. Patience, by preserving composure within, resists the impression which trouble makes from without.

21. Compassionate affections, even when they draw tears from our eyes for human misery, convey satisfaction to the heart.

22. They who have nothing to give, can often afford relief to others, by imparting what they feel.

23. Our ignorance of what is to come, and of what is really good or evil, should correct anxiety about worldly success.

24. The veil which covers from our sight the events of succeeding years, is a veil woven by the hand of mercy.

25. The best preparation for all the uncertainties of futurity, consists in a well-ordered mind, a good conscience, and a cheerful submission to the will of Heaven.

## SECTION II.

1. The chief misfortunes that befall us in life, can be traced to some vices or follies which we have committed.

2. Were we to survey the chambers of sickness and distress, we should often find them peopled with the victims of intemperance and sensuality, and with the children of vicious indolence and sloth.

3. To be wise in our own eyes, to be wise in the opinion of the world, and to be wise in the sight of our Creator, are three things so very different, as rarely to coincide.

4. Man, in his highest earthly glory, is but a reed floating on the stream of time, and forced to follow every new direction of the current.

5. The corrupted temper, and the guilty passions of the bad, frustrate the effect of every advantage which the world confers on them.

6. The external misfortunes of life, disappointments, poverty, and sickness, are light in comparison of those inward distresses of mind, occasioned by folly, by passion, and by guilt.

7. No station is so high, no power so great, no character so unblemished, as to exempt men from the attacks of rashness, malice, or envy.

8. Moral and religious instruction derives its efficacy, not so much from what men are taught to know, as from what they are brought to feel.

9. He who pretends to great sensibility towards men, and yet has no feeling for the high objects of religion, no heart to admire and adore the great Father of the universe, has reason to distrust the truth and delicacy of his sensibility.

10. When, upon rational and sober inquiry, we have established our principles, let us not suffer them to be shaken by the scoffs of the licentious, or the cavils of the sceptical.

11. When we observe any tendency to treat religion or morals with disrespect and levity, let us hold it to be a sure indication of a perverted understanding, or a depraved heart.

12. Every degree of guilt incurred by yielding to temptation, tends to debase the mind, and to weaken the generous and benevolent principles of human nature.

13. Luxury, pride, and vanity, have frequently as much influence in corrupting the sentiments of the great, as ignorance, bigotry, and prejudice, have in misleading the opinions of the multitude.

14. Mixed as the present state is, reason and religion pronounce, that generally, if not always, there is more happiness than misery, more pleasure than pain, in the condition of man.

15. Society, when formed, requires distinctions of property, diversity of conditions, subordination of ranks, and a multiplicity of occupations, in order to advance the general good.

16. That the temper, the sentiments, the morality, and, in general, the whole conduct and character of men, are influenced by the example and disposition of the persons with whom they associate, is a reflection which has long since passed into a proverb, and been ranked among the standing maxims of human wisdom, in all ages of the world.

## SECTION III.

1. The desire of improvement discovers a liberal mind, and is connected with many accomplishments, and many virtues.

2. Innocence confers ease and freedom on the mind; and leaves it open to every pleasing sensation.

3. Moderate and simple pleasures relish high with the temperate: in the midst of his studied refinements, the voluptuary languishes.

4. Gentleness corrects whatever is offensive in our manners; and, by a constant train of humane attentions, studies to alleviate the burden of common misery.

5. That gentleness which is the characteristic of a good man, has, like every other virtue, its seat in the heart: and, let me add, nothing, except what flows from the heart, can render even external manners truly pleasing.

6. Virtue, to become either vigorous or useful, must be habitually active: not breaking forth occasionally with a transient lustre, like the blaze of a comet; but regular in its returns, like the light of day: not like the aromatic gale, which sometimes feasts the sense; but like the ordinary breeze, which purifies the air, and renders it healthful.

7. The happiness of every man depends more upon the state of his own mind, than upon any one external circumstance: nay, more than upon all external things put together.

8. In no station, in no period, let us think ourselves secure from the dangers which spring from our passions. Every age, and every station they beset; from youth to gray hairs, and from the peasant to the prince.

9. Riches and pleasures are the chief temptations to criminal deeds. Yet those riches, when obtained, may very possibly overwhelm us with unforeseen miseries. Those pleasures may cut short our health and life.

10. He who is accustomed to turn aside from the world, and commune with himself in retirement, will, sometimes at least, hear the truths which the multitude do not tell him. A more sound instructer will lift his voice, and awaken within the heart those latent suggestions, which the world had overpowered and suppressed.

11. Amusement often becomes the business, instead of the relaxation, of young persons: it is then highly pernicious.

12. He that waits for an opportunity, to do much at once, may breathe out his life in idle wishes; and regret, in the last hour, his useless intentions and barren zeal.

13. The spirit of true religion breathes mildness and affability. It gives a native, unaffected ease to the behaviour. It is social, kind, and cheerful: far removed from that gloomy and illiberal superstition, which clouds the brow, sharpens the temper, dejects the spirit, and teaches men to fit themselves for another world, by neglecting the concerns of this.

14. Reveal none of the secrets of thy friend. Be faithful to his interests. Forsake him not in danger. Abhor the thought of acquiring any advantage by his prejudice.

15. Man, always prosperous, would be giddy and insolent : always afflicted, would be sullen or despondent. Hopes and fears, joy and sorrow, are, therefore, so blended in his life, as both to give room for worldly pursuits, and to recall, from time to time, the admonitions of conscience.

## SECTION IV.

1. TIME once past never returns: the moment which is lost, is lost for ever.

2. There is nothing on earth so stable, as to assure us of undisturbed rest; nor so powerful, as to afford us constant protection.

3. The house of feasting too often becomes an avenue to the house of mourning. Short, to the licentious, is the interval between them.

4. It is of great importance to us, to form a proper estimate of human life; without either loading it with imaginary evils, or expecting from it greater advantages than it is able to yield.

5. Among all our corrupt passions, there is a strong and intimate connection. When any one of them is adopted into our family, it seldom quits until it has fathered upon us all its kindred.

6. Charity, like the sun, brightens every object on which it shines; a censorious disposition casts every character into the darkest shade it will bear.

7. Many men mistake the love, for the practice of virtue; and are not so much good men as the friends of goodness.

8. Genuine virtue has a language that speaks to every heart throughout the world. It is a language which is understood by all. In every region, every climate, the homage paid to it is the same. In no one sentiment were ever mankind more generally agreed.

9. The appearances of our security are frequently deceitful.

10. When our sky seems most settled and serene, in some unobserved quarter gathers the little black cloud in which the tempest ferments, and prepares to discharge itself on our head.

11. The man of true fortitude may be compared to the castle built on a rock, which defies the attacks of surrounding waters: the man of a feeble and timorous spirit, to a hut placed on the shore, which every wind shakes, and every wave overflows.

12. Nothing is so inconsistent with self-possession as violent anger. It overpowers reason; confounds our ideas; distorts the appearance, and blackens the colour of every object. By the storms

which it raises within, and by the mischiefs which it occasions without, it generally brings on the passionate and revengeful man, greater misery than he can bring on the object of his resentment.

13. The palace of virtue has, in all ages, been represented as placed on the summit of a hill; in the ascent of which, labour is requisite, and difficulties are to be surmounted; and where a conductor is needed, to direct our way, and to aid our steps.

14. In judging of others, let us always think the best, and employ the spirit of charity and candour. But in judging of ourselves, we ought to be exact and severe.

15. Let him, who desires to see others happy, make haste to give while his gift can be enjoyed; and remember, that every moment of delay takes away something from the value of his benefaction. And let him who proposes his own happiness reflect, that while he forms his purpose, the day rolls on, and "the night cometh, when no man can work."

16. To sensual persons, hardly any thing is what it appears to be: and what flatters most, is always farthest from reality. There are voices which sing around them; but whose strains allure to ruin. There is a banquet spread, where poison is in every dish. There is a couch which invites them to repose; but to slumber upon it, is death.

17. If we would judge whether a man is really happy, it is not solely to his houses and lands, to his equipage and his retinue we are to look. Unless we could see farther, and discern what joy, or what bitterness, his heart feels, we can pronounce little concerning him.

18. The book is well written; and I have perused it with pleasure and profit. It shows, first, that true devotion is rational and well founded; next, that it is of the highest importance to every other part of religion and virtue; and, lastly, that it is most conducive to our happiness.

19. There is certainly no greater felicity, than to be able to look back on a life usefully and virtuously employed; to trace our own progress in existence, by such tokens as excite neither shame nor sorrow. It ought therefore to be the care of those who wish to pass the last hours with comfort, to lay up such a treasure of pleasing ideas, as shall support the expenses of that time, which is to depend wholly upon the fund already acquired.

## SECTION V.

1. WHAT avails the show of external liberty, to one who has lost the government of himself?

2. He that cannot live well to-day, (says Martial,) will be less qualified to live well to-morrow.

3. Can we esteem that man prosperous, who is raised to a situation which flatters his passions, but which corrupts his principles, disorders his temper, and finally oversets his virtue?

4. What misery does the vicious man secretly endure!—Adversity! how blunt are all the arrows of thy quiver in comparison with those of guilt!

5. When we have no pleasure in goodness, we may with certainty conclude the reason to be, that our pleasure is all derived from an opposite quarter.

6. How strangely are the opinions of men altered, by a change in their condition!

7. How many have had reason to be thankful, for being disappointed in designs which they earnestly pursued, but which, if successfully accomplished, they have afterwards seen would have occasioned their ruin!

8. What are the actions which afford in the remembrance a rational satisfaction? Are they the pursuits of sensual pleasure, the riots of jollity, or the displays of show and vanity? No: I appeal to your hearts, my friends, if what you recollect with most pleasure, are not the innocent, the virtuous, the honourable parts of your past life.

9. The present employment of time should frequently be an object of thought. About what are we now busied? What is the ultimate scope of our present pursuits and cares? Can we justify them to ourselves? Are they likely to produce any thing that will survive the moment, and bring forth some fruit for futurity?

10. Is it not strange (says an ingenious writer,) that some persons should be so delicate as not to bear a disagreeable picture in the house, and yet, by their behaviour, force every face they see about them, to wear the gloom of uneasiness and discontent?

11. If we are now in health, peace and safety; without any particular or uncommon evils to afflict our condition; what more can we reasonably look for in this vain and uncertain world? How little can the greatest prosperity add to such a state? Will any future situation ever make us happy, if now, with so few causes of grief, we imagine ourselves miserable? The evil lies in the state of our mind, not in our condition of fortune; and by no alteration of circumstances is likely to be remedied.

12. When the love of unwarrantable pleasures, and of vicious companions, is allowed to amuse young persons, to engross their time, and to stir up their passions; the day of ruin,—let them take heed, and beware! the day of irrecoverable ruin begins to draw nigh. Fortune is squandered; health is broken; friends are offended, affronted, estranged; aged parents, perhaps, sent afflicted and mourning to the dust.

13. On whom does time hang so heavily, as on the slothful and lazy? To whom are the hours so lingering? Who are so often devoured with spleen, and obliged to fly to every expedient, which can help them to get rid of themselves? Instead of producing tranquillity, indolence produces a fretful restlessness of mind; gives rise to cravings which are never satisfied; nourishes a sickly, effeminate delicacy, which sours and corrupts every pleasure.

## SECTION VI.

1. WE have seen the husbandman scattering his seed upon the furrowed ground! It springs up, is gathered into his barns, and crowns his labours with joy and plenty.—Thus the man who distributes his fortune with generosity and prudence, is amply repaid by the gratitude of those whom he obliges, by the approbation of his own mind, and by the favour of Heaven.

2. Temperance, by fortifying the mind and body, leads to happiness: intemperance, by enervating them, ends generally in misery.

3. Title and ancestry render a good man more illustrious; but an

ill one, more contemptible. Vice is infamous, though in a prince; and virtue honourable, though in a peasant.

4. An elevated genius, employed in little things, appears (to use the simile of Longinus) like the sun in his evening declination: he remits his splendour, but retains his magnitude; and pleases more, though he dazzles less.

5. If envious people were to ask themselves, whether they would exchange their entire situations with the persons envied, (I mean their minds, passions, notions, as well as their persons, fortunes, and dignities,)—I presume the self-love, common to human nature, would generally make them prefer their own condition.

6. We have obliged some persons:—very well!—what would we have more? Is not the consciousness of doing good, a sufficient reward?

7. Do not hurt yourselves or others, by the pursuit of pleasure. Consult your whole nature. Consider yourselves not only as sensitive, but as rational beings; not only as rational, but social; not only as social, but immortal.

8. Art thou poor?—Show thyself active and industrious, peaceable and contented. Art thou wealthy?—Show thyself beneficent and charitable, condescending and humane.

9. Though religion removes not all the evils of life, though it promises no continuance of undisturbed prosperity, (which indeed it were not salutary for man always to enjoy,) yet, if it mitigates the evils which necessarily belong to our state, it may justly be said to give "rest to them who labour and are heavy laden."

10. What a smiling aspect does the love of parents and children, of brothers and sisters, of friends and relations, give to every surrounding object, and every returning day! With what a lustre does it gild even the small habitation, where this placid intercourse dwells! where such scenes of heartfelt satisfaction succeed uninterruptedly to one another!

11. How many clear marks of benevolent intention appear every where around us! What a profusion of beauty and ornament is poured forth on the face of nature! What a magnificent spectacle presented to the view of man! What supply contrived for his wants! What a variety of objects set before him, to gratify his senses, to employ his understanding, to entertain his imagination, to cheer and gladden his heart!

12. The hope of future happiness is a perpetual source of consolation to good men. Under trouble, it sooths their minds; amidst temptation, it supports their virtue; and, in their dying moments, enables them to say, "O death! where is thy sting? O grave! where is thy victory?"

## SECTION VII.

1. AGESILAUS, king of Sparta, being asked, "What things he thought most proper for boys to learn," answered, "Those which they ought to practise when they come to be men." A wiser than Agesilaus has inculcated the same sentiment: "Train up a child in the way he should go, and when he is old he will not depart from it."

2. An Italian philosopher expressed in his motto, that "time was his estate." An estate indeed which will produce nothing

without cultivation; but which will always abundantly repay the labours of industry, and satisfy the most extensive desires, if no part of it be suffered to lie waste by negligence, to be overrun with noxious plants, or laid out for show, rather than use.

3. When Aristotle was asked, "What a man could gain by telling a falsehood," he replied, "Not to be credited when he speaks the truth."

4. L'Estrange, in his Fables, tells us that a number of frolicsome boys were one day watching frogs, at the side of a pond; and that, as any of them put their heads above the water, they pelted them down again with stones. One of the frogs, appealing to the humanity of the boys, made this striking observation; "Children, you do not consider, that though this may be sport to you, it is death to us."

5. Sully, the great statesman of France, always retained at his table, in his most prosperous days, the same frugality to which he had been accustomed in early life. He was frequently reproached, by the courtiers, for this simplicity; but he used to reply to them, in the words of an ancient philosopher: "If the guests are men of sense, there is sufficient for them: if they are not, I can very well dispense with their company."

6. Socrates, though primarily attentive to the culture of his mind, was not negligent of his external appearance. His cleanliness resulted from those ideas of order and decency which governed all his actions; and the care which he took of his health, from his desire to preserve his mind free and tranquil.

7. Eminently pleasing and honourable was the friendship between David and Jonathan. "I am distressed for thee, my brother Jonathan," said the plaintive and surviving David; "very pleasant hast thou been to me: thy love for me was wonderful; passing the love of women."

8. Sir Philip Sidney, at the battle near Zutphen, was wounded by a musket ball, which broke the bone of his thigh. He was carried about a mile and a half, to the camp; and being faint with the loss of blood, and probably parched with thirst through the heat of the weather, he called for drink. It was immediately brought to him: but, as he was putting the vessel to his mouth, a poor wounded soldier, who happened at that instant to be carried by him, looked up to it with wishful eyes. The gallant and generous Sidney took the bottle from his mouth, and delivered it to the soldier, saying, "Thy necessity is yet greater than mine."

9. Alexander the Great demanded of a pirate, whom he had taken, by what right he infested the seas? "By the same right," replied he, "that Alexander enslaves the world. But I am called a robber, because I have only one small vessel; and he is styled a conqueror, because he commands great fleets and armies." We too often judge of men by the splendour, and not by the merit of their actions.

10. Antoninus Pius, the Roman Emperor, was an amiable and good man. When any of his courtiers attempted to inflame him with a passion for military glory, he used to answer: "That he more desired the preservation of one subject, than the destruction of a thousand enemies."

11. Men are too often ingenious in making themselves misera-

ble, by aggravating to their own fancy, beyond bounds, all the evils which they endure. They compare themselves with none but those whom they imagine to be more happy; and complain, that upon them alone has fallen the whole load of human sorrows. Would they look with a more impartial eye on the world, they would see themselves surrounded with sufferers; and find that they are only drinking out of that mixed cup, which Providence has prepared for all.—"I will restore thy daughter again to life," said the eastern sage, to a prince who grieved immoderately for the loss of a beloved child, "provided thou art able to engrave on her tomb, the names of three persons who have never mourned.' The prince made inquiry after such persons; but found the inquiry vain, and was silent.

## SECTION VIII.

1. He that hath no rule over his own spirit, is like a city that is broken down, and without walls.

2. A soft answer turneth away wrath; but grievous words stir up anger.

3. Better is a dinner of herbs where love is, than a stalled ox and hatred therewith.

4. Pride goeth before destruction; and a haughty spirit before a fall.

5. Hear counsel, and receive instruction, that thou mayest be truly wise.

6. Faithful are the wounds of a friend; but the kisses of an enemy are deceitful. Open rebuke is better than secret love.

7. Seest thou a man wise in his own conceit? There is more hope of a fool than of him.

8. He that is slow to anger, is better than the mighty; and he that ruleth his spirit, than he that taketh a city.

9. He that hath pity on the poor, lendeth to the Lord; that which he hath given, will he pay him again.

10. If thine enemy be hungry, give him bread to eat; and if he be thirsty, give him water to drink.

11. He that planted the ear, shall he not hear? He that formed the eye, shall he not see?

12. I have been young, and now I am old; yet have I never seen the righteous forsaken, nor his seed begging bread.

13. It is better to be a door-keeper in the house of the Lord, than to dwell in the tents of wickedness.

14. I have seen the wicked in great power; and spreading himself like a green bay-tree. Yet he passed away: I sought him, but he could not be found.

15. Happy is the man that findeth wisdom. Length of days is in her right hand; and in her left hand, riches and honour. Her ways are ways of pleasantness, and all her paths are peace.

16. How good and how pleasant it is for brethren to dwell together in unity! It is like precious ointment: Like the dew of Hermon, and the dew that descended upon the mountains of Zion.

17. The sluggard will not plough by reason of the cold; he shall therefore beg in harvest, and have nothing.

18. I went by the field of the slothful, and by the vineyard of the man void of understanding: and lo! it was all grown over

with thorns; nettles had covered its face; and the stone wall was broken down. Then I saw, and considered it well. I looked upon it, and received instruction.

19. Honourable age is not that which standeth in length of time; nor that which is measured by number of years:—But wisdom is the gray hair to man; and an unspotted life is old age.

20. Solomon, my son, know thou the God of thy fathers; and serve him with a perfect heart, and with a willing mind. If thou seek him, he will be found of thee; but if thou forsake him, he will cast thee off for ever.

## SECTION IX.

1. THAT every day has its pains and sorrows is universally experienced, and almost universally confessed. But let us not attend only to mournful truths: if we look impartially about us, we shall find, that every day has likewise its pleasures and its joys.

2. We should cherish sentiments of charity towards all men. The Author of all good nourishes much piety and virtue in hearts that are unknown to us; and beholds repentance ready to spring up among many, whom we consider as reprobates.

3. No one ought to consider himself as insignificant in the sight of his Creator. In our several stations, we are all sent forth to be labourers in the vineyard of our heavenly Father. Every man has his work allotted, his talent committed to him; by the due improvement of which he may, in one way or other, serve God, promote virtue, and be useful in the world.

4. The love of praise should be preserved under proper subordination to the principle of duty. In itself, it is a useful motive to action; but when allowed to extend its influence too far, it corrupts the whole character, and produces guilt, disgrace, and misery. To be entirely destitute of it, is a defect. To be governed by it, is depravity. The proper adjustment of the several principles of action in human nature is a matter that deserves our highest attention. For when any one of them becomes either too weak or too strong, it endangers both our virtue and our happiness.

5. The desires and passions of a vicious man, having once obtained an unlimited sway, trample him under their feet. They make him feel that he is subject to various, contradictory, and imperious masters, who often pull him different ways. His soul is rendered the receptacle of many repugnant and jarring dispositions; and resembles some barbarous country, cantoned out into different principalities, which are continually waging war on one another.

6. Diseases, poverty, disappointment, and shame, are far from being, in every instance, the unavoidable doom of man. They are much more frequently the offspring of his own misguided choice. Intemperance engenders disease, sloth produces poverty, pride creates disappointments, and dishonesty exposes to shame. The ungoverned passions of men betray them into a thousand follies; their follies into crimes; and their crimes into misfortunes.

7. When we reflect on the many distresses which abound in human life; on the scanty proportion of happiness which any man is here allowed to enjoy; on the small difference which the diversity of fortune makes on that scanty proportion; it is surprising, that envy should ever have been a prevalent passion among men, much

more that it should have prevailed among Christians. Where so much is suffered in common, little room is left for envy. There is more occasion for pity and sympathy, and inclination to assist each other.

8. At our first setting out in life, when yet unacquainted with the world and its snares, when every pleasure enchants with its smile, and every object shines with the gloss of novelty, let us beware of the seducing appearances which surround us; and recollect what others have suffered from the power of headstrong desire. If we allow any passion, even though it be esteemed innocent, to acquire an absolute ascendant, our inward peace will be impaired. But if any, which has the taint of guilt, take early possession of our mind, we may date, from that moment, the ruin of our tranquillity.

9. Every man has some darling passion, which generally affords the first introduction to vice. The irregular gratifications, into which it occasionally seduces him, appear under the form of venial weaknesses; and are indulged, in the beginning, with scrupulousness and reserve. But, by longer practice, these restraints weaken, and the power of habit grows. One vice brings in another to its aid. By a sort of natural affinity they connect and entwine themselves together; till their roots come to be spread wide and deep over all the soul.

## SECTION X.

1. Whence arises the misery of this present world? It is not owing to our cloudy atmosphere, our changing seasons, and inclement skies. It is not owing to the debility of our bodies, or to the unequal distribution of the goods of fortune. Amidst all disadvantages of this kind, a pure, a steadfast, and enlightened mind, possessed of strong virtue, could enjoy itself in peace, and smile at the impotent assaults of fortune and the elements. It is within ourselves that misery has fixed its seat. Our disordered hearts, our guilty passions, our violent prejudices, and misplaced desires, are the instruments of the trouble which we endure. These sharpen the darts which adversity would otherwise point in vain against us.

2. While the vain and the licentious are revelling in the midst of extravagance and riot, how little do they think of those scenes of sore distress which are passing at that moment throughout the world; multitudes struggling for a poor subsistence, to support the wife and children whom they love, and who look up to them with eager eyes for that bread which they can hardly procure; multitudes groaning under sickness in desolate cottages, untended and unmourned; many, apparently in a better situation of life, pining away in secret with concealed griefs; families weeping over the beloved friends whom they have lost, or in all the bitterness of anguish, bidding those who are just expiring the last adieu.

3. Never adventure on too near an approach to what is evil. Familiarize not yourselves with it, in the slightest instances, without fear. Listen with reverence to every reprehension of conscience; and preserve the most quick and accurate sensibility to right and wrong. If ever your moral impressions begin to decay, and your natural abhorrence of guilt to lessen, you have ground to dread that the ruin of virtue is fast approaching.

4. By disappointments and trials the violence of our passions is tamed, and our minds are formed to sobriety and reflection. In the varieties of life, occasioned by the vicissitudes of worldly fortune, we are inured to habits both of the active and the suffering virtues. How much soever we complain of the vanity of the world, facts plainly show, that if its vanity were less, it could not answer the purpose of salutary discipline. Unsatisfactory as it is, its pleasures are still too apt to corrupt our hearts. How fatal then must the consequences have been, had it yielded us more complete enjoyment? If, with all its troubles, we are in danger of being too much attached to it, how entirely would it have seduced our affections, if no troubles had been mingled with its pleasures?

5. In seasons of distress or difficulty, to abandon ourselves to dejection, carries no mark of a great or a worthy mind. Instead of sinking under trouble, and declaring "that his soul is weary of life," it becomes a wise and a good man, in the evil day, with firmness to maintain his post; to bear up against the storm; to have recourse to those advantages which, in the worst of times, are always left to integrity and virtue; and never to give up the hope that better days may yet arise.

6. How many young persons have at first set out in the world with excellent dispositions of heart; generous, charitable, and humane; kind to their friends, and amiable among all with whom they had intercourse! And yet, how often have we seen all those fair appearances unhappily blasted in the progress of life, merely through the influence of loose and corrupting pleasures: and those very persons, who promised once to be blessings to the world, sunk down, in the end, to be the burden and nuisance of society!

7. The most common propensity of mankind, is, to store futurity with whatever is agreeable to them; especially in those periods of life, when imagination is lively, and hope is ardent. Looking forward to the year now beginning, they are ready to promise themselves much, from the foundations of prosperity which they have laid; from the friendships and connexions which they have secured; and from the plans of conduct which they have formed. Alas! how deceitful do all these dreams of happiness often prove! While many are saying in secret to their hearts, "To-morrow shall be as this day, and more abundantly," we are obliged in return to say to them; "Boast not yourselves of to-morrow; for you know not what a day may bring forth!"

## CHAPTER II.

### NARRATIVE PIECES.

#### SECTION I.

*No rank or possessions can make the guilty mind happy.*

1. DIONYSIUS, the tyrant of Sicily, was far from being happy, though he possessed great riches, and all the pleasures which wealth and power could procure. Damocles, one of his flatterers, deceived by those specious appearances of happiness, took occasion to compliment him on the extent of his power, his treasures,

and royal magnificence: and declared that no monarch had ever been greater or happier than Dionysius.

2. "Hast thou a mind, Damocles," says the king, "to taste this happiness; and to know, by experience, what the enjoyments are, of which thou hast so high an idea?" Damocles, with joy, accepted the offer. The king ordered that a royal banquet should be prepared, and a gilded sofa, covered with rich embroidery, placed for his favourite. Sideboards, loaded with gold and silver plate of immense value, were arranged in the apartment.

3. Pages of extraordinary beauty were ordered to attend his table, and to obey his commands with the utmost readiness, and the most profound submission. Fragrant ointments, chaplets of flowers, and rich perfumes, were added to the entertainment. The table was loaded with the most exquisite delicacies of every kind. Damocles, intoxicated with pleasure, fancied himself among superior beings.

4. But in the midst of all this happiness, as he lay indulging himself in state, he sees let down from the ceiling, exactly over his head, a glittering sword hung by a single hair. The sight of impending destruction put a speedy end to his joy and revelling. The pomp of his attendance, the glitter of the carved plate, and the delicacy of the viands, cease to afford him any pleasure.

5. He dreads to stretch forth his hand to the table. He throws off the garland of roses. He hastens to remove from his dangerous situation; and earnestly entreats the king to restore him to his former humble condition, having no desire to enjoy any longer a happiness so terrible.

6. By this device, Dionysius intimated to Damocles, how miserable he was in the midst of all his treasures; and in possession of all the honours and enjoyments which royalty could bestow.

CICERO.

## SECTION II.
*Change of external condition is often adverse to virtue.*

1. In the days of Joram, king of Israel, flourished the prophet Elisha. His character was so eminent, and his fame so widely spread, that Benhadad, the king of Syria, though an idolater, sent to consult him, concerning the issue of a distemper which threatened his life. The messenger employed on this occasion was Hazael, who appears to have been one of the princes, or chief men of the Syrian court.

2. Charged with rich gifts from the king, he presents himself before the prophet; and accosts him in terms of the highest respect. During the conference which they held together, Elisha fixed his eyes steadfastly on the countenance of Hazael; and discerning, by a prophetic spirit, his future tyranny and cruelty, he could not contain himself from bursting into a flood of tears.

3. When Hazael, in surprise, inquired into the cause of this sudden emotion, the prophet plainly informed him of the crimes and barbarities, which he foresaw that he would afterwards commit. The soul of Hazael abhorred, at this time, the thoughts of cruelty. Uncorrupted, as yet, by ambition or greatness, his indignation rose at being thought capable of the savage actions which the prophet had mentioned; and, with much warmth he replies; "But what? is thy servant a dog, that he should do this great thing?"

4. Elisha makes no return, but to point out a remarkable change, which was to take place in his condition; "The Lord hath shown me, that thou shalt be king over Syria." In course of time, all that had been predicted came to pass. Hazael ascended the throne, and ambition took possession of his heart. "He smote the children of Israel in all their coasts. He oppressed them during all the days of king Jehoahaz:" and, from what is left on record of his actions, he plainly appears to have proved, what the prophet foresaw him to be, a man of violence, cruelty, and blood.

5. In this passage of history, an object is presented, which deserves our serious attention. We behold a man who, in one state of life, could not look upon certain crimes without surprise and horror; who knew so little of himself, as to believe it impossible for him ever to be concerned in committing them; that same man, by a change of condition, and an unguarded state of mind, transformed in all his sentiments; and as he rose in greatness rising also in guilt; till at last he completed that whole character of iniquity, which he once detested. BLAIR.

## SECTION III.
### Haman; or, the misery of pride.

1. AHASUERUS, who is supposed to be the prince known among the Greek historians by the name of Artaxerxes, had advanced to the chief dignity in his kingdom, Haman, an Amalekite, who inherited all the ancient enmity of his race, to the Jewish nation. He appears, from what is recorded of him, to have been a very wicked minister. Raised to greatness without merit, he employed his power solely for the gratification of his passions.

2. As the honours which he possessed were next to royal, his pride was every day fed with that servile homage, which is peculiar to Asiatic courts; and all the servants of the king prostrated themselves before him. In the midst of this general adulation, one person only stooped not to Haman.

3. This was Mordecai the Jew; who, knowing this Amalekite to be an enemy to the people of God, and, with virtuous indignation, despising that insolence of prosperity with which he saw him lifted up, "bowed not, nor did him reverence." On this appearance of disrespect from Mordecai, Haman "was full of wrath: but he thought scorn to lay hands on Mordecai alone." Personal revenge was not sufficient to satisfy him.

4. So violent and black were his passions, that he resolved to exterminate the whole nation to which Mordecai belonged. Abusing, for his cruel purpose, the favour of his credulous sovereign, he obtained a decree to be sent forth, that, against a certain day, all the Jews throughout the Persian dominions should be put to the sword.

5. Meanwhile, confident of success, and blind to approaching ruin, he continued exulting in his prosperity. Invited by Ahasuerus to a royal banquet, which Esther the queen had prepared, "he went forth that day joyful, and with a glad heart." But behold how slight an incident was sufficient to poison his joy! As he went forth, he saw Mordecai in the king's gate; and observed, that he still refused to do him homage; "He stood not up, nor was moved for him;" although he well knew the formidable de-

signs, which Haman was preparing to execute. One private man, who despised his greatness, and disdained submission, while a whole kingdom trembled before him; one spirit, which the utmost stretch of his power could neither subdue nor humble, blasted his triumphs. His whole soul was shaken with a storm of passion. Wrath, pride, and desire of revenge, rose into fury. With difficulty he restrained himself in public; but as soon as he came to his own house, he was forced to disclose the agony of his mind.

7. He gathered together his friends and family, with Zeresh his wife. "He told them of the glory of his riches, and the multitude of his children, and of all the things wherein the king had promoted him; and how he had advanced him above the princes and servants of the king. He said, moreover, Yea, Esther the queen suffered no man to come in with the king, to the banquet that she had prepared, but myself; and to-morrow also am I invited to her with the king." After all this preamble, what is the conclusion? "Yet all this availeth me nothing, so long as I see Mordecai the Jew sitting at the king's gate."

8. The sequel of Haman's history I shall not now pursue. It might afford matter for much instruction, by the conspicuous justice of God in his fall and punishment. But contemplating only the singular situation, in which the expressions just quoted present him, and the violent agitation of his mind which they display, the following reflections naturally arise: How miserable is vice, when one guilty passion creates so much torment! how unavailing is prosperity, when in the height of it, a single disappointment can destroy the relish of all its pleasures! how weak is human nature, which, in the absence of real, is thus prone to form to itself imaginary woes!   BLAIR.

## SECTION IV.
### Lady Jane Gray.

1. THIS excellent personage was descended from the royal line of England by both her parents. She was carefully educated in the principles of the reformation; and her wisdom and virtue rendered her a shining example to her sex. But it was her lot to continue only a short period on this stage of being; for, in early life, she fell a sacrifice to the wild ambition of the duke of Northumberland; who promoted a marriage between her and his son, lord Guilford Dudley; and raised her to the throne of England, in opposition to the rights of Mary and Elizabeth.

2. At the time of their marriage, she was only about eighteen years of age, and her husband was also very young: a season of life very unequal to oppose the interested views of artful and aspiring men; who, instead of exposing them to danger, should have been the protectors of their innocence and youth.

3. This extraordinary young person, besides the solid endowments of piety and virtue, possessed the most engaging disposition, the most accomplished parts; and being of an equal age with king Edward VI. she had received all her education with him, and seemed even to possess a greater facility in acquiring every part of manly and classical literature.

4. She had attained a knowledge of the Roman and Greek languages, as well as of several modern tongues; had passed most of her time in an application to learning; and expressed a great in-

difference for other occupations and amusements usual with her sex and station.

5. Roger Ascham, tutor to the lady Elizabeth, having at one time paid her a visit, found her employed in reading Plato, while the rest of the family were engaged in a party of hunting in the park; and upon his admiring the singularity of her choice, she told him, that she "received more pleasure from that author, than others could reap from all their sport and gaiety."

6. Her heart, replete with this love of literature and serious studies, and with tenderness towards her husband, who was deserving of her affection, had never opened itself to the flattering allurements of ambition; and the information of her advancement to the throne was by no means agreeable to her. She even refused to accept the crown; pleaded the preferable right of the two princesses; expressed her dread of the consequences attending an enterprise so dangerous, not to say so criminal; and desired to remain in that private station in which she was born.

7. Overcome at last with the entreaties, rather than reasons, of her father and father-in-law, and, above all, of her husband, she submitted to their will, and was prevailed on to relinquish her own judgment. But her elevation was of very short continuance. The nation declared for queen Mary; and the lady Jane, after wearing the vain pageantry of a crown during ten days, returned to a private life, with much more satisfaction than she felt when royalty was tendered to her.

8. Queen Mary, who appears to have been incapable of generosity or clemency, determined to remove every person, from whom the least danger could be apprehended. Warning was, therefore, given to lady Jane to prepare for death; a doom which she had expected, and which the innocence of her life, as well as the misfortunes to which she had been exposed, rendered no unwelcome news to her.

9. The queen's bigoted zeal, under colour of tender mercy to the prisoner's soul, induced her to send priests, who molested her with perpetual disputation; and even a reprieve of three days was granted her, in hopes that she would be persuaded, during that time, to pay, by a timely conversion to popery, some regard to her eternal welfare.

10. Lady Jane had presence of mind, in those melancholy circumstances, not only to defend her religion by solid arguments, but, also to write a letter to her sister, in the Greek language; in which, besides sending her a copy of the Scriptures in that tongue, she exhorted her to maintain, in every fortune, a like steady perseverance.

11 On the day of her execution, her husband, lord Guilford, desired permission to see her; but she refused her consent, and sent him word, that the tenderness of their parting would overcome the fortitude of both; and would too much unbend their minds from that constancy, which their approaching end required of them. Their separation, she said, would be only for a moment; and they would soon rejoin each other in a scene, where their affections would be for ever united; and where death, disappointment, and misfortune, could no longer have access to them, or disturb their eternal felicity.

12. It had been intended to execute the lady Jane and lord Guilford together on the same scaffold, at Tower hill; but the council, dreading the compassion of the people for their youth, beauty, innocence, and noble birth, changed their orders, and gave directions that she should be beheaded within the verge of the Tower.

13. She saw her husband led to execution; and having given him from the window some token of her remembrance, she waited with tranquillity till her own appointed hour should bring her to a like fate. She even saw his headless body carried back in a cart; and found herself more confirmed by the reports, which she heard of the constancy of his end, than shaken by so tender and melancholy a spectacle.

14. Sir John Gage, constable of the Tower, when he led her to execution, desired her to bestow on him some small present, which he might keep as a perpetual memorial of her. She gave him her table-book, in which she had just written three sentences, on seeing her husband's dead body; one in Greek, another in Latin, a third in English.

15. The purport of them was, "that human justice was against his body, but the Divine Mercy would be favourable to his soul; and that if her fault deserved punishment, her youth, at least, and her imprudence, were worthy of excuse; and that God and posterity, she trusted, would show her favour." On the scaffold, she made a speech to the by-standers, in which the mildness of her disposition led her to take the blame entirely on herself, without uttering one complaint against the severity with which she had been treated.

16. She said, that her offence was, not that she had laid her hand upon the crown, but that she had not rejected it with sufficient constancy; that she had less erred through ambition than through reverence to her parents, whom she had been taught to respect and obey: that she willingly received death, as the only satisfaction which she could now make to the injured state; and though her infringement of the laws had been constrained, she would show, by her voluntary submission to their sentence, that she was desirous to atone for that disobedience, into which too much filial piety had betrayed her: that she had justly deserved this punishment for being made the instrument, though the unwilling instrument, of the ambition of others: and that the story of her life, she hoped, might at least be useful, by proving that innocence excuses not great misdeeds, if they tend any way to the destruction of the commonwealth.

17. After uttering these words, she caused herself to be disrobed by her women, and with a steady, serene countenance, submitted herself to the executioner. HUME.

## SECTION V.
### Ortogrul; or, the vanity of riches.

1. As Ortogrul of Basra was one day wandering along the streets of Bagdat, musing on the varieties of merchandise which the shops opened to his view; and observing the different occupations which busied the multitude on every side, he was awakened from the tranquillity of meditation, by a crowd that obstructed his

passage. He raised his eyes, and saw the chief vizier, who, having returned from the divan, was entering his palace.

2. Ortogrul mingled with the attendants; and being supposed to have some petition for the vizier, was permitted to enter. He surveyed the spaciousness of the apartments, admired the walls hung with golden tapestry, and the floors covered with silken carpets; and despised the simple neatness of his own little habitation.

3. "Surely," said he to himself, "this palace is the seat of happiness; where pleasure succeeds to pleasure, and discontent and sorrow can have no admission. Whatever nature has provided for the delight of sense, is here spread forth to be enjoyed. What can mortals hope or imagine, which the master of this palace has not obtained? The dishes of luxury cover his table! the voice of harmony lulls him in his bowers; he breathes the fragrance of the groves of Java, and sleeps upon the down of the cygnets of Ganges.

4. He speaks, and his mandate is obeyed; he wishes, and his wish is gratified; all, whom he sees, obey him, and all, whom he hears, flatter him. How different, Oh Ortogrul, is thy condition, who art doomed to the perpetual torments of unsatisfied desire, and who hast no amusement in thy power, that can withhold thee from thy own reflections!

5. They tell thee that thou art wise; but what does wisdom avail with poverty? None will flatter the poor; and the wise have very little power of flattering themselves. That man is surely the most wretched of the sons of wretchedness, who lives with his own faults and follies always before him; and who has none to reconcile him to himself by praise and veneration. I have long sought content, and have not found it; I will from this moment endeavour to be rich."

6. Full of his new resolution, he shut himself in his chamber for six months, to deliberate how he should grow rich. He sometimes purposed to offer himself as a counsellor to one of the kings in India; and sometimes resolved to dig for diamonds in the mines of Golconda.

7. One day, after some hours passed in violent fluctuation of opinion, sleep insensibly seized him in his chair. He dreamed that he was ranging a desert country, in search of some one that might teach him to grow rich; and as he stood on the top of a hill, shaded with cypress, in doubt whither to direct his steps, his father appeared on a sudden standing before him. "Ortogrul," said the old man, "I know thy perplexity; listen to thy father; turn thine eye on the opposite mountain."

8. Ortogrul looked, and saw a torrent tumbling down the rocks, roaring with the noise of thunder, and scattering its foam on the impending woods. "Now," said his father, "behold the valley that lies between the hills." Ortogrul looked, and espied a little well, out of which issued a small rivulet. "Tell me now," said his father, "dost thou wish for sudden affluence, that may pour upon thee like the mountain torrent; or for a slow and gradual increase, resembling the rill gliding from the well?"

9. "Let me be quickly rich," said Ortogrul; "let the golden stream be quick and violent." "Look round thee," said his father, "once again." Ortogrul looked, and perceived the channel of

the torrent dry and dusty; but following the rivulet from the well, he traced it to a wide lake, which the supply, slow and constant, kept always full. He awoke, and determined to grow rich by silent profit, and persevering industry.

10. Having sold his patrimony, he engaged in merchandise; and in twenty years purchased lands, on which he raised a house, equal in sumptuousness to that of the vizier, to which he invited all the ministers of pleasure, expecting to enjoy all the felicity which he had imagined riches able to afford. Leisure soon made him weary of himself, and he longed to be persuaded that he was great and happy. He was courteous and liberal: he gave all that approached him hopes of pleasing him, and all who should please him, hopes of being rewarded. Every art of praise was tried, and every source of adulatory fiction was exhausted.

11. Ortogrul heard his flatterers without delight, because he found himself unable to believe them. His own heart told him its frailties; his own understanding reproached him with his faults. "How long," said he, with a deep sigh, "have I been labouring in vain to amass wealth, which at last is useless! Let no man hereafter wish to be rich, who is already too wise to be flattered."

DR. JOHNSON.

## SECTION VI.
### *The hill of science.*

1. In that season of the year, when the serenity of the sky, the various fruits which cover the ground, the discoloured foliage of the trees, and all the sweet, but fading graces of inspiring autumn, open the mind to benevolence, and dispose it for contemplation, I was wandering in a beautiful and romantic country, till curiosity began to give way to weariness; and I sat down on the fragment of a rock overgrown with moss; where the rustling of the falling leaves, the dashing of waters, and the hum of the distant city, soothed my mind into a most perfect tranquillity; and sleep insensibly stole upon me, as I was indulging the agreeable reveries, which the objects around me naturally inspired.

2. I immediately found myself in a vast extended plain, in the middle of which arose a mountain higher than I had before any conception of. It was covered with a multitude of people, chiefly youth; many of whom pressed forward with the liveliest expression of ardour in their countenance, though the way was in many places steep and difficult.

3. I observed, that those, who had but just begun to climb the hill, thought themselves not far from the top; but as they proceeded, new hills were continually rising to their view; and the summit of the highest they could before discern seemed but the foot of another, till the mountain at length appeared to lose itself in the clouds.

4. As I was gazing on these things with astonishment, a friendly instructer suddenly appeared: "the mountain before thee," said he, "is the Hill of Science. On the top is the temple of Truth, whose head is above the clouds, and a veil of pure light covers her face. Observe the progress of her votaries; be silent and attentive."

5. After I had noticed a variety of objects, I turned my eye towards the multitudes who were climbing the steep ascent, and

observed among them a youth of a lively look, a piercing eye, and something fiery and irregular in all his motions. His name was Genius. He darted like an eagle up the mountain; and left his companions gazing after him with envy and admiration: but his progress was unequal, and interrupted by a thousand caprices.

6. When Pleasure warbled in the valley, he mingled in her train. When Pride beckoned towards the precipice, he ventured to the tottering edge. He delighted in devious and untried paths; and made so many excursions from the road, that his feebler companions often outstripped him. I observed that the muses beheld him with partiality; but Truth often frowned and turned aside her face.

7. While Genius was thus wasting his strength in eccentric flights, I saw a person of very different appearance, named Application. He crept along with a slow and unremitting pace, his eyes fixed on the top of the mountain, patiently removing every stone that obstructed his way, till he saw most of those below him, who had at first derided his slow and toilsome progress.

8. Indeed, there were few who ascended the hill with equal, and uninterrupted steadiness; for, besides the difficulties of the way, they were continually solicited to turn aside, by a numerous crowd of appetites, passions, and pleasures, whose importunity, when once complied with, they became less and less able to resist: and though they often returned to the path, the asperities of the road were more severely felt; the hill appeared more steep and rugged; the fruits, which were wholesome and refreshing, seemed harsh and ill tasted; their sight grew dim; and their feet tript at every little obstruction.

9. I saw, with some surprise, that the muses, whose business was to cheer and encourage those who were toiling up the ascent, would often sing in the bowers of pleasure, and accompany those who were enticed away at the call of the passions. They accompanied them, however, but a little way: and always forsook them when they lost sight of the hill. The tyrants then doubled their chains upon the unhappy captives; and led them away, without resistance, to the cells of Ignorance, or the mansions of Misery.

10. Among the innumerable seducers, who were endeavouring to draw away the votaries of Truth from the path of science, there was one, so little formidable in her appearance, and so gentle and languid in her attempts, that I should scarcely have taken notice of her, but for the numbers she had imperceptibly loaded with her chains.

11. Indolence, (for so she was called,) far from proceeding to open hostilities, did not attempt to turn their feet out of the path, but contented herself with retarding their progress; and the purpose she could not force them to abandon, she persuaded them to delay. Her touch had a power like that of the torpedo, which withered the strength of those who came within its influence. Her unhappy captives still turned their faces towards the temple, and always hoped to arrive there; but the ground seemed to slide from beneath their feet, and they found themselves at the bottom, before they suspected they had changed their place.

12. The placid serenity, which at first appeared in their countenance, changed by degrees into a melancholy languor, which was

tinged with deeper and deeper gloom, as they glided down the stream of Insignificance: a dark and sluggish water, which is curled by no breeze, and enlivened by no murmur, till it falls into a dead sea, where startled passengers are awakened by the shock, and the next moment buried in the gulf of Oblivion.

13. Of all the unhappy deserters from the paths of Science, none seemed less able to return than the followers of Indolence. The captives of Appetite and Passion would often seize the moment when their tyrants were languid or asleep, to escape from their enchantment; but the dominion of Indolence was constant and unremitted; and seldom resisted, till resistance was in vain.

14. After contemplating these things, I turned my eyes towards the top of the mountain, where the air was always pure and exhilarating, the path shaded with laurels and evergreens, and the effulgence which beamed from the face of Science seemed to shed a glory round her votaries. Happy, said I, are they who are permitted to ascend the mountain! But while I was pronouncing this exclamation, with uncommon ardour, I saw, standing beside me, a form of diviner features, and a more benign radiance.

15. "Happier," said she, "are they whom Virtue conducts to the Mansions of Content!" "What," said I, "does Virtue then reside in the vale?" "I am found," said she, "in the vale, and I illuminate the mountain. I cheer the cottager at his toil, and inspire the sage at his meditation. I mingle in the crowd of cities, and bless the hermit in his cell. I have a temple in every heart that owns my influence; and to him that wishes for me, I am already present. Science may raise thee to eminence; but I alone can guide thee to felicity!"

16. While Virtue was thus speaking, I stretched out my arms towards her, with a vehemence which broke my slumber. The chill dews were falling around me, and the shades of evening stretched over the landscape. I hastened homeward; and resigned the night to silence and meditation.  AIKEN.

## SECTION VII.

### *The journey of a day; a picture of human life.*

1. OBIDAH, the son of Abensina, left the caravansera early in the morning, and pursued his journey through the plains of Indostan. He was fresh and vigorous with rest; he was animated with hope; he was incited by desire; he walked swiftly forward over the vallies, and saw the hills gradually rising before him.

2. As he passed along, his ears were delighted with the morning song of the bird of 'paradise; he was fanned by the last flutters of the sinking breeze, and sprinkled with dew from groves of spices. He sometimes contemplated the towering height of the oak, monarch of the hills; and sometimes caught the gentle fragrance of the primrose, eldest daughter of the spring: all his senses were gratified, and all care was banished from his heart.

3. Thus he went on, till the sun approached his meridian, and the increased heat preyed upon his strength; he then looked round about him for some more commodious path. He saw, on his right hand, a grove that seemed to wave its shades as a sign of invitation; he entered it, and found the coolness and verdure irresistibly pleasant.

4. He did not, however, forget whither he was travelling; but found a narrow way, bordered with flowers, which appeared to have the same direction with the main road; and was pleased, that, by this happy experiment, he had found means to unite pleasure with business, and to gain the rewards of diligence without suffering its fatigues.

5. He, therefore, still continued to walk for a time, without the least remission of his ardour, except that he was sometimes tempted to stop by the music of the birds, which the heat had assembled in the shade; and sometimes amused himself with plucking the flowers that covered the banks on either side, or the fruits that hung upon the branches.

6. At last, the green path began to decline from its first tendency, and to wind among hills and thickets, cooled with fountains, and murmuring with waterfalls. Here Obidah paused for a time, and began to consider whether it were longer safe to forsake the known and common track; but remembering that the heat was now in its greatest violence, and that the plain was dusty and uneven, he resolved to pursue the new path, which he supposed only to make a few meanders, in compliance with the varieties of the ground, and to end at last in the common road.

7. Having thus calmed his solicitude, he renewed his pace, though he suspected that he was not gaining ground. This uneasiness of his mind inclined him to lay hold on every new object, and give way to every sensation that might sooth or divert him. He listened to every echo; he mounted every hill for a fresh prospect; he turned aside to every cascade; and pleased himself with tracing the course of a gentle river that rolled among the trees, and watered a large region with innumerable circumvolutions.

8. In these amusements, the hours passed away unaccounted; his deviations had perplexed his memory, and he knew not towards what point to travel. He stood pensive and confused, afraid to go forward lest he should go wrong, yet conscious that the time of loitering was now past. While he was thus tortured with uncertainty, the sky was overspread with clouds; the day vanished from before him; and a sudden tempest gathered round his head.

9. He was now roused by his danger to a quick and painful remembrance of his folly; he now saw how happiness is lost when ease is consulted; he lamented the unmanly impatience that prompted him to seek shelter in the grove; and despised the petty curiosity that led him on from trifle to trifle. While he was thus reflecting, the air grew blacker, and a clap of thunder broke his meditation.

10. He now resolved to do what yet remained in his power, to tread back the ground which he had passed, and try to find some issue where the wood might open into the plain. He prostrated himself on the ground, and recommended his life to the Lord of Nature. He rose with confidence and tranquillity, and pressed on with resolution. The beasts of the desert were in motion, and on every hand were heard the mingled howls of rage and fear, and ravage and expiration. All the horrors of darkness and solitude surrounded him: the winds roared in the woods; and the torrents tumbled from the hills.

11. Thus forlorn and distressed, he wandered through the wild,

without knowing whither he was going, or whether he was every moment drawing nearer to safety, or to destruction. At length, not fear, but labour, began to overcome him; his breath grew short, and his knees trembled; and he was on the point of lying down in resignation to his fate, when he beheld, through the brambles, the glimmer of a taper.

12. He advanced towards the light; and finding that it proceeded from the cottage of a hermit, he called humbly at the door, and obtained admission. The old man set before him such provisions as he had collected for himself, on which Obidah fed with eagerness and gratitude.

13. When the repast was over, "Tell me," said the hermit, "by what chance thou hast been brought hither? I have been now twenty years an inhabitant of the wilderness, in which I never saw a man before." Obidah then related the occurrences of his journey, without any concealment or palliation.

14. "Son," said the hermit, "let the errors and follies, the dangers and escape of this day, sink deep into thy heart. Remember, my son, that human life is the journey of a day. We rise in the morning of youth, full of vigour, and full of expectation; we set forward with spirit and hope, with gaiety and with diligence, and travel on a while in the direct road of piety towards the mansions of rest.

15. "In a short time, we remit our fervour, and endeavour to find some mitigation of our duty, and some more easy means of obtaining the same end. We then relax our vigour, and resolve no longer to be terrified with crimes at a distance; but rely upon our own constancy, and venture to approach what we resolve never to touch. We thus enter the bowers of ease, and repose in the shades of security.

16. "Here the heart softens, and vigilance subsides; we are then willing to inquire whether another advance cannot be made, and whether we may not, at least, turn our eyes upon the gardens of pleasure. We approach them with scruple and hesitation; we enter them, but enter timorous and trembling; and always hope to pass through them without losing the road of virtue, which, for a while, we keep in our sight, and to which we purpose to return. But temptation succeeds temptation, and one compliance prepares us for another; we in time lose the happiness of innocence, and solace our disquiet with sensual gratifications.

17. "By degrees, we let fall the remembrance of our original intention, and quit the only adequate object of rational desire. We entangle ourselves in business, immerge ourselves in luxury, and rove through the labyrinths of inconstancy; till the darkness of old age begins to invade us, and disease and anxiety obstruct our way. We then look back upon our lives with horror, with sorrow, with repentance; and wish, but too often vainly wish, that we had not forsaken the ways of virtue.

18. "Happy are they, my son, who shall learn from thy example, not to despair; but shall remember, that, though the day is past, and their strength is wasted, there yet remains one effort to be made: that reformation is never hopeless, nor sincere endeavours ever unassisted; that the wanderer may at length return after all his errors; and that he who implores strength and cou-

rage from above, shall find danger and difficulty give way before him. Go now, my son, to thy repose; commit thyself to the care of Omnipotence; and when the morning calls again to toil, begin anew thy journey and thy life." DR. JOHNSON.

## CHAPTER III.
### DIDACTIC PIECES.
### SECTION I.
*The importance of a good Education.*

1. I CONSIDER a human soul, without education, like marble in the quarry: which shows none of its inherent beauties, until the skill of the polisher fetches out the colours, makes the surface shine, and discovers every ornamental cloud, spot, and vein, that runs through the body of it. Education, after the same manner, when it works upon a noble mind, draws out to view every latent virtue and perfection, which, without such helps, are never able to make their appearance.

2. If my reader will give me leave to change the allusion so soon upon him, I shall make use of the same instance to illustrate the force of education, which Aristotle has brought to explain his doctrine of substantial forms, when he tells us that a statue lies hid in a block of marble; and that the art of the statuary only clears away the superfluous matter, and removes the rubbish. The figure is in the stone, and the sculptor only finds it.

3. What sculpture is to a block of marble, education is to a human soul. The philosopher, the saint, or the hero, the wise, the good, or the great man, very often lies hid and concealed in a plebeian, which a proper education might have disinterred, and have brought to light. I am therefore much delighted with reading the accounts of savage nations; and with contemplating those virtues which are wild and uncultivated: to see courage exerting itself in fierceness, resolution in obstinacy, wisdom in cunning, patience in sullenness and despair.

4. Men's passions operate variously, and appear in different kinds of actions, according as they are more or less rectified and swayed by reason. When one hears of negroes, who, upon the death of their masters, or upon changing their service, hang themselves upon the next tree, as it sometimes happens in our American plantations, who can forbear admiring their fidelity, though it expresses itself in so dreadful a manner?

5. What might not that savage greatness of soul, which appears in these poor wretches on many occasions, be raised to, were it rightly cultivated? And what colour of excuse can there be, for the contempt with which we treat this part of our species; that we should not put them upon the common foot of humanity; that we should only set an insignificant fine upon the man who murders them; nay, that we should, as much as in us lies, cut them off from the prospects of happiness in another world, as well as in this; and deny them that which we look upon as the proper means for attaining it?

6. It is therefore an unspeakable blessing, to be born in those

parts of the world where wisdom and knowledge flourish; though, it must be confessed, there are, even in these parts, several poor uninstructed persons, who are but little above the inhabitants of those nations of which I have been here speaking; as those who have had the advantages of a more liberal education, rise above one another by several different degrees of perfection.

7. For, to return to our statue in the block of marble, we see it sometimes only begun to be chipped, sometimes rough hewn, and but just sketched into a human figure; sometimes, we see the man appearing distinctly in all his limbs and features; sometimes, we find the figure wrought up to great elegancy; but seldom meet with any to which the hand of a Phidias or a Praxiteles could not give several nice touches and finishings.      ADDISON.

## SECTION II.
### On Gratitude.

1. THERE is not a more pleasing exercise of the mind, than gratitude. It is accompanied with so great inward satisfaction, that the duty is sufficiently rewarded by the performance. It is not, like the practice of many other virtues, difficult and painful, but attended with so much pleasure, that were there no positive command which enjoined it, nor any recompense laid up for it hereafter, a generous mind would indulge in it, for the natural gratification which it affords.

2. If gratitude is due from man to man, how much more from man to his Maker? The Supreme Being does not only confer upon us those bounties which proceed more immediately from his hand, but even those benefits which are conveyed to us by others. Every blessing we enjoy, by what means soever it may be derived upon us, is the gift of Him who is the great Author of good, and the Father of mercies.

3. If gratitude, when exerted towards one another, naturally produces a very pleasing sensation in the mind of a grateful man, it exalts the soul into rapture, when it is employed on this great object of gratitude; on this beneficent Being, who has given us every thing we already possess, and from whom we expect every thing we yet hope for.      ADDISON.

## SECTION III.
### On Forgiveness.

1. THE most plain and natural sentiments of equity concur with divine authority, to enforce the duty of forgiveness. Let him who has never in his life done wrong, be allowed the privilege of remaining inexorable. But let such as are conscious of frailties and crimes, consider forgiveness as a debt which they owe to others. Common failings are the strongest lesson of mutual forbearance. Were this virtue unknown among men, order and comfort, peace and repose, would be strangers to human life.

2. Injuries retaliated according to the exorbitant measure which passion prescribes, would excite resentment in return. The injured person would become the injurer; and thus wrongs, retaliations, and fresh injuries, would circulate in endless succession, till the world was rendered a field of blood.

3. Of all the passions which invade the human breast, revenge is the most direful. When allowed to reign with full dominion, it is

more than sufficient to poison the few pleasures which remain to man in his present state. How much soever a person may suffer from injustice, he is always in hazard of suffering more from the prosecution of revenge. The violence of an enemy cannot inflict what is equal to the torment he creates to himself, by means of the fierce and desperate passions which he allows to rage in his soul.

4. Those evil spirits who inhabit the regions of misery are represented as delighting in revenge and cruelty. But all that is great and good in the universe, is on the side of clemency and mercy. The almighty Ruler of the world, though for ages offended by the unrighteousness, and insulted by the impiety of men, is "long suffering and slow to anger."

5. His Son, when he appeared in our nature, exhibited, both in his life and his death, the most illustrious example of forgiveness which the world ever beheld. If we look into the history of mankind, we shall find that, in every age, they who have been respected as worthy, or admired as great, have been distinguished for this virtue.

6. Revenge dwells in little minds. A noble and magnanimous spirit is always superior to it. It suffers not from the injuries of men those severe shocks which others feel. Collected within itself, it stands unmoved by their impotent assaults; and with generous pity, rather than with anger, looks down on their unworthy conduct. It has been truly said, that the greatest man on earth can no sooner commit an injury, than a good man can make himself greater, by forgiving it.                                       BLAIR.

## SECTION IV.
### Motives to the practice of gentleness.

1. To promote the virtue of gentleness, we ought to view our character with an impartial eye; and to learn, from our own failings, to give that indulgence which in our turn we claim. It is pride which fills the world with so much harshness and severity. In the fulness of self-estimation, we forget what we are. We claim attentions to which we are not entitled. We are rigorous to offences, as if we had never offended; unfeeling to distress, as if we knew not what it was to suffer. From those airy regions of pride and folly, let us descend to our proper level.

2. Let us survey the natural equality on which Providence has placed man with man, and reflect on the infirmities common to all. If the reflection on natural equality and mutual offences, be insufficient to prompt humanity, let us at least remember what we are in the sight of our Creator. Have we none of that forbearance to give one another; which we all so earnestly intreat from heaven? Can we look for clemency or gentleness from our Judge, when we are so backward to show it to our own brethren?

3. Let us also accustom ourselves, to reflect on the small moment of those things, which are the usual incentives to violence and contention. In the ruffled and angry hour, we view every appearance through a false medium. The most inconsiderable point of interest, or honour, swells into a momentous object; and the slightest attack seems to threaten immediate ruin.

4. But after passion or pride has subsided, we look around in vain for the mighty mischiefs we dreaded. The fabric, which our

disturbed imagination had reared, totally disappears. But though the cause of contention has dwindled away, its consequences remain. We have alienated a friend; we have imbittered an enemy; we have sown the seeds of future suspicion, malevolence, or disgust.

5. Let us suspend our violence for a moment, when causes of discord occur. Let us anticipate that period of coolness, which, of itself, will soon arrive. Let us reflect how little we have any prospect of gaining by fierce contention; but how much of the true happiness of life we are certain of throwing away. Easily, and from the smallest chink, the bitter waters of strife are let forth; but their course cannot be foreseen; and he seldom fails of suffering most from their poisonous effect, who first allowed them to flow.

BLAIR.

## SECTION V.
*A suspicious temper the source of misery to its possessor.*

1. As a suspicious spirit is the source of many crimes and calamities in the world, so it is the spring of certain misery to the person who indulges it. His friends will be few; and small will be his comfort in those whom he possesses. Believing others to be his enemies, he will of course make them such. Let his caution be ever so great, the asperity of his thoughts will often break out in his behaviour; and in return for suspecting and hating, he will incur suspicion and hatred.

2. Besides the external evils which he draws upon himself, arising from alienated friendship, broken confidence, and open enmity, the suspicious temper itself is one of the worst evils which any man can suffer. If "in all fear there is torment," how miserable must be his state who, by living in perpetual jealousy, lives in perpetual dread!

3. Looking upon himself to be surrounded with spies, enemies, and designing men, he is a stranger to reliance and trust. He knows not to whom to open himself. He dresses his countenance in forced smiles, while his heart throbs within from apprehensions of secret treachery. Hence fretfulness and ill-humour, disgust at the world, and all the painful sensations of an irritated and imbittered mind.

4. So numerous and great are the evils arising from a suspicious disposition, that, of the two extremes, it is more eligible to expose ourselves to occasional disadvantage from thinking too well of others, than to suffer continual misery by thinking always ill of them. It is better to be sometimes imposed upon, than never to trust. Safety is purchased at too dear a rate, when, in order to secure it, we are obliged to be always clad in armour, and to live in perpetual hostility with our fellows.

5. This is, for the sake of living, to deprive ourselves of the comfort of life. The man of candour enjoys his situation, whatever it is, with cheerfulness and peace. Prudence directs his intercourse with the world; but no black suspicions haunt his hours of rest. Accustomed to view the characters of his neighbours in the most favourable light, he is like one who dwells amidst those beautiful scenes of nature, on which the eye rests with pleasure.

6. Whereas the suspicious man, having his imagination filled with all the shocking forms of human falsehood, deceit, and

treachery, resembles the traveller in the wilderness, who discerns no objects around him but such as are either dreary or terrible; caverns that open, serpents that hiss, and beasts of prey that howl. BLAIR.

## SECTION VI.
### Comforts of religion.

1. THERE are many who have passed the age of youth and beauty; who have resigned the pleasures of that smiling season; who begin to decline into the vale of years, impaired in their health, depressed in their fortunes, stript of their friends, their children, and perhaps still more tender connexions. What resource can this world afford them? It presents a dark and dreary waste, through which there does not issue a single ray of comfort.

2. Every delusive prospect of ambition is now at an end; long experience of mankind, an experience very different from what the open and generous soul of youth had fondly dreamt of, has rendered the heart almost inaccessible to new friendships. The principal sources of activity are taken away, when they for whom we labour are cut off from us; they who animated, and who sweetened all the toils of life.

3. Where then can the soul find refuge, but in the bosom of Religion? There she is admitted to those prospects of Providence and futurity, which alone can warm and fill the heart. I speak here of such as retain the feelings of humanity; whom misfortunes have softened, and perhaps rendered more delicately sensible; not of such as possess that stupid insensibility, which some are pleased to dignify with the name of Philosophy.

4. It might therefore be expected, that those philosophers, who think they stand in no need themselves of the assistance of religion to support their virtue, and who never feel the want of its consolations, would yet have the humanity to consider the very different situation of the rest of mankind; and not endeavour to deprive them of what habit, at least, if they will not allow it to be nature, has made necessary to their morals, and to their happiness.

5. It might be expected, that humanity would prevent them from breaking into the last retreat of the unfortunate, who can no longer be objects of their envy or resentment; and tearing from them their only remaining comfort. The attempt to ridicule religion may be agreeable to some, by relieving them from restraint upon their pleasures; and may render others very miserable, by making them doubt those truths, in which they were most deeply interested; but it can convey real good and happiness to no one individual. GREGORY.

## SECTION VII.
### Diffidence of our abilities, a mark of wisdom.

1. IT is a sure indication of good sense, to be diffident of it. We then, and not till then, are growing wise, when we begin to discern how weak and unwise we are. An absolute perfection of understanding, is impossible: he makes the nearest approaches to it, who has the sense to discern, and the humility to acknowledge, its imperfections.

2. Modesty always sits gracefully upon youth; it covers a multitude of faults, and doubles the lustre of every virtue which it seems to hide: the perfections of men being like those flowers

which appear more beautiful, when their leaves are a little contracted and folded up, than when they are full blown, and display themselves, without any reserve, to the view.

3. We are some of us very fond of knowledge, and apt to value ourselves upon any proficiency in the sciences: one science, however, there is, worth more than all the rest, and that is, the science of living well; which shall remain, when "tongues shall cease," and "knowledge shall vanish away."

4. As to new notions, and new doctrines, of which this age is very fruitful, the time will come, when we shall have no pleasure in them: nay, the time shall come, when they shall be exploded, and would have been forgotten, if they had not been preserved in those excellent books, which contain a confutation of them; like insects preserved for ages in amber, which otherwise would soon have returned to the common mass of things.

5. But a firm belief of Christianity, and a practice suitable to it, will support and invigorate the mind to the last; and most of all, at last, at that important hour, which must decide our hopes and apprehensions: and the wisdom, which, like our Saviour, cometh from above, will, through his merits, bring us thither. All our other studies and pursuits, however different, ought to be subservient to, and centre in, this grand point, the pursuit of eternal happiness, by being good in ourselves, and useful to the world.

SEED.

## SECTION VIII.

*On the importance of order in the distribution of our time.*

1. TIME we ought to consider as a sacred trust committed to us by God; of which we are now the depositaries, and are to render an account at the last. That portion of it which he has allotted to us, is intended partly for the concerns of this world, partly for those of the next.

2. Let each of these occupy, in the distribution of our time, that space which properly belongs to it. Let not the hours of hospitality and pleasure interfere with the discharge of our necessary affairs; and let not what we call necessary affairs, encroach upon the time which is due to devotion. To every thing there is a season, and a time for every purpose under the heaven. If we delay till to-morrow what ought to be done to-day, we overcharge the morrow with a burden which belongs not to it. We load the wheels of time, and prevent them from carrying us along smoothly.

3. He who every morning plans the transactions of the day, and follows out that plan, carries on a thread which will guide him through the labyrinth of the most busy life. The orderly arrangement of his time is like a ray of light, which darts itself through all his affairs. But, where no plan is laid, where the disposal of time is surrendered merely to the chance of incidents, all things lie huddled together in one chaos, which admits neither of distribution nor review.

4. The first requisite for introducing order into the management of time, is to be impressed with a just sense of its value. Let us consider well how much depends upon it, and how fast it flies away. The bulk of men are in nothing more capricious and inconsistent, than in their appreciation of time. When they think of it,

as the measure of their continuance on earth, they highly prize it, and with the greatest anxiety seek to lengthen it out.

5. But when they view it in separate parcels, they appear to hold it in contempt, and squander it with inconsiderate profusion. While they complain that life is short, they are often wishing its different periods at an end. Covetous of every other possession, of time only they are prodigal. They allow every idle man to be master of this property, and make every frivolous occupation welcome that can help them to consume it.

6. Among those who are so careless of time, it is not to be expected that order should be observed in its distribution. But, by this fatal neglect, how many materials of severe and lasting regret are they laying up in store for themselves! The time which they suffer to pass away in the midst of confusion, bitter repentance seeks afterwards in vain to recall. What was omitted to be done at its proper moment, arises to be the torment of some future season.

7. Manhood is disgraced by the consequences of neglected youth. Old age, oppressed by cares that belonged to a former period, labours under a burden not its own. At the close of life, the dying man beholds with anguish that his days are finishing, when his preparation for eternity is hardly commenced. Such are the effects of a disorderly waste of time, through not attending to its value. Every thing in the life of such persons is misplaced. Nothing is performed aright, from not being performed in due season.

8. But he who is orderly in the distribution of his time, takes the proper method of escaping those manifold evils. He is justly said to redeem the time. By proper management, he prolongs it. He lives much in little space; more in a few years than others do in many. He can live to God and his own soul, and at the same time attend to all the lawful interests of the present world. He looks back on the past, and provides for the future.

9. He catches and arrests the hours as they fly. They are marked down for useful purposes, and their memory remains. Whereas those hours fleet by the man of confusion like a shadow. His days and years are either blanks, of which he has no remembrance, or they are filled up with so confused and irregular a succession of unfinished transactions, that though he remembers he has been busy, yet he can give no account of the business which has employed him. BLAIR.

## SECTION IX.
*The dignity of virtue amidst corrupt examples.*

1. THE most excellent and honourable character which can adorn a man and a Christian, is acquired by resisting the torrent of vice, and adhering to the cause of God and virtue against a corrupted multitude. It will be found to hold in general, that they, who, in any of the great lines of life, have distinguished themselves for thinking profoundly, and acting nobly, have despised popular prejudices; and departed, in several things, from the common ways of the world.

2. On no occasion is this more requisite for true honour, than where religion and morality are concerned. In times of prevailing licentiousness, to maintain unblemished virtue, and uncorrupted integrity; in a public or a private cause, to stand firm by what is fair and just, amidst discouragements and opposition; despising

groundless censure and reproach; disdaining all compliance with public manners, when they are vicious and unlawful; and never ashamed of the punctual discharge of every duty towards God and man;—this is what shows true greatness of spirit, and will force approbation even from the degenerate multitude themselves.

3. "This is the man," (their conscience will oblige them to acknowledge,) "whom we are unable to bend to mean condescensions. We see it in vain either to flatter or to threaten him; he rests on a principle within, which we cannot shake. To this man we may, on any occasion, safely commit our cause. He is incapable of betraying his trust, or deserting his friend, or denying his faith."

4. It is, accordingly, this steady inflexible virtue, this regard to principle, superior to all custom and opinion, which peculiarly marked the characters of those in any age, who have shone with distinguished lustre; and has consecrated their memory to all posterity. It was this that obtained to ancient Enoch the most singular testimony of honour from heaven.

5. He continued to "walk with God," when the world apostatized from him. He pleased God, and was beloved of him; so that living among sinners, he was translated to heaven without seeing death; "Yea, speedily was he taken away, lest wickedness should have altered his understanding, or deceit beguiled his soul."

6. When Sodom could not furnish ten righteous men to save it, Lot remained unspotted amidst the contagion. He lived like an angel among spirits of darkness; and the destroying flame was not permitted to go forth, till the good man was called away, by a heavenly messenger, from his devoted city.

7. When "all flesh had corrupted their way upon the earth," then lived Noah, a righteous man, and a preacher of righteousness. He stood alone, and was scoffed by the profane crew. But they by the deluge were swept away; while on him, Providence conferred the immortal honour, of being the restorer of a better race, and the father of a new world. Such examples as these, and such honours conferred by God on them who withstood the multitude of evil doers, should often be present to our minds.

8. Let us oppose them to the numbers of low and corrupt examples, which we behold around us; and when we are in hazard of being swayed by such, let us fortify our virtue, by thinking of those who, in former times, shone like stars in the midst of surrounding darkness, and are now shining in the kingdom of heaven, as the brightness of the firmament, for ever and ever. BLAIR.

## SECTION X.

*The mortifications of vice greater than those of virtue.*

1. Though no condition of human life is free from uneasiness, yet it must be allowed, that the uneasiness belonging to a sinful course, is far greater, than what attends a course of well-doing. If we are weary of the labours of virtue, we may be assured, that the world, whenever we try the exchange, will lay upon us a much heavier load.

2. It is the outside only, of a licentious life, which is gay and smiling. Within, it conceals toil, and trouble, and deadly sorrow. For vice poisons human happiness in the spring, by introducing disorder into the heart. Those passions which it seems to in-

dulge, it only feeds with imperfect gratifications; and thereby strengthens them for preying, in the end, on their unhappy victims.

3. It is a great mistake to imagine, that the pain of self-denial is confined to virtue. He who follows the world, as much as he who follows Christ, must "take up his cross;" and to him assuredly, it will prove a more oppressive burden. Vice allows all our passions to range uncontrolled; and where each claims to be superior, it is impossible to gratify all. The predominant desire can only be indulged at the expense of its rival.

4. No mortifications which virtue exacts, are more severe than those, which ambition imposes upon the love of ease, pride upon interest, and covetousness upon vanity. Self-denial, therefore, belongs, in common, to vice and virtue; but with this remarkable difference, that the passions which virtue requires us to mortify, it tends to weaken; whereas, those which vice obliges us to deny, it, at the same time, strengthens. The one diminishes the pain of self-denial, by moderating the demand of passion; the other increases it, by rendering those demands imperious and violent.

5. What distresses that occur in the calm life of virtue, can be compared to those tortures, which remorse of conscience inflicts on the wicked; to those severe humiliations, arising from guilt combined with misfortunes, which sink them to the dust; to those violent agitations of shame and disappointment, which sometimes drive them to the most fatal extremities, and make them abhor their existence! How often, in the midst of those disastrous situations, into which their crimes have brought them, have they execrated the seductions of vice; and, with bitter regret, looked back to the day on which they first forsook the path of innocence!

BLAIR.

## SECTION XI.
### On Contentment.

1. CONTENTMENT produces, in some measure, all those effects which the alchymist usually ascribes to what he calls the philosopher's stone; and if it does not bring riches, it does the same thing, by banishing the desire of them. If it cannot remove the disquietudes arising from a man's mind, body, or fortune, it makes him easy under them. It has indeed a kindly influence on the soul of man, in respect of every being to whom he stands related.

2. It extinguishes all murmur, repining, and ingratitude, towards that Being who has allotted him his part to act in this world. It destroys all inordinate ambition, and every tendency to corruption, with regard to the community wherein he is placed. It gives sweetness to his conversation, and a perpetual serenity to all his thoughts.

3. Among the many methods which might be made use of for acquiring this virtue, I shall mention only the two following. First of all, a man should always consider how much he has more than he wants; and secondly, how much more unhappy he might be than he really is.

4. First, a man should always consider how much he has more than he wants. I am wonderfully pleased with the reply which Aristippus made to one, who condoled with him upon the loss of a farm: "Why," said he, "I have three farms still, and you have but one; so that I ought rather to be afflicted for you, than you for me."

5. On the contrary, foolish men are more apt to consider what they have lost, than what they possess; and to fix their eyes upon those who are richer than themselves, rather than on those who are under greater difficulties. All the real pleasures and conveniences of life lie in a narrow compass; but it is the humour of mankind to be always looking forward; and straining after one who has got the start of them in wealth and honour.

6. For this reason, as none can be properly called rich, who have not more than they want, there are few rich men in any of the politer nations, but among the middle sort of people, who keep their wishes within their fortunes, and have more wealth than they know how to enjoy.

7. Persons of a higher rank live in a kind of splendid poverty; and are perpetually wanting, because, instead of acquiescing in the solid pleasures of life, they endeavour to outvie one another in shadows and appearances. Men of sense have at all times beheld, with a great deal of mirth, this silly game that is playing over their heads; and, by contracting their desires, they enjoy all that secret satisfaction which others are always in quest of.

8. The truth is, this ridiculous chase after imaginary pleasures, cannot be sufficiently exposed, as it is the great source of those evils which generally undo a nation. Let a man's estate be what it may, he is a poor man, if he does not live within it; and naturally sets himself to sale to any one that can give him his price.

9. When Pittacus, after the death of his brother, who had left him a good estate, was offered a great sum of money by the king of Lydia, he thanked him for his kindness; but told him, he had already more by half than he knew what to do with. In short, content is equivalent to wealth, and luxury to poverty: or, to give the thought a more agreeable turn, "Content is natural wealth," says Socrates; to which I shall add, luxury is artificial poverty.

10. I shall therefore recommend to the consideration of those, who are always aiming at superfluous and imaginary enjoyments, and who will not be at the trouble of contracting their desires, an excellent saying of Bion the philosopher, namely, "That no man has so much care, as he who endeavours after the most happiness."

11. In the second place, every one ought to reflect how much more unhappy he might be, than he really is.—The former consideration took in all those, who are sufficiently provided with the means to make themselves easy; this regards such as actually lie under some pressure or misfortune. These may receive great alleviation, from such a comparison as the unhappy person may make between himself and others; or between the misfortune which he suffers, and greater misfortunes which might have befallen him.

12. I like the story of the honest Dutchman, who, upon breaking his leg by a fall from the main-mast, told the standers by, it was a great mercy that it was not his neck. To which, since I am got into quotations, give me leave to add the saying of an old philosopher, who, after having invited some of his friends to dine with him, was ruffled by a person that came into the room in a passion, and threw down the table that stood before them: "Every one," says he, "has his calamity; and he is a happy man that has no greater than this."

13. We find an instance to the same purpose, in the life of doc

tor Hammond, written by bishop Fell. As this good man was troubled with a complication of distempers, when he had the gout upon him, he used to thank God that it was not the stone; and when he had the stone, that he had not both these distempers on him at the same time.

14. I cannot conclude this essay without observing, that there never was any system besides that of Christianity, which could effectually produce in the mind of man the virtue I have been hitherto speaking of. In order to make us contented with our condition, many of the present philosophers tell us, that our discontent only hurts ourselves, without being able to make any alteration in our circumstances; others, that whatever evil befalls us is derived to us by a fatal necessity, to which superior beings themselves are subject; while others, very gravely, tell the man who is miserable, that it is necessary he should be so, to keep up the harmony of the universe; and that the scheme of Providence would be troubled and perverted, were he otherwise.

15. These, and the like considerations, rather silence than satisfy a man. They may show him that his discontent is unreasonable, but they are by no means sufficient to relieve it. They rather give despair than consolation. In a word, a man might reply to one of these comforters, as Augustus did to his friend, who advised him not to grieve for the death of a person whom he loved, because his grief could not fetch him again: "It is for that very reason," said the emperor, "that I grieve."

16. On the contrary, religion bears a more tender regard to human nature. It prescribes to every miserable man the means of bettering his condition: nay, it shows him, that bearing his afflictions as he ought to do, will naturally end in the removal of them. It makes him easy here, because it can make him happy hereafter.

ADDISON.

## SECTION XII.
*Rank and riches afford no ground for envy.*

1. OF all the grounds of envy among men, superiority in rank and fortune is the most general. Hence, the malignity which the poor commonly bear to the rich, as engrossing to themselves all the comforts of life. Hence, the evil eye with which persons of inferior station scrutinize those who are above them in rank; and if they approach to that rank, their envy is generally strongest against such as are just one step higher than themselves.

2. Alas! my friends, all this envious disquietude, which agitates the world, arises from a deceitful figure which imposes on the public view. False colours are hung out: the real state of men is not what it seems to be. The order of society requires a distinction of ranks to take place: but in point of happiness, all men come much nearer to equality than is commonly imagined; and the circumstances, which form any material difference of happiness among them, are not of that nature which renders them grounds of envy.

3. The poor man possesses not, it is true, some of the conveniences and pleasures of the rich; but, in return he is free from many embarrassments to which they are subject. By the simplicity and uniformity of his life, he is delivered from that variety of cares, which perplex those who have great affairs to manage, in-

tricate plans to pursue, many enemies, perhaps, to encounter in the pursuit.

4. In the tranquillity of his small habitation, and private family, he enjoys a peace which is often unknown at courts. The gratifications of nature, which are always the most satisfactory, are possessed by him to their full extent; and if he be a stranger to the refined pleasures of the wealthy, he is unacquainted also with the desire of them, and by consequence, feels no want.

5. His plain meal satisfies his appetite, with a relish probably higher than that of the rich man, who sits down to his luxurious banquet. His sleep is more sound; his health more firm; he knows not what spleen, languor, and listlessness are. His accustomed employments or labours are not more oppressive to him, than the labour of attendance on courts and the great, the labours of dress, the fatigue of amusements, the very weight of idleness, frequently are to the rich.

6. In the mean time, all the beauty of the face of nature, all the enjoyments of domestic society, all the gaiety and cheerfulness of an easy mind, are as open to him as to those of the highest rank. The splendour of retinue, the sound of titles, the appearances of high respect, are indeed soothing, for a short time, to the great. But, become familiar, they are soon forgotten. Custom effaces their impression. They sink into the rank of those ordinary things, which daily recur, without raising any sensation of joy.

7. Let us cease, therefore, from looking up with discontent and envy to those, whom birth or fortune has placed above us. Let us adjust the balance of happiness fairly. When we think of the enjoyments we want, we should think also of the troubles from which we are free. If we allow their just value to the comforts we possess, we shall find reason to rest satisfied, with a very moderate, though not an opulent and splendid, condition of fortune. Often, did we know the whole, we should be inclined to pity the state of those whom we now envy. BLAIR.

## SECTION XIII.
*Patience under provocations our interest as well as duty.*

1. The wide circle of human society is diversified by an endless variety of characters, dispositions, and passions. Uniformity is, in no respect, the genius of the world. Every man is marked by some peculiarity which distinguishes him from another: and no where can two individuals be found, who are exactly and in all respects, alike. Where so much diversity obtains, it cannot but happen, that in the intercourse which men are obliged to maintain, their tempers will often be ill adjusted to that intercourse; will jar, and interfere with each other.

2. Hence, in every station, the highest as well as the lowest, and in every condition of life, public, private, and domestic, occasions of irritation frequently arise. We are provoked, sometimes, by the folly and levity of those with whom we are connected; sometimes, by their indifference or neglect; by the incivility of a friend, the haughtiness of a superior, or the insolent behaviour of one in lower station.

3. Hardly a day passes, without somewhat or other occurring, which serves to ruffle the man of impatient spirit. Of course, such a man lives in a continual storm. He knows not what it is to

enjoy a train of good humour. Servants, neighbours, friends, spouse, and children, all, through the unrestrained violence of his temper, become sources of disturbance and vexation to him. In vain is affluence; in vain are health and prosperity. The least trifle is sufficient to discompose his mind, and poison his pleasures. His very amusements are mixed with turbulence and passion.

4. I would beseech this man to consider, of what small moment the provocations which he receives, or at least imagines himself to receive, are really in themselves; but of what great moment he makes them, by suffering them to deprive him of the possession of himself. I would beseech him, to consider, how many hours of happiness he throws away, which a little more patience would allow him to enjoy: and how much he puts it in the power of the most insignificant persons to render him miserable.

5. "But who can expect," we hear him exclaim, "that he is to possess the insensibility of a stone? How is it possible for human nature to endure so many repeated provocations? or to bear calmly with so unreasonable behaviour?"—My brother! if thou canst bear with no instances of unreasonable behaviour, withdraw thyself from the world. Thou art no longer fit to live in it. Leave the intercourse of men. Retreat to the mountain, and the desert; or shut thyself up in a cell. For here, in the midst of society, *offences must come.*

6. We might as well expect, when we behold a calm atmosphere, and a clear sky, that no clouds were ever to rise, and no winds to blow, as that our life were long to proceed, without receiving provocations from human frailty. The careless and the imprudent, the giddy and the fickle, the ungrateful and the interested, every where meet us. They are the briers and thorns, with which the paths of human life are beset. He only, who can hold his course among them with patience and equanimity, he who is prepared to bear what he must expect to happen, is worthy of the name of a man.

7. If we preserved ourselves composed but for a moment, we should perceive the insignificancy of most of those provocations which we magnify so highly. When a few suns more have rolled over our heads, the storm will, of itself, have subsided; the cause of our present impatience and disturbance will be utterly forgotten. Can we not then, anticipate this hour of calmness to ourselves; and begin to enjoy the peace which it will certainly bring?

8. If others have behaved improperly, let us leave them to their own folly, without becoming the victim of their caprice, and punishing ourselves on their account.—Patience, in this exercise of it, cannot be too much studied by all who wish their life to flow in a smooth stream. It is the reason of a man, in opposition to the passion of a child. It is the enjoyment of peace, in opposition to uproar and confusion. BLAIR.

## SECTION XIV.
*Moderation in our wishes recommended*

1. THE active mind of man seldom or never rests satisfied with its present condition, how prosperous soever. Originally formed for a wider range of objects, for a higher sphere of enjoyments, it finds itself, in every situation of fortune, straitened and confined. Sensible of deficiency in its state, it is ever sending forth the fond

desire, the aspiring wish, after something beyond what is enjoyed at present.

2. Hence, that restlessness which prevails so generally among mankind. Hence, that disgust of pleasures which they have tried; that passion for novelty; that ambition of rising to some degree of eminence or felicity, of which they have formed to themselves an indistinct idea. All which may be considered as indications of a certain native, original greatness in the human soul, swelling beyond the limits of its present condition; and pointing to the higher objects for which it was made. Happy, if these latent remains of our primitive state, served to direct our wishes towards their proper destination, and to lead us into the path of true bliss.

3. But in this dark and bewildered state, the aspiring tendency of our nature unfortunately takes an opposite direction, and feeds a very misplaced ambition. The flattering appearances which here present themselves to sense; the distinctions which fortune confers; the advantages and pleasures which we imagine the world to be capable of bestowing, fill up the ultimate wish of most men. These are the objects which engross their solitary musings, and stimulate their active labours; which warm the breasts of the young, animate the industry of the middle aged, and often keep alive the passions of the old, until the very close of life.

4. Assuredly, there is nothing unlawful in our wishing to be freed from whatever is disagreeable, and to obtain a fuller enjoyment of the comforts of life. But when these wishes are not tempered by reason, they are in danger of precipitating us into much extravagance and folly. Desires and wishes are the first springs of action. When they become exorbitant, the whole character is likely to be tainted.

5. If we suffer our fancy to create to itself worlds of ideal happiness, we shall discompose the peace and order of our minds, and foment many hurtful passions. Here, then, let moderation begin its reign; by bringing within reasonable bounds the wishes that we form. As soon as they become extravagant, let us check them, by proper reflections on the fallacious nature of those objects, which the world hangs out to allure desire.

6. You have strayed, my friends, from the road which conducts to felicity; you have dishonoured the native dignity of your souls, in allowing your wishes to terminate on nothing higher than worldly ideas of greatness or happiness. Your imagination roves in a land of shadows. Unreal forms deceive you. It is no more than a phantom, an illusion of happiness, which attracts your fond admiration; nay, an illusion of happiness, which often conceals much real misery.

7. Do you imagine that all are happy, who have attained to those summits of distinction, towards which your wishes aspire? Alas! how frequently has experience shown, that where roses were supposed to bloom, nothing but briers and thorns grew! Reputation, beauty, riches, grandeur, nay, royalty itself, would, many a time, have been gladly exchanged by the possessors, for that more quiet and humble station, with which you are now dissatisfied.

8. With all that is splendid and shining in the world, it is decreed that there should mix many deep shades of wo. On the ele-

vated situations of fortune, the great calamities of life chiefly fall. There, the storm spends its violence, and there, the thunder breaks; while, safe and unhurt, the inhabitants of the vale remain below;—Retreat, then, from those vain and pernicious excursions of extravagant desire.

9. Satisfy yourselves with what is rational and attainable. Train your minds to moderate views of human life, and human happiness. Remember, and admire, the wisdom of Agur's petition: "Remove far from me vanity and lies. Give me neither poverty nor riches. Feed me with food convenient for me: lest I be full and deny thee; and say, who is the Lord? or lest I be poor, and steal, and take the name of my God in vain." BLAIR.

## SECTION XV.
*Omniscience and omnipresence of the* DEITY, *the source of consolation to good men.*

1. I WAS yesterday, about sunset, walking in the open fields, till the night insensibly fell upon me. I at first amused myself with all the richness and variety of colours, which appeared in the western parts of heaven. In proportion as they faded away and went out, several stars and planets appeared one after another, till the whole firmament was in a glow.

2. The blueness of the ether was exceedingly heightened and enlivened, by the season of the year, and the rays of all those luminaries that passed through it. The galaxy appeared in its most beautiful white. To complete the scene, the full moon rose, at length, in that clouded majesty, which Milton takes notice of; and opened to the eye a new picture of nature, which was more finely shaded, and disposed among softer lights than that which the sun had before discovered to us.

3. As I was surveying the moon walking in her brightness, and taking her progress among the constellations, a thought arose in me, which I believe very often perplexes and disturbs men of serious and contemplative natures. David himself fell into it in that reflection; "When I consider the heavens, the work of thy fingers; the moon and the stars which thou hast ordained; what is man that thou art mindful of him, and the son of man that thou regardest him!"

4. In the same manner, when I considered that infinite host of stars, or, to speak more philosophically, of suns, which were then shining upon me; with those innumerable sets of planets or worlds, which were moving round their respective suns; when I still enlarged the idea, and supposed another heaven of suns and worlds, rising still above this which we discovered; and these still enlightened by a superior firmament of luminaries, which are planted at so great a distance, that they may appear to the inhabitants of the former, as the stars do to us: in short, while I pursued this thought, I could not but reflect on that little insignificant figure which I myself bore amidst the immensity of God's works.

5. Were the sun, which enlightens this part of the creation, with all the host of planetary worlds that move above him, utterly extinguished and annihilated, they would not be missed, more than a grain of sand upon the sea-shore. The space they possess is so exceedingly little in comparison of the whole, it would scarcely make a blank in the creation. The chasm would be impercep-

tible to an eye, that could take in the whole compass of nature, and pass from one end of the creation to the other; as it is possible there may be such a sense in ourselves hereafter, or in creatures which are at present more exalted than ourselves. By the help of glasses, we see many stars, which we do not discover with our naked eyes; and the finer our telescopes are, the more still are our discoveries.

6. Huygenius carries this thought so far, that he does not think it impossible there may be stars, whose light has not yet travelled down to us, since their first creation. There is no question that the universe has certain bounds set to it; but when we consider that it is the work of Infinite Power, prompted by Infinite Goodness, with an infinite space to exert itself in, how can our imaginations set any bounds to it?

7. To return, therefore, to my first thought, I could not but look upon myself with secret horror, as a being that was not worth the smallest regard of one who had so great a work under his care and superintendency. I was afraid of being overlooked amidst the immensity of nature; and lost among that infinite variety of creatures, which, in all probability, swarm through all these immeasurable regions of matter.

8. In order to recover myself from this mortifying thought, I considered that it took its rise from those narrow conceptions, which we are apt to entertain of the Divine Nature. We ourselves cannot attend to many different objects at the same time. If we are careful to inspect some things, we must of course neglect others. This imperfection which we observe in ourselves, is an imperfection that cleaves, in some degree, to creatures of the highest capacities, as they are creatures, that is, beings of finite and limited natures.

9. The presence of every created being is confined to a certain measure of space; and consequently his observation is stinted to a certain number of objects. The sphere in which we move, and act, and understand, is of a wider circumference to one creature, than another, according as we rise one above another in the scale of existence. But the widest of these our spheres has its circumference.

10. When, therefore, we reflect on the Divine Nature, we are so used and accustomed to this imperfection in ourselves, that we cannot forbear, in some measure, ascribing it to HIM, in whom there is no shadow of imperfection. Our reason indeed assures us, that his attributes are infinite; but the poorness of our conceptions is such, that it cannot forbear setting bounds to every thing it contemplates, till our reason comes again to our succour, and throws down all those little prejudices, which rise in us unawares, and are natural to the mind of man.

11. We shall therefore utterly extinguish this melancholy thought, of our being overlooked by our Maker, in the multiplicity of his works, and the infinity of those objects among which he seems to be incessantly employed, if we consider, in the first place, that he is omnipresent; and in the second, that he is omniscient.

12. If we consider him in his omnipresence, his being passes through, actuates, and supports, the whole frame of nature. His creation, in every part of it, is full of him. There is nothing he

has made, which is either so distant, so little, or so inconsiderable, that he does not essentially reside in it. His substance is within the substance of every being, whether material or immaterial, and as intimately present to it, as that being is to itself.

13. It would be an imperfection in him, were he able to move out of one place into another; or to withdraw himself from any thing he has created, or from any part of that space which he diffused and spread abroad to infinity. In short, to speak of him in the language of the old philosophers, he is a being whose centre is every where, and his circumference no where.

14. In the second place, he is omniscient as well as omnipresent. His omniscience, indeed, necessarily and naturally flows from his omnipresence. He cannot but be conscious of every motion that arises in the whole material world, which he thus essentially pervades; and of every thought that is stirring in the intellectual world, to every part of which he is thus intimately united.

15. Were the soul separated from the body, and should it with one glance of thought start beyond the bounds of the creation; should it for millions of years, continue its progress through infinite space, with the same activity, it would still find itself within the embrace of its Creator, and encompassed by the immensity of the Godhead.

16. In this consideration of the Almighty's omnipresence and omniscience, every uncomfortable thought vanishes. He cannot but regard every thing that has being, especially such of his creatures who fear they are not regarded by him. He is privy to all their thoughts, and to that anxiety of heart in particular, which is apt to trouble them on this occasion; for, as it is impossible he should overlook any of his creatures, so we may be confident that he regards with an eye of mercy, those who endeavour to recommend themselves to his notice; and in unfeigned humility of heart, think themselves unworthy that he should be mindful of them.

ADDISON.

## CHAPTER IV.
### ARGUMENTATIVE PIECES.
### SECTION I.
*Happiness is founded in rectitude of conduct.*

1. ALL men pursue good, and would be happy, if they knew how: not happy for minutes, and miserable for hours; but happy, if possible, through every part of their existence. Either, therefore, there is a good of this steady, durable kind, or there is not. If not, then all good must be transient and uncertain; and if so, an object of the lowest value, which can little deserve our attention or inquiry.

2. But if there be a better good, such a good as we are seeking, like every other thing, it must be derived from some cause; and that cause must either be external, internal, or mixed; in as much as, except these three, there is no other possible. Now a steady, durable good, cannot be derived from an external cause; since all derived from externals must fluctuate as they fluctuate.

3. By the same rule, it cannot be derived from a mixture of the

two; because the part which is external, will proportionably destroy its essence. What then remains but the cause internal? the very cause which we have supposed, when we place the sovereign good in mind,—in rectitude of conduct. HARRIS.

## SECTION II.
### *Virtue and piety man's highest interest.*

1. I FIND myself existing upon a little spot, surrounded every way by an immense unknown expansion.—Where am I? What sort of place do I inhabit? Is it exactly accommodated in every instance to my convenience? Is there no excess of cold, none of heat, to offend me? Am I never annoyed by animals, either of my own, or a different kind? Is every thing subservient to me, as though I had ordered all myself? No—nothing like it—the farthest from it possible.

2. The world appears not, then, originally made for the private convenience of me alone?—It does not. But is it not possible so to accommodate it, by my own particular industry? If to accommodate man and beast, heaven and earth, if this be beyond me, it is not possible. What consequence then follows; or can there be any other than this—If I seek an interest of my own detached from that of others, I seek an interest which is chimerical, and which can never have existence.

3. How then must I determine? Have I no interest at all? If I have not, I am stationed here to no purpose. But why no interest? Can I be contented with none but one separate and detached? Is a social interest, joined with others, such an absurdity as not to be admitted? The bee, the beaver, and the tribes of herding animals, are sufficient to convince me, that the thing is somewhere at least possible.

4. How, then, am I assured that it is not equally true of man? Admit it; and what follows? If so, then honour and justice are my interest; then the whole train of moral virtues are my interest; without some portion of which, not even thieves can maintain society.

5. But, farther still—I stop not here—I pursue this social interest as far as I can trace my several relations. I pass from my own stock, my own neighbourhood, my own nation, to the whole race of mankind, as dispersed throughout the earth. Am I not related to them all, by the mutual aids of commerce, by the general intercourse of arts and letters, by that common nature of which we all participate?

6. Again—I must have food and clothing. Without a proper genial warmth, I instantly perish. Am I not related, in this view, to the very earth itself; to the distant sun, from whose beams I derive vigour? to that stupendous course and order of the infinite host of heaven, by which the times and seasons ever uniformly pass on?

7. Were this order once confounded, I could not probably survive a moment; so absolutely do I depend on this common general welfare. What, then, have I to do, but to enlarge virtue into piety? Not only honour and justice, and what I owe to man, is my interest; but gratitude also, acquiescence, resignation, adoration, and all I owe to this great polity, and its great Governor our common Parent. HARRIS.

## SECTION III.
*The injustice of an uncharitable spirit.*

1. A SUSPICIOUS, uncharitable spirit is not only inconsistent with all social virtue and happiness, but it is also, in itself, unreasonable and unjust. In order to form sound opinions concerning characters and actions, two things are especially requisite, information and impartiality. But such as are most forward to decide unfavourably, are commonly destitute of both. Instead of possessing, or even requiring, full information, the grounds on which they proceed are frequently the most slight and frivolous.

2. A tale, perhaps, which the idle have invented, the inquisitive have listened to, and the credulous have propagated; or a real incident which rumour, in carrying it along, has exaggerated and disguised, supplies them with materials of confident assertion, and decisive judgment. From an action they presently look into the heart, and infer the motive. This supposed motive they conclude to be the ruling principle; and pronounce at once concerning the whole character.

3. Nothing can be more contrary both to equity and to sound reason, than this precipitate judgment. Any man who attends to what passes within himself, may easily discern what a complicated system the human character is; and what a variety of circumstances must be taken into the account, in order to estimate it truly. No single instance of conduct whatever, is sufficient to determine it.

4. As from one worthy action, it were credulity, not charity, to conclude a person to be free from all vice; so from one which is censurable, it is perfectly unjust to infer that the author of it is without conscience, and without merit. If we knew all the attending circumstances, it might appear in an excusable light; nay, perhaps, under a commendable form. The motives of the actor may have been entirely different from those which we ascribe to him; and where we suppose him impelled by bad design, he may have been prompted by conscience and mistaken principle.

5. Admitting the action to have been in every view criminal, he may have been hurried into it through inadvertency and surprise. He may have sincerely repented; and the virtuous principle may have now regained its full vigour. Perhaps this was the corner of frailty; the quarter on which he lay open to the incursions of temptation; while the other avenues of his heart were firmly guarded by conscience.

6. It is therefore evident, that no part of the government of temper deserves attention more, than to keep our minds pure from uncharitable prejudices, and open to candour and humanity in judging of others. The worst consequences, both to ourselves and to society, follow from the opposite spirit. BLAIR.

## SECTION IV.
*The misfortunes of men mostly chargeable on themselves.*

1. WE find man placed in a world, where he has by no means the disposal of the events that happen. Calamities sometimes befall the worthiest and the best, which it is not in their power to prevent, and where nothing is left them, but to acknowledge, and to submit to, the high hand of Heaven. For such visitations of trial, many good and wise reasons can be assigned, which the present subject leads me not to discuss.

## ARGUMENTATIVE PIECES.

2. But though those unavoidable calamities make a part, yet they make not the chief part, of the vexations and sorrows that distress human life. A multitude of evils beset us, for the source of which we must look to another quarter.—No sooner has any thing in the health, or in the circumstances of men, gone cross to their wish, than they begin to talk of the unequal distribution of the good things of this life; they envy the condition of others; they repine at their own lot, and fret against the Ruler of the world.

3. Full of these sentiments, one man pines under a broken constitution. But let us ask him, whether he can, fairly and honestly, assign no cause for this but the unknown decree of heaven? Has he duly valued the blessing of health, and always observed the rules of virtue and sobriety? Has he been moderate in his life, and temperate in all his pleasures? If now he is only paying the price of his former, perhaps his forgotten indulgences, has he any title to complain, as if he were suffering unjustly?

4. Were we to survey the chambers of sickness and distress, we should often find them peopled with the victims of intemperance and sensuality, and with the children of vicious indolence and sloth. Among the thousands who languish there, we should find the proportion of innocent sufferers to be small. We should see faded youth, premature old age, and the prospect of an untimely grave, to be the portion of multitudes, who, in one way or other, have brought those evils on themselves; while yet these martyrs of vice and folly have the assurance to arraign the hard fate of man, and to "fret against the Lord."

5. But you, perhaps, complain of hardships of another kind; of the injustice of the world; of the poverty which you suffer, and the discouragements under which you labour; of the crosses and disappointments of which your life has been doomed to be full.—Before you give too much scope to your discontent, let me desire you to reflect impartially upon your past train of life.

6. Have not sloth or pride, or ill temper, or sinful passions, misled you often from the path of sound and wise conduct? Have you not been wanting to yourselves in improving those opportunities which Providence offered you, for bettering and advancing your state? If you have chosen to indulge your humour, or your taste, in the gratifications of indolence or pleasure, can you complain because others, in preference to you, have obtained those advantages which naturally belong to useful labours, and honourable pursuits?

7. Have not the consequences of some false steps, into which your passions, or your pleasures, have betrayed you, pursued you through much of your life; tainted, perhaps, your characters, involved you in embarrassments, or sunk you into neglect?—It is an old saying, that every man is the artificer of his own fortune in the world. It is certain, that the world seldom turns wholly against a man, unless through his own fault. "Religion is," in general, "profitable unto all things."

8. Virtue, diligence, and industry, joined with good temper and prudence, have ever been found the surest road to prosperity; and where men fail of attaining it, their want of success is far oftener owing to their having deviated from that road, than to their having encountered insuperable bars in it. Some, by being too artful,

forfeit the reputation of probity. Some, by being too open, are accounted to fail in prudence. Others, by being fickle and changeable, are distrusted by all.

9. The case commonly is, that men seek to ascribe their disappointments to any cause, rather than to their own misconduct; and when they can devise no other cause, they lay them to the charge of Providence. Their folly leads them into vices; their vices into misfortunes; and in their misfortunes they "murmur against Providence."

10. They are doubly unjust towards their Creator. In their prosperity, they are apt to ascribe their success to their own diligence, rather than to his blessing: and in their adversity, they impute their distresses to his providence, not to their own misbehaviour. Whereas, the truth is the very reverse of this. "Every good and every perfect gift cometh from above;" and of evil and misery, man is the author to himself.

11. When, from the condition of individuals, we look abroad to the public state of the world, we meet with more proofs of the truth of this assertion. We see great societies of men torn in pieces by intestine dissensions, tumults, and civil commotions. We see mighty armies going forth, in formidable array, against each other, to cover the earth with blood, and to fill the air with the cries of widows and orphans. Sad evils these are, to which this miserable world is exposed.

12. But are these evils, I beseech you, to be imputed to God? Was it he who sent forth slaughtering armies into the field, or who filled the peaceful city with massacres and blood? Are these miseries any other than the bitter fruit of men's violent and disorderly passions? Are they not clearly to be traced to the ambition and vices of princes, to the quarrels of the great, and to the turbulence of the people?—Let us lay them entirely out of the account, in thinking of Providence; and let us think only of the "foolishness of man."

13. Did man control his passions, and form his conduct according to the dictates of wisdom, humanity, and virtue, the earth would no longer be desolated by cruelty; and human societies would live in order, harmony, and peace. In those scenes of mischief and violence which fill the world, let man behold, with shame, the picture of his vices, his ignorance, and folly. Let him be humbled by the mortifying view of his own perverseness; but let not his "heart fret against the Lord." BLAIR.

### SECTION V.
#### On disinterested friendship.

1. I AM informed that certain Greek writers (philosophers, it seems, in the opinion of their countrymen) have advanced some very extraordinary positions relating to friendship; as, indeed, what subject is there, which these subtle geniuses have not tortured with their sophistry?

2. The authors to whom I refer, dissuade their disciples from entering into any strong attachments, as unavoidably creating supernumerary disquietudes to those who engage in them; and, as every man has more than sufficient to call forth his solicitude, in the course of his own affairs, it is a weakness, they contend, anxiously to involve himself in the concerns of others.

3. They recommend it also, in all connexions of this kind, to hold the bands of union extremely loose; so as always to have it in one's power to straiten or relax them, as circumstances and situations shall render most expedient. They add, as a capital article of their doctrine, that, "to live exempt from cares, is an essential ingredient to constitute human happiness: but an ingredient, however, which he, who voluntarily distresses himself with cares, in which he has no necessary and personal interest, must never hope to possess."

4. I have been told likewise, that there is another set of pretended philosophers, of the same country, whose tenets, concerning this subject, are of a still more illiberal and ungenerous cast. The proposition they attempt to establish, is, that "friendship is an affair of self-interest entirely; and that the proper motive for engaging in it, is, not in order to gratify the kind and benevolent affections, but for the benefit of that assistance and support which are to be derived from the connexion."

5. Accordingly they assert, that those persons are most disposed to have recourse to auxiliary alliances of this kind, who are least qualified by nature, or fortune, to depend upon their own strength and powers: the weaker sex, for instance, being generally more inclined to engage in friendships, than the male part of our species; and those who are depressed by indigence, or labouring under misfortunes, than the wealthy and the prosperous.

6. Excellent and obliging sages, these, undoubtedly! To strike out the friendly affections from the moral world, would be like extinguishing the sun in the natural; each of them being the source of the best and most grateful satisfactions, that Heaven has conferred on the sons of men. But I should be glad to know, what the real value of this boasted exemption from care, which they promise their disciples, justly amounts to? an exemption flattering to self-love, I confess; but which, upon many occurrences in human life, should be rejected with the utmost disdain.

7. For nothing, surely, can be more inconsistent with a well-poised and manly spirit, than to decline engaging in any laudable action, or to be discouraged from persevering in it, by an apprehension of the trouble and solicitude, with which it may probably be attended.

8. Virtue herself, indeed, ought to be totally renounced, if it be right to avoid every possible means that may be productive of uneasiness: for who, that is actuated by her principles, can observe the conduct of an opposite character, without being affected with some degree of secret dissatisfaction?

9. Are not the just, the brave, and the good, necessarily exposed to the disagreeable emotions of dislike and aversion, when they respectively meet with instances of fraud, of cowardice, or of villany? It is an essential property of every well-constituted mind, to be affected with pain, or pleasure, according to the nature of those moral appearances that present themselves to observation.

10. If sensibility, therefore, be not incompatible with true wisdom, (and it surely is not, unless we suppose that philosophy deadens every finer feeling of our nature,) what just reason can be assigned, why the sympathetic sufferings which may result from friendship, should be a sufficient inducement for banishing that generous affection from the human breast?

11. Extinguish all emotions of the heart, and what difference will remain, I do not say between man and brute, but between man and a mere inanimate clod? Away then with those austere philosophers, who represent virtue as hardening the soul against all the softer impressions of humanity!

12. The fact, certainly, is much otherwise. A truly good man is, upon many occasions, extremely susceptible of tender sentiments; and his heart expands with joy, or shrinks with sorrow, as good or ill fortune accompanies his friend. Upon the whole, then, it may fairly be concluded, that, as in the case of virtue, so in that of friendship, those painful sensations, which may sometimes be produced by the one, as well as by the other, are equally insufficient grounds for excluding either of them from taking possession of our bosoms.

13. They who insist that "utility is the first and prevailing motive, which induces mankind to enter into particular friendships," appear to me to divest the association of its most amiable and engaging principle. For to a mind rightly disposed, it is not so much the benefits received, as the affectionate zeal from which they flow, that gives them their best and most valuable recommendation.

14. It is so far indeed from being verified by fact, that a sense of our wants is the original cause of forming these amicable alliances; that, on the contrary, it is observable, that none have been more distinguished in their friendships than those, whose power and opulence, but, above all, whose superior virtue, (a much firmer support,) have raised them above every necessity of having recourse to the assistance of others.

15. The true distinction then, in this question, is, that "although friendship is certainly productive of utility, yet utility is not the primary motive of friendship." Those selfish sensualists, therefore, who, lulled in the lap of luxury, presume to maintain the reverse, have surely no claim to attention; as they are neither qualified by reflection, nor experience, to be competent judges of the subject.

16. Is there a man upon the face of the earth, who would deliberately accept of all the wealth, and all the affluence this world can bestow, if offered to him upon the severe terms of his being unconnected with a single mortal whom he could love, or by whom he should be beloved? This would be to lead the wretched life of a detested tyrant, who, amidst perpetual suspicions and alarms, passes his miserable days a stranger to every tender sentiment; and utterly precluded from the heart-felt satisfactions of friendship.

*Melmoth's translation of Cicero's Lælius.*

### SECTION VI.
*On the immortality of the soul.*

1. I WAS yesterday walking alone, in one of my friend's woods; and lost myself in it very agreeably, as I was running over, in my mind, the several arguments that establish this great point; which is the basis of morality, and the source of all the pleasing hopes, and secret joys, that can arise in the heart of a reasonable creature.

2. I considered those several proofs drawn—First, from the nature of the soul itself, and particularly its immateriality; which, though not absolutely necessary to the eternity of its duration, has, I think, been evinced to almost a demonstration.

3. Secondly, from its passions and sentiments; as, particularly,

from its love of existence; its horror of annihilation; and its hopes of immortality; with that secret satisfaction which it finds in the practice of virtue; and that uneasiness which follows upon the commission of vice.—Thirdly, from the nature of the Supreme Being, whose justice, goodness, wisdom, and veracity, are all concerned in this point.

4. But among these, and other excellent arguments for the immortality of the soul, there is one drawn from the perpetual progress of the soul to its perfection, without a possibility of ever arriving at it; which is a hint that I do not remember to have seen opened and improved by others, who have written on this subject, though it seems to me to carry a very great weight with it.

5. How can it enter into the thoughts of man, that the soul, which is capable of immense perfections, and of receiving new improvements to all eternity, shall fall away into nothing, almost as soon as it is created? Are such abilities made for no purpose? A brute arrives at a point of perfection, that he can never pass: in a few years he has all the endowments he is capable of; and were he to live ten thousand more, would be the same thing he is at present.

6. Were a human soul thus at a stand in her accomplishments; were her faculties to be full blown, and incapable of farther enlargements; I could imagine she might fall away insensibly, and drop at once into a state of annihilation. But can we believe a thinking being that is in a perpetual progress of improvement, and travelling on from perfection to perfection, after having just looked abroad into the works of her Creator, and made a few discoveries of his infinite goodness, wisdom, and power, must perish at her first setting out, and in the very beginning of her inquiries?

7. Man, considered only in his present state, seems sent into the world merely to propagate his kind. He provides himself with a successor; and immediately quits his post to make room for him. He does not seem born to enjoy life, but to deliver it down to others. This is not surprising to consider in animals, which are formed for our use, and which can finish their business in a short life.

8. The silk-worm, after having spun her task, lays her eggs and dies. But a man cannot take in his full measure of knowledge, has not time to subdue his passions, establish his soul in virtue, and come up to the perfection of his nature, before he is hurried off the stage. Would an infinitely wise Being make such glorious creatures for so mean a purpose? Can he delight in the production of such abortive intelligences, such short-lived reasonable beings? Would he give us talents that are not to be exerted? capacities that are never to be gratified?

9. How can we find that wisdom which shines through all his works, in the formation of man, without looking on this world as only a nursery for the next; and without believing that the several generations of rational creatures, which rise up and disappear in such quick successions, are only to receive their first rudiments of existence here, and afterwards to be transplanted into a more friendly climate, where they may spread and flourish to all eternity?

10. There is not, in my opinion, a more pleasing and triumphant consideration in religion, than this of the perpetual progress, which the soul makes towards the perfection of its nature, without

ever arriving at a period in it. To look upon the soul as going on from strength to strength; to consider that she is to shine for ever with new accessions of glory, and brighten to all eternity; that she will be still adding virtue to virtue, and knowledge to knowledge; carries in it something wonderfully agreeable to that ambition, which is natural to the mind of man. Nay, it must be a prospect pleasing to God himself, to see his creation for ever beautifying in his eyes; and drawing nearer to him, by greater degrees of resemblance.

11. Methinks this single consideration, of the progress of a finite spirit to perfection, will be sufficient to extinguish all envy in inferior natures, and all contempt in superior. That cherub, which now appears as a god to a human soul, knows very well that the period will come about in eternity, when the human soul shall be as perfect as he himself now is: nay, when she shall look down upon that degree of perfection as much as she now falls short of it. It is true, the higher nature still advances, and by that means preserves his distance and superiority in the scale of being; but he knows that, how high soever the station is of which he stands possessed at present, the inferior nature will, at length, mount up to it; and shine forth in the same degree of glory.

12. With what astonishment and veneration, may we look into our own souls, where there are such hidden stores of virtue and knowledge, such inexhausted sources of perfection! We know not yet what we shall be; nor will it ever enter into the heart of man, to conceive the glory that will be always in reserve for him. The soul, considered with its Creator, is like one of those mathematical lines, that may draw nearer to another for all eternity, without a possibility of touching it: and can there be a thought so transporting, as to consider ourselves in these perpetual approaches to HIM, who is the standard not only of perfection, but of happiness? ADDISON.

## CHAPTER V.
### DESCRIPTIVE PIECES.
### SECTION I.
#### The Seasons.

1. AMONG the great blessings and wonders of the creation, may be classed the regularities of times and seasons. Immediately after the flood, the sacred promise was made to man, that seed-time and harvest, cold and heat, summer and winter, day and night, should continue to the very end of all things. Accordingly, in obedience to that promise, the rotation is constantly presenting us with some useful and agreeable alteration; and all the pleasing novelty of life arises from these natural changes: nor are we less indebted to them for many of its solid comforts.

2. It has been frequently the task of the moralist and poet, to mark, in polished periods, the particular charms and conveniences of every change; and, indeed, such discriminate observations upon natural variety, cannot be undelightful; since the blessing which every month brings along with it, is a fresh instance of the wisdom and bounty of that Providence, which regulates the

glories of the year. We glow as we contemplate; we feel a propensity to adore, whilst we enjoy.

3. In the time of seed-sowing, it is the season of *confidence:* the grain which the husbandman trusts to the bosom of the earth shall, haply, yield its seven-fold rewards. Spring presents us with a scene of lively *expectation.* That which was before sown, begins now to discover signs of successful vegetation. The labourer observes the change, and anticipates the harvest; he watches the progress of nature, and smiles at her influence: while the man of contemplation walks forth with the evening, amidst the fragrance of flowers, and promises of plenty; nor returns to his cottage till darkness closes the scene upon his eye. Then cometh the harvest, when the large wish is satisfied, and the granaries of nature are loaded with the means of life, even to a luxury of abundance.

4. The powers of language are unequal to the description of this happy season. It is the carnival of nature: sun and shade, coolness and quietude, cheerfulness and melody, love and gratitude, unite to render every scene of summer delightful. The division of light and darkness is one of the kindest efforts of Omnipotent Wisdom. Day and night yield us contrary blessings; and, at the same time, assist each other, by giving fresh lustre to the delights of both. Amidst the glare of day, and bustle of life, how could we sleep? Amidst the gloom of darkness, how could we labour?

5. How wise, how benignant, then, is the proper division! The hours of light are adapted to activity; and those of darkness, to rest. Ere the day is passed, exercise and nature prepare us for the pillow; and by the time that the morning returns, we are again able to meet it with a smile. Thus, every season has a charm peculiar to itself; and every moment affords some interesting innovation. MELMOTH.

## SECTION II.

*The cataract of Niagara, in Canada, North America.*

1. THIS amazing fall of water is made by the river St. Lawrence, in its passage from lake Erie into the lake Ontario. The St. Lawrence is one of the largest rivers in the world; and yet the whole of its waters is discharged in this place, by a fall of a hundred and fifty feet perpendicular. It is not easy to bring the imagination to correspond to the greatness of the scene.

2. A river extremely deep and rapid, and that serves to drain the waters of almost all North America into the Atlantic Ocean, is here poured precipitately down a ledge of rocks, that rises, like a wall, across the whole bed of its stream. The river, a little above, is near three quarters of a mile broad; and the rocks, where it grows narrower, are four hundred yards over.

3. Their direction is not straight across, but hollowing inwards like a horse-shoe: so that the cataract, which bends to the shape of the obstacle, rounding inwards, presents a kind of theatre the most tremendous in nature. Just in the middle of this circular wall of waters, a little island, that has braved the fury of the current, presents one of its points, and divides the stream at top into two parts; but they unite again long before they reach the bottom.

4. The noise of the fall is heard at the distance of several leagues; and the fury of the waters, at the termination of their fall, is in-

conceivable. The dashing produces a mist that rises to the very clouds; and which forms a most beautiful rainbow, when the sun shines. It will be readily supposed, that such a cataract entirely destroys the navigation of the stream; and yet some Indians in their canoes, as it is said, have ventured down it with safety.*

GOLDSMITH.

## SECTION III.
### *The grotto of Antiparos.*

1. Of all the subterranean caverns now known, the grotto of Antiparos is the most remarkable, as well for its extent, as for the beauty of its sparry incrustations. This celebrated cavern was first explored by one Magni, an Italian traveller, about one hundred years ago, at Antiparos, an inconsiderable island of the Archipelago.

2. "Having been informed," says he, "by the natives of Paros, that, in the little island of Antiparos, which lies about two miles from the former, a gigantic statue was to be seen at the mouth of a cavern in that place, it was resolved that we (the French consul and himself) should pay it a visit. In pursuance of this resolution, after we had landed on the island, and walked about four miles through the midst of beautiful plains, and sloping woodlands, we at length came to a little hill, on the side of which yawned a most horrid cavern, that, by its gloom, at first struck us with terror, and almost repressed curiosity.

3. "Recovering the first surprise, however, we entered boldly; and had not proceeded above twenty paces, when the supposed statue of the giant presented itself to our view. We quickly perceived, that what the ignorant natives had been terrified at as a giant, was nothing more than a sparry concretion, formed by the water dropping from the roof of the cave, and by degrees hardening into a figure, which their fears had formed into a monster.

4. "Incited by this extraordinary appearance, we were induced to proceed still further, in quest of new adventures in this subterranean abode. As we proceeded, new wonders offered themselves; the spars, formed into trees and shrubs, presented a kind of petrified grove; some white, some green; and all receding in due perspective. They struck us with the more amazement, as we knew them to be mere productions of nature, who, hitherto in solitude, had, in her playful moments, dressed the scene, as if for her own amusement."

5. "We had as yet seen but a few of the wonders of the place; and we were introduced only into the portico of this amazing temple. In one corner of this half illuminated recess, there appeared an opening of about three feet wide, which seemed to lead to a place totally dark, and which one of the natives assured us contained nothing more than a reservoir of water. Upon this information, we made an experiment, by throwing down some stones, which rumbling along the sides of the descent for some time, the sound seemed at last quashed in a bed of water.

---

* This *venturing down in safety*, is a report, bearing upon its front its own refutation: that it should ever have found a place in the brain or the book of the elegant historian, is a matter of surprise. Canoes and other vessels, with passengers, are, indeed, sometimes unfortunately drawn down the awful declivity, but seldom a vestige of either is ever afterwards seen. The sturdy mountain oak, and the towering pine, frequently take the *desperate leap*, and for ever disappear.

6. "In order, however, to be more certain, we sent in a Levantine mariner, who, by the promise of a good reward, ventured, with a flambeau in his hand, into this narrow aperture. After continuing within it for about a quarter of an hour, he returned, bearing in his hand, some beautiful pieces of white spar, which art could neither equal nor imitate. Upon being informed by him that the place was full of these beautiful incrustations, I ventured in once more with him, about fifty paces, anxiously and cautiously descending, by a steep and dangerous way.

7. "Finding, however, that we came to a precipice which led into a spacious amphitheatre, (if I may so call it,) still deeper than any other part, we returned, and being provided with a ladder, flambeau, and other things to expedite our descent, our whole company, man by man, ventured into the same opening; and descending one after another, we at last saw ourselves all together in the most magnificent part of the cavern."

## SECTION IV.
*The grotto of Antiparos, continued.*

1. "Our candles being now all lighted up, and the whole place completely illuminated, never could the eye be presented with a more glittering, or a more magnificent scene. The whole roof hung with solid icicles, transparent as glass, yet solid as marble. The eye could scarcely reach the lofty and noble ceiling; the sides were regularly formed with spars; and the whole presented the idea of a magnificent theatre, illuminated with an immense profusion of lights.

2. "The floor consisted of solid marble; and, in several places, magnificent columns, thrones, altars, and other objects, appeared, as if nature had designed to mock the curiosities of art. Our voices, upon speaking or singing, were redoubled to an astonishing loudness; and upon the firing of a gun, the noise and reverberations were almost deafening.

3. "In the midst of this grand amphitheatre rose a concretion of about fifteen feet high, that, in some measure, resembled an altar; from which, taking the hint, we caused mass to be celebrated there. The beautiful columns that shot up round the altar, appeared like candlesticks; and many other natural objects represented the customary ornaments of this rite."

4. "Below even this spacious grotto, there seemed another cavern; down which I ventured with my former mariner, and descended about fifty paces by means of a rope. I at last arrived at a small spot of level ground, where the bottom appeared different from that of the amphitheatre, being composed of soft clay, yielding to the pressure, and in which I thrust a stick to the depth of six feet. In this however, as above, numbers of the most beautiful crystals were formed; one of which, particularly, resembled a table.

5. "Upon our egress from this amazing cavern, we perceived a Greek inscription upon a rock at the mouth, but so obliterated by time, that we could not read it distinctly. It seemed to import that one Antipater, in the time of Alexander, had come hither; but whether he penetrated into the depths of the cavern, he does not think fit to inform us."—This account of so beautiful and striking a scene, may serve to give us some idea of the subterraneous wonders of nature. GOLDSMITH.

## SECTION V.
### Earthquake at Catanea.

1. ONE of the earthquakes most particularly described in history, is that which happened in the year 1693; the damages of which were chiefly felt in Sicily, but its motion was perceived in Germany, France, and England. It extended to a circumference of two thousand six hundred leagues; chiefly affecting the sea coasts, and great rivers; more perceivable also upon the mountains than in the valleys.

2. Its motions were so rapid, that persons who lay at their length, were tossed from side to side, as upon a rolling billow. The walls were dashed from their foundations; and no fewer than fifty-four cities, with an incredible number of villages, were either destroyed or greatly damaged. The city of Catanea, in particular, was utterly overthrown. A traveller who was on his way thither, perceived, at the distance of some miles, a black cloud, like night, hanging over the place.

3. The sea, all of a sudden, began to roar; mount Ætna to send forth great spires of flame; and soon after a shock ensued, with a noise as if all the artillery in the world had been at once discharged. Our traveller being obliged to alight instantly, felt himself raised a foot from the ground; and turning his eyes to the city, he with amazement saw nothing but a thick cloud of dust in the air.

4. The birds flew about astonished; the sun was darkened; the beasts ran howling from the hills; and although the shock did not continue above three minutes, yet near nineteen thousand of the inhabitants of Sicily perished in the ruins. Catanea, to which city the describer was travelling, seemed the principal scene of ruin; its place only was to be found; and not a footstep of its former magnificence was to be seen remaining. GOLDSMITH.

## SECTION VI.
### Creation.

1. IN the progress of the Divine works and government, there arrived a period, in which this earth was to be called into existence. When the signal moment, predestined from all eternity, was come, the Deity arose in his might; and with a word created the world. —What an illustrious moment was that, when, from non-existence, there sprang at once into being, this mighty globe, on which so many millions of creatures now dwell!

2. No preparatory measures were required. No long circuit of means was employed. "He spake; and it was done: he commanded; and it stood fast. The earth was at first without form, and void; and darkness was on the face of the deep." The Almighty surveyed the dark abyss; and fixed bounds to the several divisions of nature. He said, "Let there be light; and there was light."

3. Then appeared the sea, and the dry land. The mountains rose; and the rivers flowed. The sun and moon began their course in the skies. Herbs and plants clothed the ground. The air, the earth, and the waters, were stored with their respective inhabitants. At last, man was made after the image of God.

4. He appeared, walking with countenance erect; and received his Creator's benediction, as the Lord of this new world. The

Almighty beheld his work when it was finished; and pronounced it GOOD. Superior beings saw with wonder this new accession to existence. "The morning stars sang together; and all the sons of God shouted for joy." BLAIR.

## SECTION VII.
### Charity.

1. CHARITY is the same with benevolence or love; and is the term uniformly employed in the New Testament, to denote all the good affections which we ought to bear towards one another. It consists not in speculative ideas of general benevolence, floating in the head, and leaving the heart, as speculations too often do, untouched and cold. Neither is it confined to that indolent good nature, which makes us rest satisfied with being free from inveterate malice, or ill-will to our fellow-creatures, without prompting us to be of service to any.

2. True charity is an active principle. It is not properly a single virtue; but a disposition residing in the heart, as a fountain whence all the virtues of benignity, candour, forbearance, generosity, compassion, and liberality, flow, as so many native streams. From general good-will to all, it extends its influence particularly to those with whom we stand in nearest connexion, and who are directly with in the sphere of our good offices.

3. From the country or community to which we belong, it descends to the smaller associations of neighbourhood, relations, and friends; and spreads itself over the whole circle of social and domestic life. I mean not that it imports a promiscuous, undistinguished affection, which gives every man an equal title to our love. Charity, if we should endeavour to carry it so far, would be rendered an impracticable virtue; and would resolve itself into mere words, without affecting the heart.

4. True charity attempts not to shut our eyes to the distinction between good and bad men; nor to warm our hearts equally to those who befriend, and those who injure us. It reserves our esteem for good men, and our complacency for our friends. Towards our enemies it inspires forgiveness, humanity, and a solicitude for their welfare. It breathes universal candour, and liberality of sentiment. It forms gentleness of temper, and dictates affability of manners.

5. It prompts corresponding sympathies with them who rejoice, and them who weep. It teaches us to slight and despise no man. Charity is the comforter of the afflicted, the protector of the oppressed, the reconciler of differences, the intercessor for offenders. It is faithfulness in the friend, public spirit in the magistrate, equity and patience in the judge, moderation in the sovereign, and loyalty in the subject.

6. In parents, it is care and attention; in children, it is reverence and submission. In a word, it is the soul of social life. It is the sun that enlivens and cheers the abodes of men. It is "like the dew of Hermon," says the Psalmist, "and the dew that descended on the mountains of Zion, where the Lord commanded the blessing, even life for evermore." BLAIR

## SECTION VIII.
### Prosperity is redoubled to a good man.

1. NONE but the temperate, the regular, and the virtuous, know how to enjoy prosperity. They bring to its comforts the

manly relish of a sound uncorrupted mind. They stop at the proper point, before enjoyment degenerates into disgust, and pleasure is converted into pain. They are strangers to those complaints which flow from spleen, caprice, and all the fantastical distresses of a vitiated mind. While riotous indulgence enervates both the body and the mind, purity and virtue heighten all the powers of human fruition.

2. Feeble are all pleasures in which the heart has no share. The selfish gratifications of the bad, are both narrow in their circle, and short in their duration. But prosperity is redoubled to a good man, by his generous use of it. It is reflected back upon him from every one whom he makes happy. In the intercourse of domestic affection, in the attachment of friends, the gratitude of dependents, the esteem and good-will of all who know him, he sees blessings multiplied round him, on every side.

3. "When the ear heard me, then it blessed me; and when the eye saw me, it gave witness to me: because I delivered the poor that cried, the fatherless, and him that had none to help him. The blessing of him that was ready to perish came upon me, and I caused the widow's heart to sing with joy. I was eyes to the blind, and feet was I to the lame: I was a father to the poor; and the cause which I knew not I searched out."

4. Thus, while the righteous man flourishes like a tree planted by the rivers of water, he brings forth also his fruit in its season: and that fruit he brings forth, not for himself alone. He flourishes, not like a tree in some solitary desert, which scatters its blossoms to the wind, and communicates neither fruit nor shade to any living thing: but like a tree in the midst of an inhabited country, which to some affords friendly shelter, to others fruit; which is not only admired by all for its beauty; but blessed by the traveller for the shade, and by the hungry for the sustenance, it hath given. BLAIR.

## SECTION IX.
### On the beauties of the Psalms.

1. GREATNESS confers no exemption from the cares and sorrows of life: its share of them frequently bears a melancholy proportion to its exaltation. This the monarch of Israel experienced. He sought in piety, that peace which he could not find in empire; and alleviated the disquietudes of state, with the exercises of devotion. His invaluable Psalms convey those comforts to others, which they afforded to himself.

2. Composed upon particular occasions, yet designed for general use; delivered out as services for Israelites under the Law, yet no less adapted to the circumstances of Christians under the Gospel; they present religion to us in the most engaging dress; communicating truths which philosophy could never investigate, in a style which poetry can never equal; while history is made the vehicle of prophecy, and creation lends all its charms to paint the glories of redemption.

3. Calculated alike to profit and to please, they inform the understanding, elevate the affections, and entertain the imagination. Indited under the influence of HIM, to whom all hearts are known, and all events foreknown, they suit mankind in all situations; grateful as the manna which descended from above, and conformed itself to every palate.

4. The fairest productions of human wit, after a few perusals, like gathered flowers, wither in our hands, and lose their fragrancy: but these unfading plants of paradise become, as we are accustomed to them, still more and more beautiful; their bloom appears to be daily heightened; fresh odours are emitted, and new sweets extracted from them. He who has once tasted their excellences, will desire to taste them again; and he who tastes them oftenest, will relish them best.

5. And now, could the author flatter himself, that any one would take half the pleasure in reading his work, which he has taken in writing it, he would not fear the loss of his labour. The employment detached him from the bustle and hurry of life, the din of politics, and the noise of folly. Vanity and vexation flew away for a season; care and disquietude came not near his dwelling. He arose, fresh as the morning, to his task; the silence of the night invited him to pursue it; and he can truly say, that food and rest were not preferred before it.

6. Every psalm improved infinitely upon his acquaintance with it, and no one gave him uneasiness but the last: for then he grieved that his work was done. Happier hours than those which have been spent in these meditations on the songs of Sion, he never expects to see in this world. Very pleasantly did they pass; they moved smoothly and swiftly along: for when thus engaged, he counted no time. They are gone, but they have left a relish and a fragrance upon the mind; and the remembrance of them is sweet.                                                                   HORNE.

## SECTION X.
### *Character of* ALFRED, *king of England.*

1. THE merit of this prince, both in private and public life, may, with advantage, be set in opposition to that of any monarch or citizen, which the annals of any age, or any nation, can present to us. He seems, indeed, to be the complete model of that perfect character, which, under the denomination of a sage or wise man, the philosophers have been fond of delineating, rather as a fiction of their imagination, than in hopes of ever seeing it reduced to practice: so happily were all his virtues tempered together; so justly were they blended: and so powerfully did each prevent the other from exceeding its proper bounds.

2. He knew how to conciliate the most enterprising spirit, with the coolest moderation; the most obstinate perseverance, with the easiest flexibility; the most severe justice, with the greatest lenity; the greatest rigour in command, with the greatest affability of deportment; the highest capacity and inclination for science, with the most shining talents for action.

3. Nature also, as if desirous that so bright a production of her skill should be set in the fairest light, had bestowed on him all bodily accomplishments; vigour of limbs, dignity of shape and air, and a pleasant, engaging, and open countenance. By living in that barbarous age, he was deprived of historians worthy to transmit his fame to posterity; and we wish to see him delineated in more lively colours, and with more particular strokes, that we might at least perceive some of those small specks and blemishes, from which, as a man, it is impossible he could be entirely exempted.
                                                                   HUME

## SECTION XI.
### *Character of* QUEEN ELIZABETH.

1. THERE are few personages in history, who have been more exposed to the calumny of enemies, and the adulation of friends, than queen Elizabeth; and yet there scarcely is any, whose reputation has been more certainly determined by the unanimous consent of posterity. The unusual length of her administration, and the strong features of her character, were able to overcome all prejudices; and, obliging her detractors to abate much of their invectives, and her admirers somewhat of their panegyrics, have, at last, in spite of political factions, and what is more, of religious animosities, produced a uniform judgment with regard to her conduct.

2. Her vigour, her constancy, her magnanimity, her penetration, vigilance, and address, are allowed to merit the highest praises; and appear not to have been surpassed by any person who ever filled a throne: a conduct less rigorous, less imperious, more sincere, more indulgent to her people, would have been requisite to form a perfect character. By the force of her mind, she controlled all her more active, and stronger qualities, and prevented them from running into excess.

3. Her heroism was exempted from all temerity; her frugality from avarice; her friendship from partiality; her enterprise from turbulency and a vain ambition. She guarded not herself, with equal care, or equal success, from less infirmities; the rivalship of beauty, the desire of admiration, the jealousy of love, and the sallies of anger.

4. Her singular talents for government, were founded equally on her temper and on her capacity. Endowed with a great command over herself, she soon obtained an uncontrolled ascendency over the people. Few sovereigns of England succeeded to the throne in more difficult circumstances; and none ever conducted the government with so uniform success and felicity.

5. Though unacquainted with the practice of toleration, the true secret for managing religious factions, she preserved her people, by her superior prudence, from those confusions in which theological controversy had involved all the neighbouring nations; and though her enemies were the most powerful princes of Europe, the most active, the most enterprising, the least scrupulous, she was able, by her vigour, to make deep impressions on their state; her own greatness meanwhile remaining untouched and unimpaired.

6. The wise ministers and brave men who flourished during her reign, share the praise of her success; but, instead of lessening the applause due to her, they make great addition to it. They owed, all of them, their advancement to her choice; they were supported by her constancy; and, with all their ability, they were never able to acquire an undue ascendency over her.

7. In her family, in her court, in her kingdom, she remained equally mistress. The force of the tender passions was great over her, but the force of her mind was still superior: and the combat which her victory visibly cost her, serves only to display the firmness of her resolution, and the loftiness of her ambitious sentiments.

8. The fame of this princess, though it has surmounted the prejudices both of faction and of bigotry, yet lies still exposed to another prejudice, which is more durable, because more natural;

and which, according to the different views in which we survey her, is capable either of exalting beyond measure, or diminishing, the lustre of her character. This prejudice is founded on the consideration of her sex.

9. When we contemplate her as a woman, we are apt to be struck with the highest admiration of her qualities and extensive capacity; but we are also apt to require some more softness of disposition, some greater lenity of temper, some of those amiable weaknesses by which her sex is distinguished. But the true method of estimating her merit, is, to lay aside all these considerations, and to consider her merely as a rational being placed in authority, and intrusted with the government of mankind. HUME.

## SECTION XII.
### *The slavery of vice.*

1. THE slavery produced by vice appears in the dependence under which it brings the sinner, to circumstances of external fortune. One of the favourite characters of liberty, is the independence it bestows. He who is truly a freeman is above all servile compliances, and abject subjection. He is able to rest upon himself; and while he regards his superiors with proper deference, neither debases himself by cringing to them, nor is tempted to purchase their favour by dishonourable means. But the sinner has forfeited every privilege of this nature.

2. His passions and habits render him an absolute dependent on the world, and the world's favour; on the uncertain goods of fortune, and the fickle humours of men. For it is by these he subsists, and among these his happiness is sought; according as his passions determine him to pursue pleasures, riches, or preferments. Having no fund within himself whence to draw enjoyment, his only resource is in things without. His hopes and fears all hang upon the world. He partakes in all its vicissitudes; and is moved and shaken by every wind of fortune. This is to be, in the strictest sense, a slave to the world.

3. Religion and virtue, on the other hand, confer on the mind principles of noble independence. "The upright man is satisfied from himself." He despises not the advantages of fortune, but he centres not his happiness in them. With a moderate share of them he can be contented; and contentment is felicity. Happy in his own integrity, conscious of the esteem of good men, reposing firm trust in the providence, and the promises of God, he is exempted from servile dependence on other things.

4. He can wrap himself up in a good conscience, and look forward, without terror, to the change of the world. Let all things shift around him as they please, he believes that, by the Divine ordination, they shall be made to work together in the issue for his good: and therefore, having much to hope from God, and little to fear from the world, he can be easy in every state. One who possesses within himself such an establishment of mind, is truly free.

5. But shall I call that man free, who has nothing that is his own, no property assured; whose very heart is not his own, but rendered the appendage of external things, and the sport of fortune? Is that man free, let his outward condition be ever so splendid, whom his imperious passions detain at their call, whom they send

forth at their pleasure, to drudge and toil, and to beg his only enjoyment from the casualties of the world?

6. Is he free, who must flatter and lie to compass his ends; who must bear with this man's caprice, and that man's scorn; must profess friendship where he hates, and respect, where he contemns; who is not at liberty to appear in his own colours, nor to speak his own sentiments; who dares not be honest, lest he should be poor?

7. Believe it, no chains bind so hard, no fetters are so heavy, as those which fasten the corrupted heart to this treacherous world; no dependence is more contemptible than that under which the voluptuous, the covetous, or the ambitious man, lies to the means of pleasure, gain, or power. Yet this is the boasted liberty, which vice promises, as the recompense of setting us free from the salutary restraints of virtue. BLAIR.

## SECTION XIII.
*The man of integrity.*

1. It will not take much time to delineate the character of the man of integrity, as by its nature it is a plain one, and easily understood. He is one, who makes it his constant rule to follow the road of duty, according as the word of God, and the voice of his conscience, point it out to him. He is not guided merely by affections, which may sometimes give the colour of virtue to a loose and unstable character.

2. The upright man is guided by a fixed principle of mind, which determines him to esteem nothing but what is honourable; and to abhor whatever is base or unworthy, in moral conduct. Hence we find him ever the same; at all times, the trusty friend, the affectionate relation, the conscientious man of business, the pious worshipper, the public spirited citizen.

3. He assumes no borrowed appearance. He seeks no mask to cover him; for he acts no studied part; but he is indeed what he appears to be, full of truth, candour, and humanity. In all his pursuits, he knows no path, but the fair and direct one; and would much rather fail of success, than attain it by reproachful means.

4. He never shows us a smiling countenance, while he meditates evil against us in his heart. He never praises us among our friends; and then joins in traducing us among our enemies. We shall never find one part of his character at variance with another. In his manners, he is simple and unaffected; in all his proceedings, open and consistent. BLAIR.

## SECTION XIV.
*Gentleness.*

1. I begin with distinguishing true gentleness from passive tameness of spirit, and from unlimited compliance with the manners of others. That passive tameness, which submits, without opposition, to every encroachment of the violent and assuming, forms no part of Christian duty; but, on the contrary, is destructive of general happiness and order. That unlimited complaisance, which, on every occasion, falls in with the opinions and manners of others, is so far from being a virtue, that it is itself a vice, and the parent of many vices.

2. It overthrows all steadiness of principle; and produces that sinful conformity with the world, which taints the whole charac-

ter. In the present corrupted state of human manners, always to assent and to comply, is the very worst maxim we can adopt. It is impossible to support the purity and dignity of Christian morals, without opposing the world on various occasions, even though we should stand alone.

3. That gentleness therefore which belongs to virtue, is to be carefully distinguished from the mean spirit of cowards, and the fawning assent of sycophants. It renounces no just right from fear. It gives up no important truth from flattery. It is indeed not only consistent with a firm mind, but it necessarily requires a manly spirit, and a fixed principle, in order to give it any real value. Upon this solid ground only, the polish of gentleness can with advantage be superinduced.

4. It stands opposed, not to the most determined regard for virtue and truth, but to harshness and severity, to pride and arrogance, to violence and oppression. It is properly, that part of the great virtue of charity, which makes us unwilling to give pain to any of our brethren. Compassion prompts us to relieve their wants. Forbearance prevents us from retaliating their injuries. Meekness restrains our angry passions; candour, our severe judgments.

5. Gentleness corrects whatever is offensive in our manners; and, by a constant train of humane attentions, studies to alleviate the burden of common misery. Its office, therefore, is extensive. It is not, like some other virtues, called forth only on peculiar emergencies; but it is continually in action, when we are engaged in intercourse with men. It ought to form our address, to regulate our speech, and to diffuse itself over our whole behaviour.

6. We must not, however, confound this gentle "wisdom which is from above," with that artificial courtesy, that studied smoothness of manners, which is learned in the school of the world. Such accomplishments, the most frivolous and empty may possess. Too often they are employed by the artful, as a snare; too often affected by the hard and unfeeling, as a cover to the baseness of their minds. We cannot, at the same time, avoid observing the homage, which, even in such instances, the world is constrained to pay to virtue.

7. In order to render society agreeable, it is found necessary to assume somewhat, that may at least carry its appearance. Virtue is the universal charm. Even its shadow is courted, when the substance is wanting. The imitation of its form has been reduced into an art; and, in the commerce of life, the first study of all who would either gain the esteem, or win the hearts of others, is to learn the speech, and to adopt the manners, of candour, gentleness, and humanity.

8. But that gentleness which is the characteristic of a good man, has, like every other virtue, its seat in the heart; and let me add, nothing except what flows from the heart, can render even external manners truly pleasing. For no assumed behaviour can at all times hide the real character. In that unaffected civility which springs from a gentle mind, there is a charm infinitely more powerful, than in all the studied manners of the most finished courtier.

9. True gentleness is founded on a sense of what we owe to HIM who made us, and to the common nature of which we all share.

It arises from reflection on our own failings and wants; and from just views of the condition, and the duty of man. It is native feeling, heightened and improved by principle. It is the heart which easily relents; which feels for every thing that is human; and is backward and slow to inflict the least wound.

10. It is affable in its address, and mild in its demeanour; ever ready to oblige, and willing to be obliged by others; breathing habitual kindness towards friends, courtesy to strangers, long-suffering to enemies. It exercises authority with moderation; administers reproof with tenderness; confers favours with ease and modesty. It is unassuming in opinion, and temperate in zeal. It contends not eagerly about trifles; slow to contradict, and still slower to blame; but prompt to allay dissension, and to restore peace.

11. It neither intermeddles unnecessarily with the affairs, nor pries inquisitively into the secrets of others. It delights above all things to alleviate distress; and, if it cannot dry up the falling tear, to sooth at least the grieving heart. Where it has not the power of being useful, it is never burdensome. It seeks to please, rather than to shine and dazzle; and conceals with care that superiority, either of talents or of rank, which is oppressive to those who are beneath it.

12. In a word, it is that spirit and that tenour of manners, which the gospel of Christ enjoins, when it commands us, "to bear one another's burdens; to rejoice with those who rejoice, and to weep with those who weep; to please every one his neighbour for his good; to be kind and tender-hearted; to be pitiful and courteous; to support the weak, and to be patient towards all men."—BLAIR.

## CHAPTER VI.
### PATHETIC PIECES.
#### SECTION I.

*Trial and execution of the* EARL *of* STRAFFORD, *who fell a sacrifice to the violence of the times, in the reign of* CHARLES *the First.*

1. THE earl of Strafford defended himself against the accusations of the house of Commons, with all the presence of mind, judgment, and sagacity, that could be expected from innocence and ability. His children were placed beside him, as he was thus defending his life, and the cause of his royal master. After he had, in a long and eloquent speech, delivered without premeditation, confuted all the accusations of his enemies, he thus drew to a conclusion.

2. "But, my lords, I have troubled you too long: longer than I should have done, but for the sake of these dear pledges, which a saint in heaven has left me."—Upon this he paused; dropped a tear; looked upon his children; and proceeded.—" What I forfeit for myself is a trifle: that my indiscretions should reach my posterity, wounds me to the heart.

3. "Pardon my infirmity.—Something I should have added, but I am not able: and therefore I let it pass. And now, my lords, for myself. I have long been taught, that the afflictions of this life are overpaid by that eternal weight of glory, which awaits the innocent. And so, my lords, even so, with the utmost tranquillity, I

*Chap.* 6.     PATHETIC PIECES.     77

submit myself to your judgment, whether that judgment be life or death: not my will, but thine, O God, be done!"

4. His eloquence and innocence induced those judges to pity, who were the most zealous to condemn him. The king himself went to the house of lords, and spoke for some time in his defence; but the spirit of vengeance, which had been chained for eleven years, was now roused; and nothing but his blood could give the people satisfaction. He was condemned by both houses of parliament; and nothing remained but for the king to give his consent to the bill of attainder.

5. But in the present commotions, the consent of the king would very easily be dispensed with; and imminent danger might attend his refusal. Charles, however, who loved Strafford tenderly, hesitated, and seemed reluctant; trying every expedient to put off so dreadful an office, as that of signing the warrant for his execution. While he continued in this agitation of mind, and state of suspense, his doubts were at last silenced by an act of great magnanimity in the condemned lord.

6. He received a letter from that unfortunate nobleman, desiring that his life might be made a sacrifice to obtain reconciliation between the king and his people: adding, that he was prepared to die; and that to a willing mind there could be no injury. This instance of noble generosity was but ill repaid by his master, who complied with his request. He consented to sign the fatal bill by commission; and Strafford was beheaded on Tower-hill; behaving with all that composed dignity of resolution, which was expected from his character.     GOLDSMITH.

## SECTION II.

*An eminent instance of true fortitude.*

1. ALL who have been distinguished as servants of God, or benefactors of men; all who, in perilous situations, have acted their part with such honour as to render their names illustrious through succeeding ages, have been eminent for fortitude of mind. Of this we have one conspicuous example in the apostle Paul, whom it will be instructive for us to view in a remarkable occurrence of his life.

2. After having long acted as the apostle of the Gentiles, his mission called him to go to Jerusalem, where he knew that he was to encounter the utmost violence of his enemies. Just before he set sail, he called together the elders of his favourite church at Ephesus; and, in a pathetic speech, which does great honour to his character, gave them his last farewell. Deeply affected by their knowledge of the certain dangers to which he was exposing himself, all the assembly were filled with distress, and melted into tears.

3. The circumstances were such, as might have conveyed dejection even into a resolute mind; and would have totally overwhelmed the feeble. "They all wept sore, and fell on Paul's neck, and kissed him; sorrowing most of all for the words which he spoke, that they should see his face no more."—What were then the sentiments, what was the language, of this great and good man? Hear the words which spoke his firm and undaunted mind.

4. "Behold, I go bound in the spirit, to Jerusalem, not knowing the things that shall befall me there; save that the Holy Spirit witnesseth in every city, saying, that bonds and afflictions abide me. But none of these things move me; neither count I

G 2

my life dear to myself, so that I might finish my course with joy, and the ministry which I have received of the Lord Jesus, to testify the gospel of the grace of God."

5. There was uttered the voice, there breathed the spirit, of a brave and a virtuous man. Such a man knows not what it is to shrink from danger, when conscience points out his path. In that path he is determined to walk, let the consequences be what they may. This was the magnanimous behaviour of that great apostle, when he had persecution and distress full in view.

6. Attend now to the sentiments of the same excellent man, when the time of his last suffering approached; and remark the majesty, and the ease, with which he looked on death. "I am now ready to be offered, and the time of my departure is at hand. I have fought the good fight. I have finished my course. I have kept the faith. Henceforth there is laid up for me a crown of righteousness."

7. How many years of life does such a dying moment overbalance? Who would not choose, in this manner, to go off the stage, with such a song of triumph in his mouth, rather than prolong his existence through a wretched old age, stained with sin and shame?
BLAIR.

## SECTION III.
*The good man's comfort in affliction.*

1. THE religion of Christ not only arms us with fortitude against the approach of evil; but, supposing evils to fall upon us with their heaviest pressure, it lightens the load by many consolations to which others are strangers. While bad men trace, in the calamities with which they are visited, the hand of an offended sovereign, Christians are taught to view them as the well-intended chastisements of a merciful Father.

2. They hear amidst them, that still voice which a good conscience brings to their ear: "Fear not, for I am with thee; be not dismayed, for I am thy God." They apply to themselves the comfortable promises with which the gospel abounds. They discover in these the happy issue decreed to their troubles; and wait with patience till Providence shall have accomplished its great and good designs.

3. In the mean time, Devotion opens to them its blessed and holy sanctuary: that sanctuary in which the wounded heart is healed, and the weary mind is at rest; where the cares of the world are forgotten, where its tumults are hushed, and its miseries disappear; where greater objects open to our view than any which the world presents; where a more serene sky shines, and a sweeter and calmer light beams on the afflicted heart.

4. In those moments of devotion, a pious man, pouring out his wants and sorrows to an Almighty Supporter, feels that he is not left solitary and forsaken in a vale of wo. God is with him; Christ and the holy Spirit are with him; and though he should be bereaved of every friend on earth, he can look up in heaven to a Friend that will never desert him.
BLAIR.

## SECTION IV.
*The close of life.*

1. WHEN we contemplate the close of life; the termination of man's designs and hopes; the silence that now reigns among those

who, a little while ago, were so busy, or so gay; who can avoid being touched with sensations at once awful and tender? What heart but then warms with the glow of humanity? In whose eye does not the tear gather, on revolving the fate of passing and short-lived man?

2. Behold the poor man who lays down at last the burden of his wearisome life. No more shall he groan under the load of poverty and toil. No more shall he hear the insolent calls of the master, from whom he received his scanty wages. No more shall he be raised from needful slumber on his bed of straw, nor be hurried away from his homely meal, to undergo the repeated labours of the day.

3. While his humble grave is preparing, and a few poor and decayed neighbours are carrying him thither, it is good for us to think, that this man too was our brother; that for him the aged and destitute wife, and the needy children, now weep; that, neglected as he was by the world, he possessed, perhaps, both a sound understanding, and a worthy heart; and is now carried by angels to rest in Abraham's bosom.

4. At no great distance from him, the grave is opened to receive the rich and proud man. For, as it is said with emphasis in the parable, "the rich man also died, and was buried." He also died. His riches prevented not his sharing the same fate with the poor man; perhaps, through luxury, they accelerated his doom. Then, indeed, "the mourners go about the streets;" and, while, in all the pomp and magnificence of wo, his funeral is preparing, his heirs, impatient to examine his will, are looking on one another with jealous eyes, and already beginning to dispute about the division of his substance.

5. One day, we see carried along, the coffin of the smiling infant; the flower just nipped as it began to blossom in the parent's view: and the next day, we behold the young man, or young woman, of blooming form and promising hopes, laid in an untimely grave. While the funeral is attended by a numerous unconcerned company, who are discoursing to one another about the news of the day, or the ordinary affairs of life, let our thoughts rather follow to the house of mourning, and represent to themselves what is passing there.

6. There we should see a disconsolate family, sitting in silent grief, thinking of the sad breach that is made in their little society; and with tears in their eyes, looking to the chamber that is now left vacant, and to every memorial that presents itself of their departed friend. By such attention to the woes of others, the selfish hardness of our hearts will be gradually softened, and melted down into humanity.

7. Another day, we follow to the grave, one who, in old age, and after a long career of life, has in full maturity sunk at last into rest. As we are going along to the mansion of the dead, it is natural for us to think, and to discourse, of all the changes which such a person has seen during the course of his life. He has passed, it is likely, through varieties of fortune. He has experienced prosperity, and adversity. He has seen families and kindreds rise and fall. He has seen peace and war succeeding in their turns; the face of his country undergoing many alterations; and the very city in which he dwelt, rising, in a manner, new around him.

8. After all he has beheld, his eyes are now closed for ever. He was becoming a stranger in the midst of a new succession of men. A race who knew him not, had arisen to fill the earth.—Thus passes the world away. Throughout all ranks and conditions, "one generation passeth, and another generation cometh;" and this great inn is by turns evacuated and replenished, by troops of succeeding pilgrims.

9. O vain and inconstant world! O fleeting and transient life! When will the sons of men learn to think of thee as they ought? When will they learn humanity from the afflictions of their brethren; or moderation and wisdom, from the sense of their own fugitive state? BLAIR.

## SECTION V.

*Exalted society, and the renewal of virtuous connexions, two sources of future felicity.*

1. BESIDES the felicity which springs from perfect love, there are two circumstances which particularly enhance the blessedness of that "multitude who stand before the throne;" these are, access to the most exalted society, and renewal of the most tender connexions. The former is pointed out in the Scripture, by "joining the innumerable company of angels, and the general assembly and church of the first-born; by sitting down with Abraham, and Isaac, and Jacob, in the kingdom of heaven;" a promise which opens the sublimest prospects to the human mind.

2. It allows good men to entertain the hope, that, separated from all the dregs of the human mass, from that mixed and polluted crowd in the midst of which they now dwell, they shall be permitted to mingle with prophets, patriarchs, and apostles, with all those great and illustrious spirits, who have shone in former ages as the servants of God, or the benefactors of men; whose deeds we are accustomed to celebrate; whose steps we now follow at a distance; and whose names we pronounce with veneration.

3. United to this high assembly, the blessed, at the same time, renew those ancient connexions with virtuous friends, which had been dissolved by death. The prospect of this awakens in the heart, the most pleasing and tender sentiment that perhaps can fill it, in this mortal state. For of all the sorrows which we are here doomed to endure, none is so bitter as that occasioned by the fatal stroke which separates us, in appearance for ever, from those to whom either nature or friendship had intimately joined our hearts.

4. Memory, from time to time, renews the anguish; opens the wound which seemed once to have been closed; and, by recalling joys that are past and gone, touches every spring of painful sensibility. In these agonizing moments, how relieving the thought, that the separation is only temporary, not eternal; that there is a time to come of re-union with those with whom our happiest days were spent: whose joys and sorrows once were ours; whose piety and virtue cheered and encouraged us; and from whom after we shall have landed on the peaceful shore where they dwell, no revolutions of nature shall ever be able to part us more! Such is the society of the blessed above. Of such are the multitude composed, who "stand before the throne." BLAIR.

## SECTION VI.

*The clemency and amiable character of the patriarch* JOSEPH.

1. No human character exhibited in the records of Scripture, is more remarkable and instructive than that of the patriarch Joseph. He is one whom we behold tried in all the vicissitudes of fortune; from the condition of a slave, rising to be ruler of the land of Egypt; and in every station acquiring, by his virtue and wisdom, favour with God and man. When overseer of Potiphar's house, his fidelity was proved by strong temptations, which he honourably resisted.

2. When thrown into prison by the artifices of a false woman, his integrity and prudence soon rendered him conspicuous, even in that dark mansion. When called into the presence of Pharaoh, the wise and extensive plan which he formed for saving the kingdom from the miseries of impending famine, justly raised him to a high station, wherein his abilities were eminently displayed in the public service.

3. But in his whole history, there is no circumstance so striking and interesting, as his behaviour to his brethren who had sold him into slavery. The moment in which he made himself known to them, was the most critical one of his life, and the most decisive of his character. It is such as rarely occurs in the course of human events; and is calculated to draw the highest attention of all who are endowed with any degree of sensibility of heart.

4. From the whole tenour of the narration it appears, that though Joseph, upon the arrival of his brethren in Egypt, made himself strange to them, yet from the beginning he intended to discover himself; and studied so to conduct the discovery, as might render the surprise of joy complete. For this end, by affected severity, he took measures for bringing down into Egypt all his father's children.

5. They were now arrived there; and Benjamin among the rest, who was his younger brother by the same mother, and was particularly beloved by Joseph. Him he threatened to detain; and seemed willing to allow the rest to depart. This incident renewed their distress. They all knew their father's extreme anxiety about the safety of Benjamin, and with what difficulty he had yielded to his undertaking this journey.

6. Should he be prevented from returning, they dreaded that grief would overpower the old man's spirits, and prove fatal to his life. Judah, therefore, who had particularly urged the necessity of Benjamin's accompanying his brothers, and had solemnly pledged himself to their father for his safe return, craved, upon this occasion, an audience of the governor; and gave him a full account of the circumstances of Jacob's family.

7. Nothing can be more interesting and pathetic than this discourse of Judah. Little knowing to whom he spoke, he paints in all the colours of simple and natural eloquence, the distressed situation of the aged patriarch, hastening to the close of life; long afflicted for the loss of a favourite son, whom he supposed to have been torn in pieces by a beast of prey; labouring now under anxious concern about his youngest son, the child of his old age, who alone was left alive of his mother, and whom nothing but

the calamities of severe famine could have moved a tender father to send from home, and expose to the dangers of a foreign land.

8. "If we bring him not back with us, we shall bring down the gray hairs of thy servant, our father, with sorrow, to the grave. I pray thee therefore let thy servant abide, instead of the young man, a bondman to our lord. For how shall I go up to my father, and Benjamin not with me? lest I see the evil that shall come on my father."

9. Upon this relation Joseph could no longer restrain himself. The tender ideas of his father, and his father's house, of his ancient home, his country, and his kindred, of the distress of his family, and his own exaltation, all rushed too strongly upon his mind to bear any farther concealment. "He cried, Cause every man to go out from me; and he wept aloud."

10. The tears which he shed were not the tears of grief. They were the burst of affection. They were the effusions of a heart overflowing with all the tender sensibilities of nature. Formerly he had been moved in the same manner, when he first saw his brethren before him. "His bowels yearned upon them; he sought for a place where to weep. He went into his chamber; and then washed his face and returned to them."

11. At that period his generous plans were not completed. But now, when there was no farther occasion for constraining himself, he gave free vent to the strong emotions of his heart. The first minister to the king of Egypt was not ashamed to show, that he felt as a man, and a brother. "He wept aloud; and the Egyptians, and the house of Pharaoh, heard him."

12. The first words which his swelling heart allowed him to pronounce, are the most suitable to such an affecting situation that were ever uttered;—"I am Joseph; doth my father yet live?"—What could he, what ought he, in that impassioned moment, to have said more? This is the voice of nature herself, speaking her own language; and it penetrates the heart; no pomp of expression; no parade of kindness; but strong affection hastening to utter what it strongly felt.

13. "His brethren could not answer him; for they were troubled at his presence." Their silence is as expressive of those emotions of repentance and shame, which, on this amazing discovery, filled their breasts, and stopped their utterance, as the few words which Joseph speaks, are expressive of the generous agitations which struggled for vent within him.

14. No painter could seize a more striking moment for displaying the characteristical features of the human heart, than what is here presented. Never was there a situation of more tender and virtuous joy, on the one hand; nor, on the other, of more overwhelming confusion and conscious guilt. In the simple narration of the sacred historian, it is set before us with greater energy and higher effect, than if it had been wrought up with all the colouring of the most admired modern eloquence. BLAIR.

## SECTION VII.
### ALTAMONT.

*The following account of an affecting, mournful exit, is related by Dr. Young, who was present at the melancholy scene.*

1. THE sad evening before the death of the noble youth, whose

last hours suggested the most solemn and awful reflections, I was with him. No one was present, but his physician, and an intimate whom he loved, and whom he had ruined. At my coming in, he said, "You and the physician are come too late. I have neither life nor hope. You both aim at miracles. You would raise the dead!"

2. Heaven, I said, was merciful—"Or," exclaimed he,—"I could not have been thus guilty. What has it not done to bless and to save me!—I have been too strong for Omnipotence! I have plucked down ruin."——I said, the blessed Redeemer,—"Hold! hold! you wound me!—That is the rock on which I split:—I denied his name!"

3. Refusing to hear any thing from me, or take any thing from the physician, he lay silent, as far as sudden darts of pain would permit, till the clock struck: Then with vehemence he exclaimed; "Oh! time! time! it is fit thou shouldst thus strike thy murderer to the heart!—How art thou fled for ever!—A month!—Oh, for a single week! I ask not for years! though an age were too little for the much I have to do."

4. On my saying, we could not do too much: that heaven was a blessed place——"So much the worse.—'Tis lost! 'tis lost!—Heaven is to me the severest part of hell!" Soon after, I proposed prayer,—"Pray you that can, I never prayed. I cannot pray—nor need I. Is not Heaven on my side already? It closes with my conscience. Its severest strokes but second my own."

5. Observing that his friend was much touched at this, even to tears—(who could forbear? I could not)—with a most affectionate look he said, "Keep those tears for thyself. I have undone thee.—Dost thou weep for me? that is cruel. What can pain me more?"

6. Here his friend, too much affected, would have left him.—"No, stay—thou still mayst hope; therefore hear me. How madly have I talked! How madly hast thou listened and believed! but look on my present state, as a full answer to thee, and to myself. This body is all weakness and pain; but my soul, as if stung up by torment to greater strength and spirit, is full powerful to reason; full mighty to suffer. And that, which thus triumphs within the jaws of immortality, is, doubtless, immortal—And, as for a Deity, nothing less than an Almighty could inflict what I feel."

7. I was about to congratulate this passive, involuntary confessor, on his asserting the two prime articles of his creed, extorted by the rack of nature, when he thus, very passionately exclaimed:—"No, no! let me speak on. I have not long to speak.—My much injured friend! my soul, as my body, lies in ruins; in scattered fragments of broken thought.

8. "Remorse for the past, throws my thought on the future. Worse dread of the future, strikes it back on the past. I turn, and turn, and find no ray. Didst thou feel half the mountain that is on me, thou wouldst struggle with the martyr for his stake; and bless Heaven for the flames!—that is not an everlasting flame; that is not an unquenchable fire."

9. How were we struck! yet, soon after, still more. With what an eye of distraction, what a face of despair, he cried out! "My principles have poisoned my friend; my extravagance has beggared my boy! my unkindness has murdered my wife!—And is there

another hell? Oh! thou blasphemed, yet indulgent LORD GOD! Hell itself is a refuge, if it hide me from thy frown!"

10. Soon after, his understanding failed. His terrified imagination uttered horrors not to be repeated, or ever forgotten. And ere the sun (which, I hope, has seen few like him) arose, the gay, young, noble, ingenious, accomplished, and most wretched Altamont, expired!

11. If this is a man of pleasure, what is a man of pain? How quick, how total, is the transit of such persons! In what a dismal gloom they set for ever! How short, alas! the day of their rejoicing!—For a moment they glitter—they dazzle! In a moment, where are they? Oblivion covers their memories. Ah! would it did! Infamy snatches them from oblivion. In the long living annals of infamy their triumphs are recorded.

12. Thy sufferings, poor Altamont! still bleed in the bosom of the heart-stricken friend—for Altamont had a friend. He might have had many. His transient morning might have been the dawn of an immortal day. His name might have been gloriously enrolled in the records of eternity. His memory might have left a sweet fragrance behind it, grateful to the surviving friend, salutary to the succeeding generation.

13. With what capacity was he endowed! with what advantages, for being greatly good! But with the talents of an angel, a man may be a fool. If he judges amiss in the supreme point, judging right in all else, but aggravates his folly; as it shows him wrong, though blessed with the best capacity of being right.

DR. YOUNG.

## CHAPTER VII.

### DIALOGUES.

### SECTION I

#### DEMOCRITUS AND HERACLITUS.*

*The vices and follies of men should exite compassion rather than ridicule.*

*Democritus.* I FIND it impossible to reconcile myself to a melancholy philosophy.

*Heraclitus.* And I am equally unable to approve of that vain philosophy, which teaches men to despise and ridicule one another. To a wise and feeling mind, the world appears in a wretched and painful light.

*Dem.* Thou art too much affected with the state of things; and this is a source of misery to thee.

*Her.* And I think thou art too little moved by it. Thy mirth and ridicule bespeak the buffoon, rather than the philosopher. Does it not excite thy compassion, to see mankind so frail, so blind, so far departed from the rules of virtue?

*Dem.* I am excited to laughter, when I see so much impertinence and folly.

*Her.* And yet, after all, they, who are the objects of thy ridicule,

* Democritus and Heraclitus were two ancient philosophers, the former of whom laughed, and the latter wept, at the errors and follies of mankind.

include, not only mankind in general, but the persons with whom thou livest, thy friends, thy family, nay even thyself.

*Dem.* I care very little for all the silly persons I meet with; and think I am justifiable in diverting myself with their folly.

*Her.* If they are weak and foolish, it marks neither wisdom nor humanity, to insult rather than pity them. But is it certain, that thou art not as extravagant as they are?

*Dem.* I presume that I am not; since, in every point, my sentiments are the very reverse of theirs.

*Her.* There are follies of different kinds. By constantly amusing thyself with the errors and misconduct of others, thou mayst render thyself equally ridiculous and culpable.

*Dem.* Thou art at liberty to indulge such sentiments; and to weep over me too, if thou hast any tears to spare. For my part, I cannot refrain from pleasing myself with the levities and ill conduct of the world about me. Are not all men foolish, or irregular in their lives?

*Her.* Alas! there is but too much reason to believe, they are so; and on this ground, I pity and deplore their condition. We agree in this point, that men do not conduct themselves according to reasonable and just principles: but I, who do not suffer myself to act as they do, must yet regard the dictates of my understanding and feelings, which compel me to love them; and that love fills me with compassion for their mistakes and irregularities. Canst thou condemn me for pitying my own species, my brethren, persons born in the same condition of life, and destined to the same hopes and privileges? If thou shouldst enter a hospital, where sick and wounded persons reside, would their wounds and distresses excite thy mirth? And yet, the evils of the body bear no comparison with those of the mind. Thou wouldst certainly blush at thy barbarity, if thou hadst been so unfeeling as to laugh at or despise a poor miserable being, who had lost one of his legs: and yet thou art so destitute of humanity, as to ridicule those, who appear to be deprived of the noble powers of the understanding, by the little regard which they pay to its dictates.

*Dem.* He who has lost a leg is to be pitied, because the loss is not to be imputed to himself: but he who rejects the dictates of reason and conscience, voluntarily deprives himself of their aid. The loss originates in his own folly.

*Her.* Ah! so much the more is he to be pitied! A furious maniac, who should pluck out his own eyes, would deserve more compassion than an ordinary blind man.

*Dem.* Come, let us accommodate the business. There is something to be said on each side of the question. There is every where reason for laughing, and reason for weeping. The world is ridiculous, and I laugh at it: it is deplorable, and thou lamentest over it. Every person views it in his own way, and according to his own temper. One point is unquestionable, that mankind are preposterous: to think right and to act well, we must think and act differently from them. To submit to the authority, and follow the example of the greater part of men, would render us foolish and miserable.

*Her.* All this is, indeed, true; but then, thou hast no real love or feeling for thy species. The calamities of mankind excite thy

H

mirth: and this proves that thou hast no regard for men, nor any true respect for the virtues which they have unhappily abandoned. *Fenelon, Archbishop of Cambray.*

## SECTION II.
### DIONYSIUS, PYTHIAS, AND DAMON.
*Genuine virtue commands respect, even from the bad.*

*Dionysius.* AMAZING! What do I see? It is Pythias just arrived.—It is indeed Pythias. I did not think it possible. He is come to die, and to redeem his friend!

*Pythias.* Yes, it is Pythias. I left the place of my confinement, with no other views, than to pay to Heaven the vows I had made; to settle my family concerns according to the rules of justice; and to bid adieu to my children, that I might die tranquil and satisfied.

*Dio.* But why dost thou return? Hast thou no fear of death? Is it not the character of a madman, to seek it thus voluntarily?

*Py.* I return to suffer, though I have not deserved death. Every principle of honour and goodness, forbids me to allow my friend to die for me.

*Dio.* Dost thou, then, love him better than thyself?

*Py.* No; I love him as myself. But I am persuaded that I ought to suffer death, rather than my friend; since it was Pythias whom thou hadst decreed to die. It were not just that Damon should suffer, to deliver me from the death which was designed, not for him, but for me only.

*Dio.* But thou supposest, that it is as unjust to inflict death upon thee, as upon thy friend.

*Py.* Very true; we are both perfectly innocent; and it is equally unjust to make either of us suffer.

*Dio.* Why dost thou then assert, that it were injustice to put him to death, instead of thee?

*Py.* It is unjust, in the same degree, to inflict death either on Damon or on myself; but Pythias were highly culpable to let Damon suffer that death, which the tyrant had prepared for Pythias only.

*Dio.* Dost thou then return hither, on the day appointed, with no other view, than to save the life of a friend, by losing thy own?

*Py.* I return, in regard to thee, to suffer an act of injustice which it is common for tyrants to inflict; and, with respect to Damon, to perform my duty, by rescuing him from the danger he incurred by his generosity to me.

*Dio.* And now, Damon, let me address myself to thee. Didst thou not really fear, that Pythias would never return; and that thou wouldst be put to death on his account?

*Da.* I was but too well assured, that Pythias would punctually return; and that he would be more solicitous to keep his promise, than to preserve his life. Would to heaven, that his relations and friends had forcibly detained him! He would then have lived for the comfort and benefit of good men; and I should have the satisfaction of dying for him!

*Dio.* What! Does life displease thee?

*Da.* Yes; it displeases me when I see and feel the power of a tyrant.

*Dio.* It is well! Thou shall see him no more. I will order thee to be put to death immediately.

*Py.* Pardon the feelings of a man who sympathizes with his

dying friend. But remember it was Pythias who was devoted by thee to destruction. I come to submit to it, that I may redeem my friend. Do not refuse me this consolation in my last hour.

*Dio.* I cannot endure men, who despise death, and set my power at defiance.

*Da.* Thou canst not, then, endure virtue.

*Dio.* No: I cannot endure that proud, disdainful virtue, which contemns life; which dreads no punishment; and which is insensible to the charms of riches and pleasure.

*Da.* Thou seest, however, that it is a virtue, which is not insensible to the dictates of honour, justice, and friendship.

*Dio.* Guards, take Pythias to execution. We shall see whether Damon will continue to despise my authority.

*Da.* Pythias, by returning to submit himself to thy pleasure, has merited his life, and deserved thy favour; but I have excited thy indignation, by resigning myself to thy power, in order to save him; be satisfied, then, with this sacrifice, and put me to death.

*Py.* Hold, Dionysius! remember, it was Pythias alone who offended thee: Damon could not——

*Dio.* Alas! what do I see and hear! where am I? How miserable; and how worthy to be so! I have hitherto known nothing of true virtue. I have spent my life in darkness and error. All my power and honours are insufficient to produce love. I cannot boast of having acquired a single friend, in the course of a reign of thirty years. And yet these two persons, in a private condition, love one another tenderly, unreservedly confide in each other, are mutually happy, and ready to die for each other's preservation.

*Py.* How couldst thou, who hast never loved any person, expect to have friends? If thou hadst loved and respected men, thou wouldst have secured their love and respect. Thou hast feared mankind; and they fear thee; they detest thee.

*Dio.* Damon, Pythias, condescend to admit me as a third friend, in a connexion so perfect. I give you your lives; and I will load you with riches.

*Da.* We have no desire to be enriched by thee; and, in regard to thy friendship, we cannot accept or enjoy it, till thou become good and just. Without these qualities, thou canst be connected with none but trembling slaves, and base flatterers. To be loved and esteemed by men of free and generous minds, thou must be virtuous, affectionate, disinterested, beneficent; and know how to live in a sort of equality with those who share and deserve thy friendship. *Fenelon, Archbishop of Cambray.*

## SECTION III.
### LOCKE AND BAYLE.
*Christianity defended against the cavils of scepticism.*

*Bayle.* YES, we both were philosophers; but my philosophy was the deepest. You dogmatized; I doubted.

*Locke.* Do you make doubting a proof of depth in philosophy? It may be a good beginning of it; but it is a bad end.

*Bayle.* No:—the more profound our searches are into the nature of things, the more uncertainty we shall find; and the most subtle minds see objections and difficulties in every system, which are overlooked or undiscoverable by ordinary understandings.

*Locke.* It would be better then to be no philosopher, and to continue in the vulgar herd of mankind, that one may have the convenience of thinking that one knows something. I find that the eyes which nature has given me, see many things very clearly, though some are out of their reach, or discerned but dimly. What opinion ought I to have of a physician, who should offer me an eye-water, the use of which would at first so sharpen my sight, as to carry it farther than ordinary vision; but would in the end put them out? Your philosophy is to the eyes of the mind, what I have supposed the doctor's nostrum to be to those of the body. It actually brought your own excellent understanding, which was by nature quick-sighted, and rendered more so by art and a subtilty of logic peculiar to yourself—it brought, I say, your very acute understanding to see nothing clearly; and enveloped all the great truths of reason and religion in mists of doubt.

*Bayle.* I own it did;—but your comparison is not just. I did not see well, before I used my philosophic eye-water: I only supposed I saw well; but I was in an error, with all the rest of mankind. The blindness was real, the perceptions were imaginary. I cured myself first of those false imaginations, and then I laudably endeavoured to cure other men.

*Locke.* A great cure indeed!—and do not you think that, in return for the service you did them, they ought to erect you a statue?

*Bayle.* Yes; it is good for human nature to know its own weakness. When we arrogantly presume on a strength we have not, we are always in great danger of hurting ourselves, or at least of deserving ridicule and contempt, by vain and idle efforts.

*Locke.* I agree with you, that human nature should know its own weakness; but it should also feel its strength, and try to improve it. This was my employment as a philosopher. I endeavoured to discover the real powers of the mind, to see what it could do, and what it could not; to restrain it from efforts beyond its ability; but to teach it how to advance as far as the faculties given to it by nature, with the utmost exertion and most proper culture of them, would allow it to go. In the vast ocean of philosophy, I had the line and the plummet always in my hands. Many of its depths I found myself unable to fathom; but, by caution in sounding, and the careful observations I made in the course of my voyage, I found out some truths of so much use to mankind, that they acknowledge me to have been their benefactor.

*Bayle.* Their ignorance makes them think so. Some other philosopher will come hereafter and show those truths to be falsehoods. He will pretend to discover other truths of equal importance. A later sage will arise, perhaps among men now barbarous and unlearned, whose sagacious discoveries will discredit the opinions of his admired predecessor. In philosophy, as in nature, all changes its form, and one thing exists by the destruction of another.

*Locke.* Opinions taken up without a patient investigation, depending on terms not accurately defined, and principles begged without proof, like theories to explain the phænomena of nature, built on suppositions instead of experiments, must perpetually change and destroy one another. But some opinions there are, even in matters not obvious to the common sense of mankind, which the mind has received on such rational grounds of assent, that they are as immoveable as the pillars of heaven; or (to speak philosophically) as the great laws of Nature, by which, under God, the universe is sustained. Can you seriously think, that, because the hypothesis of your countryman Descartes, which was nothing but an ingenious, well-imagined romance, has been lately exploded, the system of Newton, which is built on experiments and geometry, the two most certain methods of discovering truth, will ever fail; or that, because the whims of fanatics and the divinity of the schoolmen, cannot now be supported, the doctrines of that religion, which I, the declared enemy of all enthusiasm and false reasoning, firmly believed and maintained, will ever be shaken?

*Bayle.* If you had asked Descartes, while he was in the height of his vogue, whether his system would ever be confuted by any other philosophers, as that of Aristotle had been by his, what answer do you suppose he would have returned?

*Locke.* Come, come, you yourself know the difference between the foundations on which the credit of those systems, and that of Newton is placed. Your scepticism is more affected than real. You found it a shorter way to a great reputation, (the only wish of your heart,) to object, than to defend; to pull down, than to set up. And your talents were admirable for that kind of work. Then your huddling together in a Critical Dictionary, a pleasant tale, or obscene jest, and a grave argument against the Christian religion, a witty confutation of some absurd author, and an artful sophism to impeach some respectable truth, was particularly commodious to all our young smarts and smatterers in free-thinking. But what mischief have you not done to human society? You have endeavoured, and with some degree of success, to shake those foundations, on which the whole moral world, and the great fabric of social happiness, entirely rest. How could you, as a philosopher, in the sober hours of reflection, answer for this to your conscience, even supposing you had doubts of the truth of a system, which gives to virtue its sweetest hopes, to impenitent vice its greatest fears, and to true penitence its best consolations; which restrains even the least approaches to guilt, and yet makes those allowances for the infirmities of our nature, which the Stoic pride denied to it, but which its real imperfection, and the goodness of its infinitely benevolent Creator, so evidently require?

*Bayle.* The mind is free; and it loves to exert its freedom. Any restraint upon it is a violence done to its nature, and a tyranny, against which it has a right to rebel.

*Locke.* The mind, though free, has a governor within itself, which may and ought to limit the exercise of its freedom. That governor is reason.

*Bayle.* Yes:—but reason, like other governors, has a policy more dependent upon uncertain caprice, than upon any fixed laws. And if that reason, which rules my mind or yours, has happened to set up a favourite notion, it not only submits implicitly to it, but desires that the same respect should be paid to it by all the rest of mankind. Now I hold that any man may lawfully oppose this desire in another; and that if he is wise, he will use his utmost endeavours to check it in himself.

*Locke.* Is there not also a weakness of a contrary nature to this you are now ridiculing? Do we not often take a pleasure in show ing our own power, and gratifying our own pride, by degrading the notions set up by other men, and generally respected?

*Bayle.* I believe we do; and by this means it often happens, that, if one man builds and consecrates a temple to folly, another pulls it down.

*Locke.* Do you think it beneficial to human society, to have all temples pulled down?

*Bayle.* I cannot say that I do.

*Locke.* Yet I find not in your writings any mark of distinction, to show us which you mean to save.

*Bayle.* A true philosopher, like an impartial historian, must be of no sect.

*Locke.* Is there no medium between the blind zeal of a sectary, and a total indifference to all religion?

*Bayle.* With regard to morality, I was not indifferent.

*Locke.* How could you then be indifferent with regard to the sanctions religion gives to morality? How could you publish what tends so directly and apparently to weaken in mankind the belief of those sanctions? Was not this sacrificing the great interests of virtue to the little motives of vanity?

*Bayle.* A man may act indiscreetly, but he cannot do wrong, by declaring that, which, on a full discussion of the question, he sincerely thinks to be true.

*Locke.* An enthusiast, who advances doctrines prejudicial to society, or opposes any that are useful to it, has the strength of opinion, and the heat of a disturbed imagination, to plead in alleviation of his fault. But your cool head and sound judgment, can have no such excuse. I know very well there are passages in all your works, and those not few, where you talk like a rigid moralist. I have also heard that your character was irreproachably good. But when, in the most laboured parts of your writings, you sap the surest foundations of all moral duties; what avails it that in others, or in the conduct of your life, you appeared to respect them? How many, who have stronger passions than you had, and are desirous to get rid of the curb that restrains them, will lay hold of your scepticism, to set themselves loose from all obligations of virtue! What a misfortune is it to have made such a use of such talents! It would have been better for you and for mankind, if you had been one of the dullest of Dutch theologians, or the most credulous monk in a Portuguese convent. The riches of the mind, like those of fortune, may be employed so perversely, as to become a nuisance and pest, instead of an ornament and support, to society.

*Bayle.* You are very severe upon me.—But do you count it no merit, no service to mankind, to deliver them from the frauds and fetters of priestcraft, from the deliriums of fanaticism, and from the terrors and follies of superstition? Consider how much mischief these have done to the world! Even in the last age, what massacres, what civil wars, what convulsions of government, what confusion in society, did they produce! Nay, in that we both lived in, though much more enlightened than the former, did I not see them occasion a violent persecution in my own country? and can you blame me for striking at the root of these evils?

*Locke.* The root of these evils, you well know, was false religion: but you struck at the true. Heaven and hell are not more different, than the system of faith I defended, and that which produced the horrors of which you speak. Why would you so fallaciously confound them together in some of your writings, that it requires much more judgment, and a more diligent attention, than ordinary readers have, to separate them again, and to make the proper distinctions? This, indeed, is the great art of the most celebrated freethinkers. They recommend themselves to warm and ingenuous minds, by lively strokes of wit, and by arguments really strong, against superstition, enthusiasm, and priestcraft. But, at the same time, they insidiously throw the colours of these upon the fair face of true religion; and dress her out in their garb, with a malignant intention to render her odious or despicable, to those who have not penetration enough to discern the impious fraud. Some of them may have thus deceived themselves, as well as others. Yet it is certain, no book that ever was written by the most acute of these gentlemen, is so repugnant to priestcraft, to spiritual tyranny, to all absurd superstitions, to all that can tend to disturb or injure society, as that gospel they so much affect to despise.

*Bayle.* Mankind are so made, that, when they have been overheated, they cannot be brought to a proper temper again, till they have been over-cooled. My scepticism might be necessary, to abate the fever and phrenzy of false religion.

*Locke.* A wise prescription, indeed, to bring on a paralytical state of the mind, (for such a scepticism as yours is a palsy, which deprives the mind of all vigour, and deadens its natural and vital powers,) in order to take off a fever, which temperance, and the milk of the evangelical doctrines, would probably cure!

*Bayle.* I acknowledge that those medicines have a great power. But few doctors apply them untainted with the mixture of some harsher drugs, or some unsafe and ridiculous nostrums of their own.

*Locke.* What you now say is too true.—God has given us a most excellent physic for the soul, in all its diseases; but bad and interested physicians, or ignorant and conceited quacks, administer it so ill to the rest of mankind, that much of the benefit of it is unhappily lost. LORD LYTTELTON.

## CHAPTER VIII.
### PUBLIC SPEECHES.
#### SECTION I.
Cicero *against* Verres.

1. The time is come, Fathers, when that which has long been wished for, towards allaying the envy your order has been subject to, and removing the imputations against trials, is effectually put in your power. An opinion has long prevailed, not only here at home, but likewise in foreign countries, both dangerous to you, and pernicious to the state,—that, in prosecutions, men of wealth are always safe, however clearly convicted.

2. There is now to be brought upon his trial before you, to the confusion, I hope, of the propagators of this slanderous imputation, one whose life and actions condemn him in the opinion of all im-

partial persons; but who, according to his own reckoning and declared dependence upon his riches, is already acquitted; I mean Caius Verres. I demand justice of you, fathers, upon the robber of the public treasury, the oppressor of Asia Minor and Pamphylia, the invader of the rights and privileges of Romans, the scourge and curse of Sicily.

3. If that sentence is passed upon him which his crimes deserve, your authority, fathers, will be venerable and sacred in the eyes of the public: but if his great riches should bias you in his favour, I shall still gain one point,—to make it apparent to all the world, that what was wanting in this case, was not a criminal nor a prosecutor, but justice and adequate punishment.

4. To pass over the shameful irregularities of his youth, what does his quæstorship, the first public employment he held, what does it exhibit, but one continued scene of villanies? Cneius Carbo, plundered of the public money by his own treasurer, a consul stripped and betrayed, an army deserted and reduced to want, a province robbed, the civil and religious rights of a people violated.

5. The employment he held in Asia Minor and Pamphylia, what did it produce but the ruin of those countries? in which houses, cities, and temples, were robbed by him. What was his conduct in his prætorship here at home? Let the plundered temples, and public works neglected, that he might embezzle the money intended for carrying them on, bear witness. How did he discharge the office of a judge? Let those who suffered by his injustice answer.

6. But his prætorship in Sicily crowns all his works of wickedness, and finishes a lasting monument to his infamy. The mischiefs done by him in that unhappy country, during the three years of his iniquitous administration, are such, that many years, under the wisest and best of prætors, will not be sufficient to restore things to the condition in which he found them: for it is notorious, that, during the time of his tyranny, the Sicilians neither enjoyed the protection of their own original laws; of the regulations made for their benefit by the Roman senate, upon their coming under the protection of the commonwealth; nor of the natural and unalienable rights of men.

7. His nod has decided all causes in Sicily for these three years. And his decisions have broken all law, all precedent, all right. The sums he has, by arbitrary taxes and unheard-of impositions, extorted from the industrious poor, are not to be computed.

8. The most faithful allies of the commonwealth have been treated as enemies. Roman citizens have, like slaves, been put to death with tortures. The most atrocious criminals, for money, have been exempted from the deserved punishments; and men of the most unexceptionable characters, condemned and banished unheard.

9. The harbours, though sufficiently fortified, and the gates of strong towns, have been opened to pirates and ravagers. The soldiery and sailors, belonging to a province under the protection of the commonwealth, have been starved to death; whole fleets, to the great detriment of the province, suffered to perish. The ancient monuments of either Sicilian or Roman greatness, the statues of heroes and princes, have been carried off; and the temples stripped of their images.

10. Having, by his iniquitous sentences, filled the prisons with the most industrious and deserving of the people, he then proceeded to order numbers of Roman citizens to be strangled in the gaols: so that the exclamation, "I am a citizen of Rome!" which has often, in the most distant regions, and among the most barbarous people, been a protection, was of no service to them; but, on the contrary, brought a speedier and a more severe punishment upon them.

11. I ask now, Verres, what thou hast to advance against this charge? Wilt thou pretend to deny it? Wilt thou pretend, that any thing false, that even any thing aggravated, is alleged against thee? Had any prince, or any state, committed the same outrage against the privilege of Roman citizens, should we not think we had sufficient ground for demanding satisfaction?

12. What punishment ought, then, to be inflicted upon a tyrannical and wicked prætor, who dared, at no greater distance than Sicily, within sight of the Italian coast, to put to the infamous death of crucifixion, that unfortunate and innocent citizen, Publius Gavius Cosanus, only for his having asserted his privilege of citizenship, and declared his intention of appealing to the justice of his country, against the cruel oppressor, who had unjustly confined him in prison at Syracuse, whence he had just made his escape?

13. The unhappy man, arrested as he was going to embark for his native country, is brought before the wicked prætor. With eyes darting fury, and a countenance distorted with cruelty, he orders the helpless victim of his rage to be stripped, and rods to be brought: accusing him, but without the least shadow of evidence, or even of suspicion, of having come to Sicily as a spy.

14. It was in vain that the unhappy man cried out, "I am a Roman citizen; I have served under Lucius Pretius, who is now at Panormus, and will attest my innocence." The blood-thirsty prætor, deaf to all he could urge in his own defence, ordered the infamous punishment to be inflicted.

15. Thus, fathers, was an innocent Roman citizen publicly mangled with scourging; whilst the only words he uttered, amidst his cruel sufferings, were, "I am a Roman citizen!" With these he hoped to defend himself from violence and infamy. But of so little service was this privilege to him, that, while he was thus asserting his citizenship, the order was given for his execution,—for his execution upon the cross!

16. O liberty!—O sound once delightful to every Roman ear!—O sacred privilege of Roman citizenship!—once sacred!—now trampled upon!—But what then! Is it come to this? Shall an inferior magistrate, a governor, who holds his whole power of the Roman people, in a Roman province, within sight of Italy, bind, scourge, torture with fire and red hot plates of iron, and at last put to the infamous death of the cross, a Roman citizen?

17. Shall neither the cries of innocence expiring in agony, nor the tears of pitying spectators, nor the majesty of the Roman commonwealth, nor the fear of the justice of his country, restrain the licentious and wanton cruelty of a monster, who, in confidence of his riches, strikes at the root of liberty, and sets mankind at defiance?

18. I conclude with expressing my hopes, that your wisdom and justice, fathers, will not, by suffering the atrocious and unexam-

pled insolence of Caius Verres to escape due punishment, leave room to apprehend the danger of a total subversion of authority, and the introduction of general anarchy and confusion.

CICERO'S ORATIONS.

## SECTION II.

*Speech of* ADHERBAL *to the Roman Senate, imploring their protection against* JUGURTHA.

FATHERS!

1. It is known to you, that king Micipsa, my father, on his death-bed, left in charge to Jugurtha, his adopted son, conjunctly with my unfortunate brother Hiempsal and myself, the children of his own body, the administration of the kingdom of Numidia, directing us to consider the senate and people of Rome as proprietors of it. He charged us to use our best endeavours to be serviceable to the Roman commonwealth; assuring us, that your protection would prove a defence against all enemies; and would be instead of armies, fortifications, and treasures.

2. While my brother and I were thinking of nothing but how to regulate ourselves according to the directions of our deceased father—Jugurtha—the most infamous of mankind!—breaking through all ties of gratitude and of common humanity, and trampling on the authority of the Roman commonwealth, procured the murder of my unfortunate brother; and has driven me from my throne and native country, though he knows I inherit, from my grandfather Massinissa, and my father Micipsa, the friendship and alliance of the Romans.

3. For a prince to be reduced, by villany, to my distressful circumstances, is calamity enough; but my misfortunes are heightened by the consideration—that I find myself obliged to solicit your assistance, fathers, for the services done you by my ancestors, not for any I have been able to render you in my own person. Jugurtha has put it out of my power to deserve any thing at your hands; and has forced me to be burdensome, before I could be useful to you.

4. And yet, if I had no plea, but my undeserved misery—a once powerful prince, the descendant of a race of illustrious monarchs, now, without any fault of my own, destitute of every support, and reduced to the necessity of begging foreign assistance, against an enemy who has seized my throne and my kingdom—if my unequalled distresses were all I had to plead—it would become the greatness of the Roman commonwealth, to protect the injured, and to check the triumph of daring wickedness over helpless innocence.

5. But, to provoke your resentment to the utmost, Jugurtha has driven me from the very dominions, which the senate and people of Rome gave to my ancestors; and, from which, my grandfather, and my father, under your umbrage, expelled Syphax and the Carthaginians. Thus, fathers, your kindness to our family is defeated; and Jugurtha, in injuring me, throws contempt upon you.

6. O wretched prince! Oh cruel reverse of fortune! Oh father Micipsa! is this the consequence of thy generosity; that he, whom thy goodness raised to an equality with thy own children, should be the murderer of thy children? Must, then, the royal house of Numidia always be a scene of havoc and blood?

7. While Carthage remained, we suffered, as was to be expected, all sorts of hardships from their hostile attacks; our enemy

near; our only powerful ally, the Roman commonwealth, at a distance. When that scourge of Africa was no more, we congratulated ourselves on the prospect of established peace. But, instead of peace, behold the kingdom of Numidia drenched with royal blood! and the only surviving son of its late king, flying from an adopted murderer, and seeking that safety in foreign parts, which he cannot command in his own kingdom.

8. Whither—Oh! whither shall I fly? If I return to the royal palace of my ancestors, my father's throne is seized by the murderer of my brother. What can I there expect, but that Jugurtha should hasten to imbrue, in my blood, those hands which are now reeking with my brother's? If I were to fly for refuge, or for assistance to any other court, from what prince can I hope for protection, if the Roman commonwealth give me up? From my own family or friends I have no expectations.

9. My royal father is no more. He is beyond the reach of violence, and out of hearing of the complaints of his unhappy son. Were my brother alive, our mutual sympathy would be some alleviation. But he is hurried out of life, in his early youth, by the very hand which should have been the last to injure any of the royal family of Numidia.

10. The bloody Jugurtha has butchered all whom he suspected to be in my interest. Some have been destroyed by the lingering torment of the cross. Others have been given a prey to wild beasts; and their anguish made the sport of men more cruel than wild beasts. If there be any yet alive, they are shut up in dungeons, there to drag out a life more intolerable than death itself.

11. Look down, illustrious senators of Rome! from that height of power to which you are raised, on the unexampled distresses of a prince, who is, by the cruelty of a wicked intruder, become an outcast from all mankind. Let not the crafty insinuations of him who returns murder for adoption, prejudice your judgment. Do not listen to the wretch who has butchered the son and relations of a king, who gave him power to sit on the same throne with his own sons.

12. I have been informed, that he labours by his emissaries to prevent your determining any thing against him in his absence; pretending that I magnify my distress, and might, for him, have staid in peace in my own kingdom. But, if ever the time comes, when the due vengeance from above shall overtake him, he will then dissemble as I do. Then he, who now, hardened in wickedness, triumphs over those whom his violence has laid low, will, in his turn, feel distress, and suffer for his impious ingratitude to my father, and his blood-thirsty cruelty to my brother.

13. Oh murdered, butchered brother! Oh dearest to my heart—now gone for ever from my sight!—but why should I lament his death? He is, indeed, deprived of the blessed light of heaven, of life, and kingdom, at once, by the very person who ought to have been the first to hazard his own life, in defence of any one of Micipsa's family. But, as things are, my brother is not so much deprived of these comforts, as delivered from terror, from flight, from exile, and the endless train of miseries which render life to me a burden.

14. He lies full low, gored with wounds, and festering in his own,

blood. But he lies in peace. He feels none of the miseries which rend my soul with agony and distraction, while I am set up a spectacle to all mankind, of the uncertainty of human affairs. So far from having it in my power to punish his murderer, I am not master of the means of securing my own life. So far from being in a condition to defend my kingdom from the violence of the usurper, I am obliged to apply for foreign protection for my own person.

15. Fathers! Senators of Rome! the arbiters of nations! to you I fly for refuge from the murderous fury of Jugurtha.—By your affection for your children; by your love for your country; by your own virtues; by the majesty of the Roman commonwealth; by all that is sacred, and all that is dear to you—deliver a wretched prince from undeserved, unprovoked injury; and save the kingdom of Numidia, which is your own property, from being the prey of violence, usurpation, and cruelty. SALLUST.

## SECTION III.

*The* APOSTLE PAUL'S *noble defence before* FESTUS *and* AGRIPPA.

1. AGRIPPA said unto Paul, thou art permitted to speak for thyself.—Then Paul stretched forth his hand, and answered for himself. I think myself happy, king Agrippa, because I shall answer for myself this day before thee, concerning all the things whereof I am accused by the Jews: especially, as I know thee to be expert in all customs and questions which are among the Jews. Wherefore I beseech thee to hear me patiently.

2. My manner of life from my youth, which was at the first among my own nation at Jerusalem, know all the Jews; who knew me from the beginning, (if they would testify,) that after the straitest sect of our religion, I lived a Pharisee. And now I stand and am judged for the hope of the promise made by God to our fathers; to which promise, our twelve tribes, continually serving God day and night, hope to come: and, for this hope's sake, king Agrippa, I am accused by the Jews.

3. Why should it be thought a thing incredible with you, that God should raise the dead? I verily thought with myself, that I ought to do many things contrary to the name of Jesus of Nazareth: and this I did in Jerusalem. Many of the saints I shut up in prison, having received authority from the chief priests: and when they were put to death, I gave my voice against them. And I often punished them in every synagogue, and compelled them to blaspheme; and being exceedingly mad against them, I persecuted them even unto strange cities.

4. But as I went to Damascus, with authority and commission from the chief priests, at mid-day, O king! I saw in the way a light from heaven, above the brightness of the sun, shining round about me, and them who journeyed with me. And when we were all fallen to the earth, I heard a voice speaking to me and saying, in the Hebrew tongue, Saul, Saul, why persecutest thou me? It is hard for thee to kick against the pricks. And I said, who art thou, Lord? And he replied, I am Jesus whom thou persecutest.

5. But rise, and stand upon thy feet: for I have appeared to thee for this purpose, to make thee a minister, and a witness both of these things which thou hast seen, and of those things in which I will appear to thee; delivering thee from the people, and from the Gentiles, to whom I now send thee, to open their eyes, and to

turn them from darkness to light, and from the power of Satan to God; that they may receive forgiveness of sins, and inheritance among them who are sanctified by faith that is in me.

6. Whereupon, O king Agrippa! I was not disobedient to the heavenly vision; but showed first to them of Damascus, and at Jerusalem, and through all the coasts of Judea, and then to the Gentiles, that they should repent, and turn to God, and do works meet for repentance. For these causes, the Jews caught me in the temple; and went about to kill me. Having, however, obtained help from God, I continue to this day witnessing both to small and great, saying no other things than those which the prophets and Moses declared should come; that Christ should suffer; that he would be the first who should rise from the dead; and that he would show light to the people, and to the Gentiles.

7. And as he thus spoke for himself, Festus said, with a loud voice, "Paul, thou art beside thyself; much learning hath made thee mad." But he replied, I am not mad, most noble Festus; but speak the words of truth and soberness. For the king knoweth these things, before whom I also speak freely. I am persuaded that none of these things are hidden from him: for this thing was not done in a corner. King Agrippa, believest thou the prophets? I know that thou believest. Then Agrippa said to Paul, "Almost thou persuadest me to be a Christian." And Paul replied, "I would to God, that not only thou, but also all that hear me this day, were both almost, and altogether such as I am, except these bonds."*    ACTS XXVI.

## SECTION IV.

LORD MANSFIELD's *speech in the House of Peers, 1770, on the bill for preventing the delays of justice, by claiming the Privilege of Parliament.*

MY LORDS,

1. WHEN I consider the importance of this bill to your lordships, I am not surprised it has taken up so much of your consideration. It is a bill, indeed, of no common magnitude; it is no less than to take away from two-thirds of the legislative body of this great kingdom, certain privileges and immunities of which they have been long possessed. Perhaps there is no situation the human mind can be placed in, that is so difficult and so trying, as when it is made a judge in its own cause.

2. There is something implanted in the breast of man so attached to self, so tenacious of privileges once obtained, that in such a situation, either to discuss with impartiality, or decide with justice, has ever been held the summit of all human virtue. The bill now in question puts your lordships in this very predicament; and I have no doubt the wisdom of your decision will convince the world, that where self-interest and justice are in opposite scales, the latter will ever preponderate with your lordships.

3. Privileges have been granted to legislators in all ages, and in

---

* How happy was this great Apostle, even in the most perilous circumstances! Though under bonds and oppression, his mind was free, and raised above every fear of man. With what dignity and composure does he defend himself, and the noble cause he had espoused; whilst he displays the most compassionate and generous feelings, for those who were strangers to the sublime religion by which he was animated!

all countries. The practice is founded in wisdom; and, indeed, it is peculiarly essential to the constitution of this country, that the members of both houses should be free in their persons, in cases of civil suits: for there may come a time when the safety and welfare of this whole empire, may depend upon their attendance in parliament. I am far from advising any measure that would in future endanger the state: but the bill before your lordships has, I am confident, no such tendency; for it expressly secures the persons of members of either house in all civil suits.

4. This being the case, I confess, when I see many noble lords, for whose judgment I have a very great respect, standing up to oppose a bill which is calculated merely to facilitate the recovery of just and legal debts, I am astonished and amazed. They, I doubt not, oppose the bill upon public principles: I would not wish to insinuate, that private interest had the least weight in their determination.

5. The bill has been frequently proposed, and as frequently has miscarried: but it was always lost in the lower house. Little did I think, when it had passed the commons, that it possibly could have met with such opposition here. Shall it be said, that you, my lords, the grand council of the nation, the highest judicial and legislative body of the realm, endeavour to evade, by privilege, those very laws which you enforce on your fellow-subjects? Forbid it justice! —I am sure, were the noble lords as well acquainted as I am, with but half the difficulties and delays occasioned in the courts of justice, under pretence of privilege, they would not, nay, they could not, oppose this bill.

6. I have waited with patience to hear what arguments might be urged against this bill; but I have waited in vain: the truth is, there is no argument that can weigh against it. The justice and expediency of the bill are such as render it self-evident. It is a proposition of that nature, which can neither be weakened by argument, nor entangled with sophistry. Much, indeed, has been said by some noble lords, on the wisdom of our ancestors, and how differently they thought from us. They not only decreed, that privilege should prevent all civil suits from proceeding during the sitting of parliament, but likewise granted protection to the very servants of members. I shall say nothing on the wisdom of our ancestors; it might perhaps appear invidious: that is not necessary in the present case.

7. I shall only say, that the noble lords who flatter themselves with the weight of that reflection, should remember, that as circumstances alter, things themselves should alter. Formerly, it was not so fashionable either for masters or servants to run in debt, as it is at present. Formerly, we were not that great commercial nation we are at present; nor formerly were merchants and manufacturers members of parliament as at present. The case is now very different: both merchants and manufacturers are, with great propriety, elected members of the lower house.

8. Commerce having thus got into the legislative body of the kingdom, privilege must be done away. We all know, that the very soul and essence of trade are regular payments; and sad experience teaches us, that there are men, who will not make their regular payments without the compulsive power of the laws.

The law then ought to be equally open to all. Any exemption to particular men, or particular ranks of men, is, in a free and commercial country, a solecism of the grossest nature.

9. But I will not trouble your lordships with arguments for that, which is sufficiently evident without any. I shall only say a few words to some noble lords, who foresee much inconvenience, from the persons of their servants being liable to be arrested. One noble lord observes, That the coachman of a peer may be arrested, while he is driving his master to the House, and that, consequently, he will not be able to attend his duty in parliament. If this were actually to happen, there are so many methods by which the member might still get to the House, that I can hardly think the noble lord is serious in his objection.

10. Another noble peer said, That, by this bill, one might lose his most valuable and honest servants. This I hold to be a contradiction in terms: for he can neither be a valuable servant, nor an honest man, who gets into debt which he is neither able nor willing to pay, till compelled by the law. If my servant, by unforeseen accidents, has got into debt, and I still wish to retain him, I certainly would pay the demand. But upon no principle of liberal legislation whatever, can my servant have a title to set his creditors at defiance, while, for forty shillings only, the honest tradesman may be torn from his family, and locked up in a gaol. It is monstrous injustice! I flatter myself, however, the determination of this day will entirely put an end to all these partial proceedings for the future, by passing into a law the bill now under your lordships' consideration.

11. I come now to speak, upon what, indeed, I would have gladly avoided, had I not been particularly pointed at, for the part I have taken in this bill. It has been said, by a noble lord on my left hand, that I likewise am running the race of popularity. If the noble lord means by popularity, that applause bestowed by after-ages on good and virtuous actions, I have long been struggling in that race: to what purpose, all-trying time can alone determine.

12. But if the nobler lord means that mushroom popularity, which is raised without merit, and lost without a crime, he is much mistaken in his opinion. I defy the noble lord to point out a single action of my life, in which the popularity of the times ever had the smallest influence on my determinations. I thank God I have a more permanent and steady rule for my conduct,—the dictates of my own breast.

13. Those who have forgone that pleasing adviser, and given up their mind to be the slave of every popular impulse, I sincerely pity: I pity them still more, if their vanity leads them to mistake the shouts of a mob, for the trumpet of fame. Experience might inform them, that many, who have been saluted with the huzzas of a crowd one day, have received their execrations the next; and many, who by the popularity of their times, have been held up as spotless patriots, have, nevertheless, appeared upon the historian's page, when truth has triumphed over delusion, the assassins of liberty.

14. Why then the noble lord can think I am ambitious of present popularity, that echo of folly, and shadow of renown, I am at a loss to determine. Besides, I do not know that the bill now

before your lordships will be popular: it depends much upon the caprice of the day. It may not be popular to compel people to pay their debts; and, in that case, the present must be a very unpopular bill.

15. It may not be popular either to take away any of the privileges of parliament; for I very well remember, and many of your lordships may remember, that, not long ago, the popular cry was for the extension of privilege; and so far did they carry it at that time, that it was said, the privilege protected members even in criminal actions; nay, such was the power of popular prejudices over weak minds, that the very decisions of some of the courts were tinctured with that doctrine. It was undoubtedly an abominable doctrine. I thought so then, and I think so still: but, nevertheless, it was a popular doctrine, and came immediately from those who are called the friends of liberty; how deservedly, time will show.

16. True liberty, in my opinion, can only exist when justice is equally administered to all; to the king and to the beggar. Where is the justice then, or where is the law that protects a member of parliament, more than any other man, from the punishment due to his crimes? The laws of this country allow of no place, nor any employment, to be a sanctuary for crimes; and where I have the honour to sit as judge, neither royal favour, nor popular applause, shall protect the guilty.

17. I have now only to beg pardon for having employed so much of your lordships' time; and I am sorry a bill, fraught with so many good consequences, has not met with an abler advocate: but I doubt not your lordships' determination will convince the world, that a bill, calculated to contribute so much to the equal distribution of justice as the present, requires with your lordships but very little support.

## SECTION V.
### *An address to young persons.*

1. I INTEND, in this address, to show you the importance of beginning early to give serious attention to your conduct. As soon as you are capable of reflection, you must perceive that there is a right and a wrong in human actions. You see, that those who are born with the same advantages of fortune, are not all equally prosperous in the course of life. While some of them, by wise and steady conduct, attain distinction in the world, and pass their days with comfort and honour; others, of the same rank, by mean and vicious behaviour, forfeit the advantages of their birth; involve themselves in much misery; and end in being a disgrace to their friends, and a burden on society.

2. Early, then, may you learn, that it is not on the external condition in which you find yourselves placed, but on the part which you are to act, that your welfare or unhappiness, your honour or infamy, depends. Now, when beginning to act that part, what can be of greater moment, than to regulate your plan of conduct with the most serious attention, before you have yet committed any fatal or irretrievable errors?

3. If instead of exerting reflection for this valuable purpose, you deliver yourselves up, at so critical a time, to sloth and pleasures; if you refuse to listen to any counsellor but humour, or to attend to any pursuit except that of amusement; if you allow your

selves to float loose and careless on the tide of life, ready to receive any direction which the current of fashion may chance to give you; what can you expect to follow from such beginnings?

4. While so many around you are undergoing the sad consequences of a like indiscretion, for what reason shall not those consequences extend to you? Shall you attain success without that preparation, and escape dangers without that precaution, which are required of others? Shall happiness grow up to you, of its own accord, and solicit your acceptance, when, to the rest of mankind, it is the fruit of long cultivation, and the acquisition of labour and care?

5. Deceive not yourselves with those arrogant hopes. Whatever be your rank, Providence will not, for your sake, reverse its established order. The Author of your being hath enjoined you to "take heed to your ways; to ponder the paths of your feet; to remember your Creator in the days of your youth."

6. He hath decreed, that they only "who seek after wisdom, shall find it; that fools shall be afflicted, because of their transgressions; and that whoever refuseth instruction, shall destroy his own soul." By listening to these admonitions, and tempering the vivacity of youth with a proper mixture of serious thought, you may ensure cheerfulness for the rest of life; but by delivering yourselves up at present to giddiness and levity, you lay the foundation of lasting heaviness of heart.

7. When you look forward to those plans of life, which either your circumstances have suggested, or your friends have proposed, you will not hesitate to acknowledge, that in order to pursue them with advantage, some previous discipline is requisite. Be assured, that whatever is to be your profession, no education is more necessary to your success, than the acquirement of virtuous dispositions and habits. This is the universal preparation for every character, and every station in life.

8. Bad as the world is, respect is always paid to virtue. In the usual course of human affairs, it will be found, that a plain understanding, joined with acknowledged worth, contributes more to prosperity, than the brightest parts without probity or honour. Whether science, or business, or public life, be your aim, virtue still enters, for a principal share, into all those great departments of society. It is connected with eminence, in every liberal art; with reputation in every branch of fair and useful business; with distinction in every public station.

9. The vigour which it gives the mind, and the weight which it adds to character; the generous sentiments which it breathes; the undaunted spirit which it inspires; the ardour of diligence which it quickens; the freedom which it procures from pernicious and dishonourable avocations; are the foundations of all that is highly honourable, or greatly successful among men.

10. Whatever ornamental or engaging endowments you now possess, virtue is a necessary requisite, in order to their shining with proper lustre. Feeble are the attractions of the fairest form, if it be suspected that nothing within corresponds to the pleasing appearance without. Short are the triumphs of wit, when it is supposed to be the vehicle of malice.

11. By whatever means you may at first attract the attention,

you can hold the esteem, and secure the hearts of others, only by amiable dispositions, and the accomplishments of the mind. These are the qualities whose influence will last, when the lustre of all that once sparkled and dazzled has passed away.

12. Let not then the season of youth be barren of improvements, so essential to your future felicity and honour. Now is the seed-time of life; and according to "what you sow, you shall reap." Your character is now, under Divine assistance, of your own forming; your fate is, in some measure, put into your own hands.

13. Your nature is as yet pliant and soft. Habits have not established their dominion. Prejudices have not pre-occupied your understanding. The world has not had time to contract and debase your affections. All your powers are more vigorous, disembarrassed, and free, than they will be at any future period.

14. Whatever impulse you now give to your desires and passions, the direction is likely to continue. It will form the channel in which your life is to run; nay, it may determine its everlasting issue. Consider then the employment of this important period, as the highest trust which shall ever be committed to you; as in a great measure, decisive of your happiness, in time, and in eternity.

15. As in the succession of the seasons, each, by the invariable laws of nature, affects the productions of what is next in course; so, in human life, every period of our age, according as it is well or ill spent, influences the happiness of that which is to follow. Virtuous youth gradually brings forward accomplished and flourishing manhood; and such manhood passes of itself, without uneasiness, into respectable and tranquil old age.

16. But when nature is turned out of its regular course, disorder takes place in the moral, just as in the vegetable world. If the spring put forth no blossoms, in summer there will be no beauty, and in autumn, no fruit: so, if youth be trifled away without improvement, manhood will probably be contemptible, and old age miserable. If the beginnings of life have been "vanity," its latter end can scarcely be any other than "vexation of spirit."

17. I shall finish this address, with calling your attention to that dependence on the blessing of Heaven, which, amidst all your endeavours after improvement, you ought continually to preserve. It is too common with the young, even when they resolve to tread the path of virtue and honour, to set out with presumptuous confidence in themselves.

18. Trusting to their own abilities for carrying them successfully through life, they are careless of applying to God, or of deriving any assistance from what they are apt to reckon the gloomy discipline of religion. Alas! how little do they know the dangers which await them? Neither human wisdom, nor human virtue, unsupported by religion, is equal to the trying situations which often occur in life.

19. By the shock of temptation, how frequently have the most virtuous intentions been overthrown? Under the pressure of disaster, how often has the greatest constancy sunk? "Every good, and every perfect gift, is from above." Wisdom and virtue, as well as "riches and honour, come from God." Destitute of his favour,

you are in no better situation, with all your boasted abilities, than orphans left to wander in a trackless desert, without any guide to conduct them, or any shelter to cover them from the gathering storm.

20. Correct, then, this ill-founded arrogance. Expect not, that your happiness can be independent of Him who made you. By faith and repentance, apply to the Redeemer of the world. By piety and prayer, seek the protection of the God of heaven.

21. I conclude with the solemn words, in which a great prince delivered his dying charge to his son: words, which every young person ought to consider as addressed to himself, and to engrave deeply on his heart: "Solomon, my son, know thou the God of thy fathers; and serve him with a perfect heart, and with a willing mind. For the Lord searcheth all hearts, and understandeth all the imaginations of the thoughts. If thou seek him, he will be found of thee; but if thou forsake him, he will cast thee off for ever."

BLAIR.

## CHAPTER IX.
### PROMISCUOUS PIECES.
### SECTION I.
*Earthquake at Calabria, in the year* 1638.

1. AN account of this dreadful earthquake, is given by the celebrated father Kircher. It happened whilst he was on his journey to visit Mount Ætna, and the rest of the wonders that lie towards the South of Italy. Kircher is considered, by scholars, as one of the greatest prodigies of learning. "Having hired a boat, in company with four more, (two friars of the order of St. Francis, and two seculars,) we launched from the harbour of Messina, in Sicily; and arrived, the same day, at the promontory of Pelorus. Our destination was for the city of Euphæmia, in Calabria; where we had some business to transact; and where we designed to tarry for some time.

2. "However, Providence seemed willing to cross our design; for we were obliged to continue three days at Pelorus, on account of the weather; and though we often put out to sea, yet we were as often driven back. At length, wearied with the delay, we resolved to prosecute our voyage; and, although the sea seemed more than usually agitated, we ventured forward.

3. "The gulf of Charybdis, which we approached, seemed whirled round in such a manner, as to form a vast hollow, verging to a point in the centre. Proceeding onward, and turning my eyes to Ætna, I saw it cast forth large volumes of smoke, of mountainous sizes, which entirely covered the island, and blotted out the very shores from my view. This, together with the dreadful noise, and the sulphurous stench which was strongly perceived, filled me with apprehensions, that some more dreadful calamity was impending.

4. "The sea itself seemed to wear a very unusual appearance: they who have seen a lake in a violent shower of rain, covered all over with bubbles, will conceive some idea of its agitations. My surprise was still increased, by the calmness and serenity of the

weather; not a breeze, not a cloud, which might be supposed to put all nature thus into motion. I therefore warned my companions, that an earthquake was approaching; and, after some time, making for the shore with all possible diligence, we landed at Tropæa, happy and thankful for having escaped the threatening dangers of the sea.

5. "But our triumphs at land were of short duration; for we had scarcely arrived at the Jesuits' College, in that city, when our ears were stunned with a horrid sound, resembling that of an infinite number of chariots, driven fiercely forward; the wheels rattling, and the thongs cracking. Soon after this, a most dreadful earthquake ensued; so that the whole tract upon which we stood seemed to vibrate, as if we were in the scale of a balance that continued wavering. This motion, however, soon grew more violent; and being no longer able to keep my legs, I was thrown prostrate upon the ground. In the mean time, the universal ruin round me redoubled my amazement.

6. "The crash of falling houses, the tottering of towers, and the groans of the dying, all contributed to raise my terror and despair. On every side of me, I saw nothing but a scene of ruin; and danger threatening wherever I should fly. I recommended myself to God, as my last great refuge.

7. "At that hour, O how vain was every sublunary happiness! Wealth, honour, empire, wisdom, all mere useless sounds, and as empty as the bubbles of the deep! Just standing on the threshold of eternity, nothing but God was my pleasure; and the nearer I approached, I only loved him the more.

8. "After some time, however, finding that I remained unhurt, amidst the general concussion, I resolved to venture for safety; and running as fast as I could, I reached the shore, but almost terrified out of my reason. I did not search long here, till I found the boat in which I had landed; and my companions also, whose terrors were even greater than mine. Our meeting was not of that kind, where every one is desirous of telling his own happy escape: it was all silence, and a gloomy dread of impending terrors.

9. "Leaving this seat of desolation, we prosecuted our voyage along the coast; and the next day came to Rochetta, where we landed, although the earth still continued in violent agitations. But we had scarcely arrived at our inn, when we were once more obliged to return to the boat; and, in about half an hour, we saw the greater part of the town, and the inn at which we had put up, dashed to the ground, and burying the inhabitants beneath the ruins.

10. "In this manner, proceeding onward in our little vessel, finding no safety at land, and yet, from the smallness of our boat, having but a very dangerous continuance at sea, we at length landed at Lopizium, a castle midway between Tropæa and Euphæmia, the city to which, as I said before, we were bound. Here, wherever I turned my eyes, nothing but scenes of ruin and horror appeared; towns and castles levelled to the ground; Strombalo, though at sixty miles distance, belching forth flames in an unusual manner, and with a noise which I could distinctly hear.

11. "But my attention was quickly turned from more remote,

to contiguous danger. The rumbling sound of an approaching earthquake, which we by this time were grown acquainted with, alarmed us for the consequences; it every moment seemed to grow louder, and to approach nearer. The place on which we stood now began to shake most dreadfully; so that being unable to stand, my companions and I caught hold of whatever shrub grew next to us, and supported ourselves in that manner.

12. "After some time, this violent paroxysm ceasing, we again stood up, in order to prosecute our voyage to Euphæmia, which lay within sight. In the mean time, while we were preparing for this purpose, I turned my eyes towards the city, but could see only a frightful dark cloud, that seemed to rest upon the place. This the more surprised us, as the weather was so very serene.

13. "We waited, therefore, till the cloud had passed away: then turning to look for the city, it was totally sunk. Wonderful to tell! nothing but a dismal and putrid lake was seen where it stood. We looked about to find some one that could tell us of its sad catastrophe, but could see no person. All was become a melancholy solitude; a scene of hideous desolation.

14. "Thus proceeding pensively along, in quest of some human being that could give us a little information, we at length saw a boy sitting by the shore, and appearing stupified with terror. Of him, therefore, we inquired concerning the fate of the city; but he could not be prevailed on to give us an answer.

15. "We entreated him, with every expression of tenderness and pity to tell us; but his senses were quite wrapt up in the contemplation of the danger he had escaped. We offered him some victuals, but he seemed to loath the sight. We still persisted in our offices of kindness; but he only pointed to the place of the city, like one out of his senses; and then running up into the woods, was never heard of after. Such was the fate of the city of Euphæmia.

16. "As we continued our melancholy course along the shore, the whole coast, for the space of two hundred miles, presented nothing but the remains of cities; and men scattered, without a habitation, over the fields. Proceeding thus along, we at length ended our distressful voyage by arriving at Naples, after having escaped a thousand dangers both at sea and land." GOLDSMITH.

## SECTION II.
### *Letter from* Pliny *to* Geminius.

1. Do we not sometimes observe a sort of people, who, though they are themselves under the abject dominion of every vice, show a kind of malicious resentment against the errors of others; and are most severe upon those whom they most resemble? yet, surely a lenity of disposition, even in persons who have the least occasion for clemency themselves, is of all virtues the most becoming.

2. The highest of all characters, in my estimation, is his, who is as ready to pardon the errors of mankind, as if he were every day guilty of some himself; and, at the same time, as cautious of committing a fault, as if he never forgave one. It is a rule then which we should, upon all occasions, both private and public, most religiously observe; "to be inexorable to our own failings, while

we treat those of the rest of the world with tenderness, not excepting even such as forgive none but themselves."

3. I shall, perhaps, be asked, who it is that has given occasion to these reflections. Know then that a certain person lately—but of that when we meet—though, upon second thoughts, not even then; lest, whilst I condemn and expose his conduct, I shall act counter to that maxim I particularly recommend. Whoever therefore, and whatever he is, shall remain in silence: for though there may be some use, perhaps, in setting a mark upon the man, for the sake of example, there will be more, however, in sparing him, for the sake of humanity. Farewell. MELMOTH'S PLINY.

## SECTION III.

*Letter from* PLINY *to* MARCELLINUS, *on the death of an amiable young woman.*

1. I WRITE this under the utmost oppression of sorrow: the youngest daughter of my friend Fundanus is dead! Never surely was there a more agreeable, and more amiable young person; or one who better deserved to have enjoyed a long, I had almost said, an immortal life! She had all the wisdom of age, and discretion of a matron, joined with youthful sweetness and virgin modesty.

2. With what an engaging fondness did she behave to her father! How kindly and respectfully receive his friends! How affectionately treat all those who, in their respective offices, had the care and education of her!

3. She employed much of her time in reading, in which she discovered great strength of judgment; she indulged herself in few diversions, and those with much caution. With what forbearance, with what patience, with what courage, did she endure her last illness! She complied with all the directions of her physicians; she encouraged her sister, and her father; and, when all her strength of body was exhausted, supported herself by the single vigour of her mind. That, indeed, continued, even to her last moments, unbroken by the pain of a long illness, or the terrors of approaching death; and it is a reflection which makes the loss of her so much the more to be lamented. A loss infinitely severe! and more severe by the particular conjuncture in which it happened!

4. She was contracted to a most worthy youth; the wedding day was fixed, and we were all invited.—How sad a change from the highest joy, to the deepest sorrow! How shall I express the wound that pierced my heart, when I heard Fundanus himself, (as grief is ever finding out circumstances to aggravate its affliction,) ordering the money he had designed to lay out upon clothes and jewels for her marriage, to be employed in myrrh and spices for her funeral!

5. He is a man of great learning and good sense, who has applied himself, from his earliest youth, to the noblest and most elevated studies: but all the maxims of fortitude which he has received from books, or advanced himself, he now absolutely rejects; and every other virtue of his heart gives place to all a parent's tenderness. We shall excuse, we shall even approve his sorrow, when we consider what he has lost. He has lost a daughter who resembled him in his manners, as well as his person; and exactly copied out all her father.

6. If his friend Marcellinus shall think proper to write to him, upon the subject of so reasonable a grief, let me remind him not to use the rougher arguments of consolation, and such as seem to carry a sort of reproof with them; but those of kind and sympathizing humanity.

7. Time will render him more open to the dictates of reason: for as a fresh wound shrinks back from the hand of the surgeon, but by degrees submits to, and even requires the means of its cure; so a mind, under the first impressions of a misfortune, shuns and rejects all arguments of consolation; but at length, if applied with tenderness, calmly and willingly acquiesces in them. Farewell.

MELMOTH'S PLINY.

## SECTION IV.
*On discretion.*

1. I HAVE often thought, if the minds of men were laid open, we should see but little difference between that of a wise man, and that of a fool. There are infinite reveries, numberless extravagances, and a succession of vanities, which pass through both. The great difference is, that the first knows how to pick and cull his thoughts for conversation, by suppressing some, and communicating others; whereas the other lets them all indifferently fly out in words. This sort of discretion, however, has no place in private conversation between intimate friends. On such occasions, the wisest men very often talk like the weakest; for indeed talking with a friend is nothing else than *thinking aloud*.

2. Tully has therefore very justly exposed a precept, delivered by some ancient writers, That a man should live with his enemy in such a manner, as might leave him room to become his friend; and with his friend, in such a manner, that, if he became his enemy, it should not be in his power to hurt him. The first part of this rule, which regards our behaviour towards an enemy, is indeed very reasonable, as well as very prudential; but the latter part of it, which regards our behaviour towards a friend, savours more of cunning than of discretion: and would cut a man off from the greatest pleasures of life, which are the freedoms of conversation with a bosom friend. Besides that, when a friend is turned into an enemy, the world is just enough to accuse the perfidiousness of the friend, rather than the indiscretion of the person who confided in him.

3. Discretion does not only show itself in words, but in all the circumstances of action; and is like an under-agent of Providence, to guide and direct us in the ordinary concerns of life. There are many more shining qualities in the mind of man, but there is none so useful as discretion. It is this, indeed, which gives a value to all the rest; which sets them at work in their proper times and places; and turns them to the advantage of the person who is possessed of them. Without it, learning is pedantry, and wit impertinence; virtue itself looks like weakness; the best parts only qualify a man to be more sprightly in errors, and active to his own prejudice.

4. Discretion does not only make a man the master of his own parts, but of other men's. The discreet man finds out the talents of those he converses with; and knows how to apply them to proper uses. Accordingly, if we look into particular communities and

divisions of men, we may observe, that it is the discreet man, not the witty, nor the learned, nor the brave, who guides the conversation, and gives measures to society. A man with great talents, but void of discretion, is like Polyphemus in the fable, strong and blind; endued with an irresistible force, which, for want of sight, is of no use to him.

5. Though a man has all other perfections, yet if he wants discretion, he will be of no great consequence in the world; on the contrary, if he has this single talent in perfection, and but a common share of others, he may do what he pleases in his particular station of life.

6. At the same time that I think discretion the most useful talent a man can be master of, I look upon cunning to be the accomplishment of little, mean, ungenerous minds. Discretion points out the noblest ends to us; and pursues the most proper and laudable methods of attaining them: cunning has only private selfish aims; and sticks at nothing which may make them succeed.

7. Discretion has large and extended views; and, like a well-formed eye, commands a whole horizon: cunning is a kind of short-sightedness, that discovers the minutest objects which are near at hand, but is not able to discern things at a distance. Discretion, the more it is discovered, gives a greater authority to the person who possesses it: cunning, when it is once detected, loses its force, and makes a man incapable of bringing about even those events which he might have done, had he passed only for a plain man.

8. Discretion is the perfection of reason; and a guide to us in all the duties of life: cunning is a kind of instinct, that only looks out after our immediate interest and welfare. Discretion is only found in men of strong sense and good understandings: cunning is often to be met with in brutes themselves; and in persons who are but the fewest removes from them. In short, cunning is only the mimic of discretion; and it may pass upon weak men, in the same manner as vivacity is often mistaken for wit, and gravity, for wisdom.

9. The cast of mind which is natural to a discreet man, makes him look forward into futurity, and consider what will be his condition millions of ages hence, as well as what it is at present. He knows that the misery or happiness which is reserved for him in another world, loses nothing of its reality by being placed at so great a distance from him. The objects do not appear little to him because they are remote. He considers, that those pleasures and pains which lie hid in eternity, approach nearer to him every moment; and will be present with him in their full weight and measure, as much as those pains and pleasures which he feels at this very instant. For this reason, he is careful to secure to himself that which is the proper happiness of his nature, and the ultimate design of his being.

10. He carries his thoughts to the end of every action; and considers the most distant, as well as the most immediate effects of it. He supersedes every little prospect of gain and advantage which offers itself here, if he does not find it consistent with his views of an hereafter. In a word, his hopes are full of immortality; his schemes are large and glorious; and his conduct suitable to one who knows his true interest, and how to pursue it by proper methods. ADDISON.

## SECTION V.

### On the government of our thoughts.

1. A MULTITUDE of cases occur, in which we are no less accountable for what we think, than for what we do. As, first, when the introduction of any train of thought depends upon ourselves, and is our voluntary act, by turning our attention towards such objects, awakening such passions, or engaging in such employments, as we know must give a peculiar determination to our thoughts. Next, when thoughts, by whatever accident they may have been originally suggested, are indulged with deliberation and complacency.

2. Though the mind has been passive in their reception, and, therefore, free from blame; yet, if it be active in their continuance, the guilt becomes its own. They may have intruded at first, like unbidden guests; but if when entered, they are made welcome, and kindly entertained, the case is the same as if they had been invited from the beginning.

3. If we are thus accountable to God for thoughts either voluntarily introduced, or deliberately indulged, we are no less so, in the last place, for those which find admittance into our hearts from supine negligence, from total relaxation of attention, from allowing our imagination to rove with entire license, "like the eyes of the fool, towards the end of the earth."

4. Our minds are, in this case, thrown open to folly and vanity. They are prostituted to every evil thing which pleases to take possession. The consequences must all be charged to our account; and in vain we plead excuse from human infirmity. Hence it appears, that the great object at which we are to aim in governing our thoughts, is, to take the most effectual measures for preventing the introduction of such as are sinful; and for hastening their expulsion, if they shall have introduced themselves without consent of the will.

5. But when we descend into our breasts, and examine how far we have studied to keep this object in view, who can tell, "how oft he hath offended?" In no article of religion or morals are men more culpably remiss, than in the unrestrained indulgence they give to fancy; and that too, for the most part, without remorse. Since the time that reason began to exert her powers, thought, during our waking hours, has been active in every breast, without a moment's suspension or pause.

6. The current of ideas has been always flowing. The wheels of the spiritual engine have circulated with perpetual motion. Let me ask, what has been the fruit of this incessant activity, with the greater part of mankind? Of the innumerable hours that have been employed in thought, how few are marked with any permanent or useful effect? How many have either passed away in idle dreams; or have been abandoned to anxious discontented musings, to unsocial and malignant passions, or to irregular and criminal desires?

7. Had I power to lay open that storehouse of iniquity which the hearts of too many conceal; could I draw out and read to them a list of all the imaginations they have devised, and all the passions they have indulged in secret; what a picture of men should I present to themselves! What crimes would th

pear to have perpetrated in secrecy, which to their most intimate companions they durst not reveal!

8. Even when men imagine their thoughts to be innocently employed, they too commonly suffer them to run out into extravagant imaginations, and chimerical plans of what they would wish to attain, or choose to be, if they could frame the course of things according to their desire. Though such employments of fancy come not under the same description with those which are plainly criminal, yet wholly unblamable they seldom are. Besides the waste of time which they occasion, and the misapplication which they indicate of those intellectual powers that were given to us for much nobler purposes, such romantic speculations lead us always into the neighbourhood of forbidden regions.

9. They place us on dangerous ground. They are, for the most part, connected with some one bad passion; and they always nourish a giddy and frivolous turn of thought. They unfit the mind for applying with vigour to rational pursuits, or for acquiescing in sober plans of conduct. From that ideal world in which it allows itself to dwell, it returns to the commerce of men, unbent and relaxed, sickly and tainted, averse to discharging the duties, and sometimes disqualified even for relishing the pleasures of ordinary life. BLAIR.

## SECTION VI.
*On the evils which flow from unrestrained passions.*

1. WHEN man revolted from his Maker, his passions rebelled against himself; and, from being originally the ministers of reason, have become the tyrants of the soul. Hence, in treating of this subject, two things may be assumed as principles: first, that through the present weakness of the understanding, our passions are often directed towards improper objects; and next, that even when their direction is just, and their objects are innocent, they perpetually tend to run into excess; they always hurry us towards their gratification, with a blind and dangerous impetuosity. On these two points then turns the whole government of our passions: first, to ascertain the proper objects of their pursuit; and next, to restrain them in that pursuit, when they would carry us beyond the bounds of reason.

2. If there is any passion which intrudes itself unseasonably into our mind, which darkens and troubles our judgment, or habitually discomposes our temper; which unfits us for properly discharging the duties, or disqualifies us for cheerfully enjoying the comforts of life, we may certainly conclude it to have gained a dangerous ascendant. The great object which we ought to propose to ourselves is, to acquire a firm and steadfast mind, which the infatuation of passion shall not seduce, nor its violence shake; which, resting on fixed principles, shall, in the midst of contending emotions, remain free, and master of itself; able to listen calmly to the voice of conscience, and prepared to obey its dictates without hesitation.

3. To obtain, if possible, such command of passion, is one of the highest attainments of the rational nature. Arguments to show its importance crowd upon us from every quarter. If there be any fertile source of mischief to human life, it is, beyond doubt, the misrule of passion. It is this which poisons the enjoyment of individuals, overturns the order of society, and strews the path of life with so many miseries, as to render it indeed the vale of tears.

**4.** All those great scenes of public calamity, which we behold with astonishment and horror, have originated from the source of violent passions. These have overspread the earth with bloodshed. These have pointed the assassin's dagger, and filled the poisoned bowl. These, in every age, have furnished too copious materials for the orator's pathetic declamation, and for the poet's tragical song. When from public life we descend to private conduct, though passion operates not there in so wide and destructive a sphere, we shall find its influence to be no less baneful.

**5.** I need not mention the black and fierce passions, such as envy, jealousy, and revenge, whose effects are obviously noxious, and whose agitations are immediate misery. But take any of the licentious and sensual kind. Suppose it to have unlimited scope; trace it throughout its course; and we shall find that gradually, as it rises, it taints the soundness, and troubles the peace, of his mind over whom it reigns; that, in its progress, it engages him in pursuits which are marked either with danger or with shame; that, in the end, it wastes his fortune, destroys his health, or debases his character; and aggravates all the miseries in which it has involved him, with the concluding pangs of bitter remorse. Through all the stages of this fatal course, how many have heretofore run? What multitudes do we daily behold pursuing it, with blind and headlong steps? BLAIR.

## SECTION VII.

*On the proper state of our temper, with respect to one another.*

**1.** It is evident, in the general, that if we consult either public welfare or private happiness, Christian charity ought to regulate our disposition in mutual intercourse. But as this great principle admits of several diversified appearances, let us consider some of the chief forms under which it ought to show itself in the usual tenor of life.

**2.** What, first, presents itself to be recommended, is a peaceable temper; a disposition averse to give offence, and desirous of cultivating harmony, and amicable intercourse in society. This supposes yielding and condescending manners, unwillingness to contend with others about trifles, and, in contests that are unavoidable, proper moderation of spirit.

**3.** Such a temper is the first principle of self-enjoyment. It is the basis of all order and happiness among mankind. The positive and contentious, the rude and quarrelsome, are the bane of society. They seem destined to blast the small share of comfort which nature has here allotted to man. But they cannot disturb the peace of others, more than they break their own. The hurricane rages first in their own bosom, before it is let forth upon the world. In the tempests which they raise, they are always tost; and frequently it is their lot to perish.

**4.** A peaceable temper must be supported by a candid one, or a disposition to view the conduct of others with fairness and impartiality. This stands opposed to a jealous and suspicious temper, which ascribes every action to the worst motive, and throws a black shade over every character. If we would be happy in ourselves, or in our connexions with others, let us guard against this malignant spirit. Let us study that charity " which thinketh no evil;" that temper which, without degenerating into credulity, will dispose us to be just; and which can allow us to observe an error, without imputing it as a crime. Thus we shall be kept free from that continual irritation, which imaginary injuries raise in a suspicious breast; and shall walk among men as our brethren, not as our enemies.

5. But to be peaceable, and to be candid, is not all that is required of a good man. He must cultivate a kind, generous, and sympathizing temper, which feels for distress, wherever it is beheld; which enters into the concerns of his friends with ardour; and to all with whom he has intercourse, is gentle, obliging, and humane. How amiable appears such a disposition, when contrasted with a malicious or envious temper, which wraps itself up in its own narrow interest, looks with an evil eye on the success of others, and, with an unnatural satisfaction, feeds on their disappointments or miseries! How little does he know of the true happiness of life, who is a stranger to that intercourse of good offices and kind affections, which, by a pleasing charm, attaches men to one another, and circulates joy from heart to heart!

6. We are not to imagine, that a benevolent temper finds no exercise, unless when opportunities offer of performing actions of high generosity, or of extensive utility. These may seldom occur. The condition of the greater part of mankind in a good measure, precludes them. But, in the ordinary round of human affairs, many occasions daily present themselves, of mitigating the vexations which others suffer; of soothing their minds; of aiding their interest; of promoting their cheerfulness, or ease. Such occasions may relate to the smaller incidents of life.

7. But let us remember, that of small incidents the system of human life is chiefly composed. The attentions which respect these, when suggested by real benignity of temper, are often more material to the happiness of those around us, than actions which carry the appearance of greater dignity and splendour. No wise or good man ought to account any rules of behaviour as below his regard, which tend to cement the great brotherhood of mankind in comfortable union. Particularly amidst that familiar intercourse which belongs to domestic life, all the virtues of temper find an ample range.

8. It is very unfortunate, that within that circle, men too often think themselves at liberty, to give unrestrained vent to the caprice of passion and humour. Whereas there, on the contrary, more than any where else, it concerns them to attend to the government of their heart; to check what is violent in their tempers, and to soften what is harsh in their manners. For there the temper is formed. There, the real character displays itself. The forms of the world disguise men when abroad. But within his own family, every man is known to be what he truly is.

9. In all our intercourse then with others, particularly in that which is closest and most intimate, let us cultivate a peaceable, a candid, a gentle, and friendly temper. This is the temper to which, by repeated injunctions, our holy religion seeks to form us. This was the temper of Christ. This is the temper of Heaven.

BLAIR.

## SECTION VIII.
*Excellence of the holy Scriptures.*

1. Is it bigotry to believe the sublime truths of the Gospel, with full assurance of faith? I glory in such bigotry. I would not part with it for a thousand worlds. I congratulate the man who is possessed of it: for, amidst all the vicissitudes and calamities of the present state, that man enjoys an inexhaustible fund of consolation, of which it is not in the power of fortune to deprive him.

2. There is not a book on earth, so favourable to all the kind, and all the sublime affections; or so unfriendly to hatred and persecution, to tyranny, to injustice, and every sort of malevolence, as the Gospel. It breathes nothing throughout, but mercy, benevolence, and peace.

3. Poetry is sublime, when it awakens in the mind any great and good affection, as piety, or patriotism. This is one of the noblest effects of the art. The Psalms are remarkable, beyond all other writings, for their power of inspiring devout emotions. But it is not in this respect only, that they are sublime. Of the divine nature, they contain the most magnificent descriptions, that the soul of man can comprehend. The hundred and fourth Psalm, in particular, displays the power and goodness of Providence, in creating and preserving the world, and the various tribes of animals in it, with such majestic brevity and beauty, as it is vain to look for in any human composition.

4. Such of the doctrines of the Gospel as are level to human capacity, appear to be agreeable to the purest truth, and the soundest morality. All the genius and learning of the heathen world; all the penetration of Pythagoras, Socrates, and Aristotle, had never been able to produce such a system of moral duty, and so rational an account of Providence and of man, as are to be found in the New Testament. Compared, indeed, with this, all other moral and theological wisdom

Loses, discountenanc'd, and like folly shows.   BEATTIE.

## SECTION IX.
*Reflections occasioned by a review of the blessings, pronounced by Christ on his disciples, in his sermon on the mount.*

1. What abundant reason have we to thank God, that this large and instructive discourse of our blessed Redeemer, is so particularly recorded by the sacred historian. Let every one that "hath ears to hear," attend to it: for surely no man ever spoke as our Lord did on this occasion. Let us fix our minds in a posture of humble attention, that we may "receive the law from his mouth."

2. He opened it with blessings, repeated and most important blessings. But on whom are they pronounced? and whom are we taught to think the happiest of mankind? The meek and the humble; the penitent and the merciful; the peaceful and the pure; those that hunger and thirst after righteousness; those that labour, but faint not, under persecution! Lord! how different are thy maxims from those of the children of this world!

3. They call the proud happy; and admire the gay, the rich, the powerful, and the victorious. But let a vain world take its gaudy trifles, and dress up the foolish creatures that pursue them. May our souls share in that happiness, which the Son of God came

to recommend and to procure! May we obtain mercy of the Lord; may we be owned as his children; enjoy his presence; and inherit his kingdom! With these enjoyments, and these hopes, we will cheerfully welcome the lowest, or the most painful circumstances.

4. Let us be animated to cultivate those amiable virtues, which are here recommended to us; this humility and meekness; this penitent sense of sin; this ardent desire after righteousness; this compassion and purity; this peacefulness and fortitude of soul; and, in a word, this universal goodness which becomes us, as we sustain the character of "the salt of the earth," and "the light of the world."

5. Is there not reason to lament, that we answer the character no better? Is there not reason to exclaim with a good man in former times, "Blessed Lord! either these are not thy words, or we are not Christians!" Oh, season our hearts more effectually with thy grace! Pour forth that divine oil on our lamps! Then shall the flame brighten; then shall the ancient honours of thy religion be revived; and multitudes be awakened and animated, by the lustre of it, "to glorify our Father in heaven."

DODDRIDGE.

## SECTION X.
*Schemes of life often illusory.*

1. OMAR, the son of Hassan, had passed seventy-five years in honour and prosperity. The favour of three successive califs had filled his house with gold and silver; and whenever he appeared, the benedictions of the people proclaimed his passage.

2. Terrestrial happiness is of short continuance. The brightness of the flame is wasting its fuel; the fragrant flower is passing away in its own odours. The vigour of Omar began to fail; the curls of beauty fell from his head; strength departed from his hands; and agility from his feet. He gave back to the calif the keys of trust, and the seals of secrecy; and sought no other pleasure for the remains of life, than the converse of the wise, and the gratitude of the good.

3. The powers of his mind were yet unimpaired. His chamber was filled by visitants, eager to catch the dictates of experience, and officious to pay the tribute of admiration. Caled, the son of the viceroy of Egypt, entered every day early, and retired late. He was beautiful and eloquent: Omar admired his wit, and loved his docility. "Tell me," said Caled, "thou to whose voice nations have listened, and whose wisdom is known to the extremities of Asia, tell me how I may resemble Omar the prudent. The arts by which thou hast gained power and preserved it, are to thee no longer necessary or useful; impart to me the secret of thy conduct, and teach me the plan upon which thy wisdom has built thy fortune."

4. "Young man," said Omar, "it is of little use to form plans of life. When I took my first survey of the world, in my twentieth year, having considered the various conditions of mankind, in the hour of solitude I said thus to myself, leaning against a cedar, which spread its branches over my head: 'Seventy years are allowed to man; I have yet fifty remaining.

5. "Ten years I will allot to the attainment of knowledge, and ten I will pass in foreign countries; I shall be learned, and therefore

shall be honoured; every city will shout at my arrival, and every student will solicit my friendship. Twenty years thus passed, will store my mind with images, which I shall be busy, through the rest of my life, in combining and comparing. I shall revel in inexhaustible accumulations of intellectual riches; I shall find new pleasures for every moment; and shall never more be weary of myself.

6. "I will not, however, deviate too far from the beaten track of life; but will try what can be found in female delicacy. I will marry a wife beautiful as the Houries, and wise as Zobeide: with her I will live twenty years within the suburbs of Bagdat, in every pleasure that wealth can purchase, and fancy can invent.

7. "I will then retire to a rural dwelling; pass my days in obscurity and contemplation; and lie silently down on the bed of death. Through my life it shall be my settled resolution, that I will never depend upon the smile of princes; that I will never stand exposed to the artifices of courts; I will never pant for public honours, nor disturb my quiet with the affairs of state.' Such was my scheme of life, which I impressed indelibly upon my memory.

8. "The first part of my ensuing time was to be spent in search of knowledge, and I know not how I was diverted from my design. I had no visible impediments without, nor any ungovernable passions within. I regarded knowledge as the highest honour, and the most engaging pleasure; yet day stole upon day, and month glided after month, till I found that seven years of the first ten had vanished, and left nothing behind them.

9. "I now postponed my purpose of travelling; for why should I go abroad, while so much remained to be learned at home? I immured myself for four years, and studied the laws of the empire. The fame of my skill reached the judges; I was found able to speak upon doubtful questions; and was commanded to stand at the footstool of the calif. I was heard with attention; I was consulted with confidence; and the love of praise fastened on my heart.

10. "I still wished to see distant countries; listened with rapture to the relations of travellers; and resolved some time to ask my dismission, that I might feast my soul with novelty: but my presence was always necessary; and the stream of business hurried me along. Sometimes I was afraid lest I should be charged with ingratitude: but I still proposed to travel, and therefore would not confine myself by marriage.

11. "In my fiftieth year, I began to suspect that the time of travelling was past; and thought it best to lay hold on the felicity yet in my power, and indulge myself in domestic pleasures.' But at fifty no man easily finds a woman beautiful as the Houries, and wise as Zobeide. I inquired and rejected, consulted and deliberated, till the sixty-second year made me ashamed of wishing to marry. I had now nothing left but retirement; and for retirement I never found a time, till disease forced me from public employment.

12. "Such was my scheme, and such has been its consequence. With an insatiable thirst for knowledge, I trifled away the years of improvement; with a restless desire of seeing different countries, I have always resided in the same city; with the highest expectation of connubial felicity, I have lived unmarried; and with unalterable resolutions of contemplative retirement, I am going to die within the walls of Bagdat." DR. JOHNSON

## SECTION XI.
### *The pleasures of virtuous sensibility.*

1. THE good effects of true sensibility on general virtue and happiness, admit of no dispute. Let us consider its effect on the happiness of him who possesses it, and the various pleasures to which it gives him access. If he is master of riches or influence, it affords him the means of increasing his own enjoyment, by relieving the wants, or increasing the comforts of others. If he commands not these advantages, yet all the comforts, which he sees in the possession of the deserving, become in some sort his, by his rejoicing in the good which they enjoy.

2. Even the face of nature yields a satisfaction to him, which the insensible can never know. The profusion of goodness, which he beholds poured forth on the universe, dilates his heart with the thought, that innumerable multitudes around him are blest and happy. When he sees the labours of men appearing to prosper, and views a country flourishing in wealth and industry; when he beholds the spring coming forth in its beauty, and reviving the decayed face of nature; or in autumn beholds the fields loaded with plenty, and the year crowned with all its fruits; he lifts his affections with gratitude to the great Father of all, and rejoices in the general felicity and joy.

3. It may indeed be objected, that the same sensibility lays open the heart to be pierced with many wounds, from the distresses which abound in the world; exposes us to frequent suffering from the participation which it communicates of the sorrows, as well as of the joys of friendship. But let it be considered, that the tender melancholy of sympathy, is accompanied with a sensation, which they who feel it would not exchange for the gratifications of the selfish. When the heart is strongly moved by any of the kind affections, even when it pours itself forth in virtuous sorrow, a secret attractive charm mingles with the painful emotion; there is a joy in the midst of grief.

4. Let it be farther considered, that the griefs which sensibility introduces, are counterbalanced by pleasures which flow from the same source. Sensibility heightens in general the human powers, and is connected with acuteness in all our feelings. If it makes us more alive to some painful sensations, in return, it renders the pleasing ones more vivid and animated.

5. The selfish man languishes in his narrow circle of pleasures. They are confined to what affects his own interest. He is obliged to repeat the same gratifications, till they become insipid. But the man of virtuous sensibility moves in a wider sphere of felicity. His powers are much more frequently called forth into occupations of pleasing activity. Numberless occasions open to him of indulging his favourite taste, by conveying satisfaction to others. Often it is in his power, in one way or other, to sooth the afflicted heart, to carry some consolation into the house of wo.

6. In the scenes of ordinary life, in the domestic and social intercourses of men, the cordiality of his affections cheers and gladdens him. Every appearance, every description of innocent happiness, is enjoyed by him. Every native expression of kindness and affection among others, is felt by him, even though he be not the

object of it. In a circle of friends enjoying one another, he is as happy as the happiest.

7. In a word, he lives in a different sort of world, from what the selfish man inhabits. He possesses a new sense that enables him to behold objects which the selfish cannot see. At the same time, his enjoyments are not of that kind which remain merely on the surface of the mind. They penetrate the heart. They enlarge and elevate, they refine and ennoble it. To all the pleasing emotions of affection, they add the dignified consciousness of virtue.

8. Children of men! men formed by nature to live and to feel as brethren! how long will ye continue to estrange yourselves from one another by competitions and jealousies, when in cordial union ye might be so much more blest? How long will ye seek your happiness in selfish gratifications alone, neglecting those purer and better sources of joy, which flow from the affections and the heart? BLAIR.

## SECTION XII.
### On the true honour of man.

1. THE proper honour of man arises not from some of those splendid actions and abilities, which excite high admiration. Courage and prowess, military renown, signal victories and conquests, may render the name of a man famous, without rendering his character truly honourable. To many brave men, to many heroes renowned in story, we look up with wonder. Their exploits are recorded. Their praises are sung. They stand as on an eminence above the rest of mankind. Their eminence, nevertheless, may not be of that sort, before which we bow with inward esteem and respect. Something more is wanted for that purpose, than the conquering arm, and the intrepid mind.

2. The laurels of the warrior must at all times be dyed in blood, and bedewed with the tears of the widow and the orphan. But if they have been stained by rapine and inhumanity; if sordid avarice has marked his character; or low and gross sensuality has degraded his life; the great hero sinks into a little man. What, at a distance, or on a superficial view, we admired, becomes mean, perhaps odious, when we examine it more closely. It is like the Colossal statue, whose immense size struck the spectator afar off with astonishment; but when nearly viewed, it appears disproportioned, unshapely, and rude.

3. Observations of the same kind may be applied to all the reputation derived from civil accomplishments; from the refined politics of the statesman; or the literary efforts of genius and erudition. These bestow, and within certain bounds, ought to bestow, eminence and distinction on men. They discover talents which in themselves are shining; and which become highly valuable, when employed in advancing the good of mankind. Hence, they frequently give rise to fame. But a distinction is to be made between fame and true honour.

4. The statesman, the orator, or the poet, may be famous; while yet the man himself is far from being honoured. We envy his abilities. We wish to rival them. But we would not choose to be classed with him who possesses them. Instances of this sort are too often found in every record of ancient or modern history.

5. From all this it follows, that in order to discern where man's

true honour lies, we must look, not to any adventitious circumstance of fortune; not to any single sparkling quality; but to the whole of what forms a man; what entitles him, as such, to rank high among that class of beings to which he belongs; in a word, we must look to the mind and the soul.

6. A mind superior to fear, to selfish interest and corruption; a mind governed by the principles of uniform rectitude and integrity; the same in prosperity and adversity; which no bribe can seduce, nor terror overawe; neither by pleasure melted into effeminacy, nor by distress sunk into dejection: such is the mind which forms the distinction and eminence of man.

7. One, who in no situation of life, is either ashamed or afraid of discharging his duty, and acting his proper part with firmness and constancy; true to the God whom he worships, and true to the faith in which he professes to believe; full of affection to his brethren of mankind; faithful to his friends, generous to his enemies, warm with compassion to the unfortunate; self-denying to little private interests and pleasures, but zealous for public interest and happiness; magnanimous, without being proud; humble, without being mean; just, without being harsh; simple in his manners, but manly in his feelings; on whose words we can entirely rely; whose countenance never deceives us; whose professions of kindness are the effusions of his heart: one, in fine, whom, independent of any views of advantage, we would choose for a superior, could trust in as a friend, and could love as a brother—this is the man, whom in our heart, above all others, we do, we must honour. BLAIR.

## SECTION XIII.
*The influence of devotion on the happiness of life.*

1. WHATEVER promotes and strengthens virtue, whatever calms and regulates the temper, is a source of happiness. Devotion produces these effects in a remarkable degree. It inspires composure of spirit, mildness, and benignity; weakens the painful, and cherishes the pleasing emotions; and, by these means, carries on the life of a pious man in a smooth and placid tenor.

2. Besides exerting this habitual influence on the mind, devotion opens a field of enjoyments, to which the vicious are entire strangers; enjoyments the more valuable, as they peculiarly belong to retirement, when the world leaves us; and to adversity, when it becomes our foe. These are the two seasons, for which every wise man would most wish to provide some hidden store of comfort.

3. For let him be placed in the most favourable situation which the human state admits, the world can neither always amuse him, nor always shield him from distress. There will be many hours of vacuity, and many of dejection, in his life. If he be a stranger to God, and to devotion, how dreary will the gloom of solitude often prove! With what oppressive weight will sickness, disappointment, or old age, fall upon his spirits!

4. But for those pensive periods, the pious man has a relief prepared. From the tiresome repetition of the common vanities of life, or from the painful corrosion of its cares and sorrows, devotion transports him into a new region; and surrounds him there with such objects, as are the most fitted to cheer the dejection, to calm the tumults, and to heal the wounds of his heart.

5. If the world has been empty and delusive, it gladdens him with the prospect of a higher and better order of things, about to arise. If men have been ungrateful and base, it displays before him the faithfulness of that Supreme Being, who, though every other friend fail, will never forsake him.

6. Let us consult our experience, and we shall find, that the two greatest sources of inward joy, are, the exercise of love directed towards a deserving object, and the exercise of hope terminating on some high and assured happiness. Both these are supplied by devotion; and therefore we have no reason to be surprised, if, on some occasions, it fills the hearts of good men with a satisfaction not to be expressed.

7. The refined pleasures of a pious mind are, in many respects, superior to the coarse gratifications of sense. They are pleasures which belong to the highest powers and best affections of the soul; whereas the gratifications of sense reside in the lowest region of our nature. To the latter, the soul stoops below its native dignity. The former, raise it above itself. The latter, leave always a comfortless, often a mortifying, remembrance behind them. The former, are reviewed with applause and delight.

8. The pleasures of sense resemble a foaming torrent, which, after a disorderly course, speedily runs out, and leaves an empty and offensive channel. But the pleasures of devotion resemble the equable current of a pure river, which enlivens the fields through which it passes, and diffuses verdure and fertility along its banks.

9. To thee, O Devotion! we owe the highest improvement of our nature, and much of the enjoyment of our life. Thou art the support of our virtue, and the rest of our souls, in this turbulent world. Thou composest the thoughts. Thou calmest the passions. Thou exaltest the heart. Thy communications, and thine only, are imparted to the low, no less than to the high; to the poor, as well as to the rich.

10. In thy presence, worldly distinctions cease; and under thy influence, worldly sorrows are forgotten. Thou art the balm of the wounded mind. Thy sanctuary is ever open to the miserable; inaccessible only to the unrighteous and impure. Thou beginnest on earth the temper of heaven. In thee, the hosts of angels and blessed spirits eternally rejoice. BLAIR.

## SECTION XIV.

*The planetary and terrestrial worlds comparatively considered.*

1. To us, who dwell on its surface, the earth is by far the most extensive orb that our eyes can any where behold: it is also clothed with verdure, distinguished by trees, and adorned with a variety of beautiful decorations; whereas, to a spectator placed on one of the planets, it wears a uniform aspect; looks all luminous; and no larger than a spot. To beings who dwell at still greater distances, it entirely disappears.

2. That which we call alternately the morning and the evening star, (as in one part of the orbit she rides foremost in the procession of night, in the other ushers in and anticipates the dawn,) is a planetary world. This planet, and the four others that so wonderfully vary their mystic dance, are in themselves dark bodies, and shine only by reflection; have fields, and seas, and skies, of

their own; are furnished with all accommodations for animal subsistence, and are supposed to be the abodes of intellectual life; all which, together with our earthly habitation, are dependent on that grand dispenser of Divine munificence, the sun; receive their light from the distribution of his rays, and derive their comfort from his benign agency.

3. The sun, which seems to perform its daily stages through the sky, is in this respect fixed and immoveable: it is the great axle of heaven, about which the globe we inhabit, and other more spacious orbs, wheel their stated courses. The sun, though seemingly smaller than the dial it illuminates, is abundantly larger than this whole earth, on which so many lofty mountains rise, and such vast oceans roll. A line extending from side to side through the centre of that resplendent orb, would measure more than eight hundred thousand miles: a girdle formed to go round its circumference, would require a length of millions. Were its solid contents to be estimated, the account would overwhelm our understanding, and be almost beyond the power of language to express.

4. Are we startled at these reports of philosophy! Are we ready to cry out in a transport of surprise, " How mighty is the Being who kindled so prodigious a fire; and keeps alive, from age to age, so enormous a mass of flame!" let us attend our philosophical guides, and we shall be brought acquainted with speculations more enlarged and more inflaming.

5. This sun with all its attendant planets, is but a very little part of the grand machine of the universe: every star, though in appearance no bigger than the diamond that glitters upon a lady's ring, is really a vast globe, like the sun in size and in glory; no less spacious, no less luminous, than the radiant source of day. So that every star, is not barely a world, but the centre of a magnificent system; has a retinue of worlds, irradiated by its beams, and revolving round its attractive influence, all which are lost to our sight in unmeasurable wilds of ether.

6. That the stars appear like so many diminutive, and scarcely distinguishable points, is owing to their immense and inconceivable distance. Immense and inconceivable indeed it is, since a ball, shot from the loaded cannon, and flying with unabated rapidity, must travel, at this impetuous rate, almost seven hundred thousand years, before it could reach the nearest of these twinkling luminaries.

7. While, beholding this vast expanse, I learn my own extreme meanness, I would also discover the abject littleness of all terrestrial things. What is the earth, with all her ostentatious scenes, compared with this astonishing grand furniture of the skies? What, but a dim speck, hardly perceivable in the map of the universe?

8. It is observed by a very judicious writer, that if the sun himself, which enlightens this part of the creation, were extinguished, and all the host of planetary worlds, which move about him, were annihilated, they would not be missed by an eye that can take in the whole compass of nature, any more than a grain of sand upon the sea-shore. The bulk of which they consist, and the space which they occupy, are so exceedingly little in comparison of the whole, that their loss would scarcely leave a blank in the immensity of God's works.

9. If then, not our globe only, but this whole system, be so very diminutive, what is a kingdom or a country? What are a few lordships, or the so much admired patrimonies of those who are styled wealthy? When I measure them with my own little pittance, they swell into proud and bloated dimensions: but when I take the universe for my standard, how scanty is their size! how contemptible their figure! They shrink into pompous nothings. ADDISON.

## SECTION XV.

*On the power of custom, and the uses to which it may be applied.*

1. THERE is not a common saying, which has a better turn of sense in it, than what we often hear in the mouths of the vulgar, that 'Custom is a second nature.' It is indeed able to form the man anew; and give him inclinations and capacities altogether different from those he was born with.

2. A person who is addicted to play or gaming, though he took but little delight in it at first, by degrees contracts so strong an inclination towards it, and gives himself up so entirely to it, that it seems the only end of his being. The love of a retired or busy life will grow upon a man insensibly, as he is conversant in the one or the other, till he is utterly unqualified for relishing that to which he has been for some time disused.

3. Nay, a man may smoke, or drink, or take snuff, till he is unable to pass away his time without it; not to mention how our delight in any particular study, art, or science, rises and improves, in proportion to the application which we bestow upon it. Thus, what was at first an exercise, becomes at length an entertainment. Our employments are changed into diversions. The mind grows fond of those actions it is accustomed to; and is drawn with reluctancy from those paths in which it has been used to walk.

4. If we attentively consider this property of human nature, it may instruct us in very fine moralities. In the first place, I would have no man discouraged with that kind of life, or series of action, in which the choice of others, or his own necessities, may have engaged him. It may perhaps be very disagreeable to him, at first; but use and application will certainly render it not only less painful, but pleasing and satisfactory.

5. In the second place, I would recommend to every one, the admirable precept, which Pythagoras is said to have given to his disciples, and which that philosopher must have drawn from the observation I have enlarged upon: "Pitch upon that course of life which is the most excellent, and custom will render it the most delightful."

6. Men, whose circumstances will permit them to choose their own way of life, are inexcusable if they do not pursue that which their judgment tells them is the most laudable. The voice of reason is more to be regarded, than the bent of any present inclination: since, by the rule above-mentioned, inclination will at length come over to reason, though we can never force reason to comply with inclination.

7. In the third place, this observation may teach the most sensual and irreligious man, to overlook those hardships and difficulties, which are apt to discourage him from the prosecution of a virtuous life. "The gods," said Hesiod, "have placed labour before vir-

tue; the way to her is at first rough and difficult, but grows more smooth and easy the farther we advance in it." The man who proceeds in it with steadiness and resolution, will, in a little time, find that "her ways are ways of pleasantness, and that all her paths are peace."

8. To enforce this consideration, we may further observe, that the practice of religion will not only be attended with that pleasure which naturally accompanies those actions to which we are habituated, but with those supernumerary joys of heart, that rise from the consciousness of such a pleasure; from the satisfaction of acting up to the dictates of reason; and from the prospect of a happy immortality.

9. In the fourth place, we may learn from this observation which we have made on the mind of man, to take particular care, when we are once settled in a regular course of life, how we too frequently indulge ourselves in even the most innocent diversions and entertainments; since the mind may insensibly fall off from the relish of virtuous actions, and by degrees, exchange that pleasure which it takes in the performance of its duty, for delights of a much inferior and an unprofitable nature.

10. The last use which I shall make of this remarkable property in human nature, of being delighted with those actions to which it is accustomed, is, to show how absolutely necessary it is for us to gain habits of virtue in this life, if we would enjoy the pleasures of the next. The state of bliss we call heaven, will not be capable of affecting those minds which are not thus qualified for it: we must, in this world, gain a relish for truth and virtue, if we would be able to taste that knowledge and perfection, which are to make us happy in the next. The seeds of those spiritual joys and raptures, which are to rise up and flourish in the soul to all eternity, must be planted in it during this its present state of probation. In short, heaven is not to be looked upon only as the reward, but as the natural effect of a religious life. ADDISON.

## SECTION XVI.

*The pleasures resulting from a proper use of our faculties.*

1. HAPPY that man, who, unembarrassed by vulgar cares, master of himself, his time, and fortune, spends his time in making himself wiser; and his fortune, in making others (and therefore himself) happier: who, as the will and understanding are the two ennobling faculties of the soul, thinks himself not complete, till his understanding is beautified with the valuable furniture of knowledge, as well as his will enriched with every virtue; who has furnished himself with all the advantages to relish solitude and enliven conversation; who when serious, is not sullen; and when cheerful, not indiscreetly gay; whose ambition is, not to be admired for a false glare of greatness, but to be beloved for the gentle and sober lustre of his wisdom and goodness.

2. The greatest minister of state has not more business to do, in a public capacity, than he, and indeed every other man, may find in the retired and still scenes of life. Even in his private walks, every thing that is visible convinces him there is present a Being invisible. Aided by natural philosophy, he reads plain legible traces of the Divinity in every thing he meets: he sees the Deity

in every tree, as well as Moses did in the burning bush, though not in so glaring a manner: and when he sees him, he adores him with the tribute of a grateful heart. SEED.

## SECTION XVII.
### Description of candour.

1. TRUE candour is altogether different from that guarded, inoffensive language, and that studied openness of behaviour, which we so frequently meet with among men of the world. Smiling, very often, is the aspect, and smooth are the words, of those who inwardly are the most ready to think evil of others. That candour which is a Christian virtue, consists, not in fairness of speech, but in fairness of heart.

2. It may want the blandishment of external courtesy, but supplies its place with a humane and generous liberality of sentiment. Its manners are unaffected, and its professions cordial. Exempt, on one hand, from the dark jealousy of a suspicious mind, it is no less removed, on the other, from that easy credulity which is imposed on by every specious pretence. It is perfectly consistent with extensive knowledge of the world, and with due attention to our own safety.

3. In that various intercourse, which we are obliged to carry on with persons of every different character, suspicion, to a certain degree, is a necessary guard. It is only when it exceeds the bounds of prudent caution, that it degenerates into vice. There is a proper mean between undistinguished credulity, and universal jealousy, which a sound understanding discerns, and which the man of candour studies to preserve.

4. He makes allowance for the mixture of evil with good, which is to be found in every human character. He expects none to be faultless; and he is unwilling to believe that there is any without some commendable qualities. In the midst of many defects, he can discover a virtue. Under the influence of personal resentment, he can be just to the merit of an enemy.

5. He never lends an open ear to those defamatory reports and dark suggestions, which, among the tribes of the censorious, circulate with so much rapidity, and meet with so ready acceptance. He is not hasty to judge; and he requires full evidence before he will condemn.

6. As long as an action can be ascribed to different motives, he holds it as no mark of sagacity to impute it always to the worst. Where there is just ground for doubt, he keeps his judgment undecided; and, during the period of suspense, leans to the most charitable construction which an action can bear. When he must condemn, he condemns with regret; and without those aggravations which the severity of others adds to the crime. He listens calmly to the apology of the offender, and readily admits every extenuating circumstance, which equity can suggest.

7. How much soever he may blame the principles of any sect or party, he never confounds, under one general censure, all who belong to that party or sect. He charges them not with such consequences of their tenets, as they refuse and disavow. From one wrong opinion, he does not infer the subversion of all sound principles; nor from one bad action, conclude that all regard to conscience is overthrown.

8. When he "beholds the mote in his brother's eye," he remembers "the beam in his own." He commiserates, human frailty; and judges of others according to the principles, by which he would think it reasonable that they should judge of him. In a word, he views men and actions in the clear sunshine of charity and good nature; and not in that dark and sullen shade which jealousy and party-spirit throw over all characters. BLAIR.

## SECTION XVIII.
*On the imperfection of that happiness which rests solely on worldly pleasures.*

1. THE vanity of human pleasures, is a topic which might be embellished with the pomp of much description. But I shall studiously avoid exaggeration, and only point out a threefold vanity in human life, which every impartial observer cannot but admit; disappointment in pursuit, dissatisfaction in enjoyment, uncertainty in possession.

2. First, disappointment in pursuit. When we look around us on the world, we every where behold a busy multitude, intent on the prosecution of various designs, which their wants or desires have suggested. We behold them employing every method which ingenuity can devise; some the patience of industry, some the boldness of enterprise, others the dexterity of stratagem, in order to compass their ends.

3. Of this incessant stir and activity, what is the fruit? In comparison of the crowd who have toiled in vain, how small is the number of the successful? Or rather where is the man who will declare, that in every point he has completed his plan, and attained his utmost wish?

4. No extent of human abilities has been able to discover a path which, in any line of life, leads unerringly to success. "The race is not always to the swift, nor the battle to the strong, nor riches to men of understanding." We may form our plans with the most profound sagacity, and with the most vigilant caution may guard against dangers on every side. But some unforeseen occurrence comes across, which baffles our wisdom, and lays our labours in the dust.

5. Were such disappointments confined to those who aspire at engrossing the higher departments of life, the misfortune would be less. The humiliation of the mighty, and the fall of ambition from its towering height, little concern the bulk of mankind. These are objects on which, as on distant meteors, they gaze from afar, without drawing personal instruction from events so much above them.

6. But, alas! when we descend into the regions of private life, we find disappointment and blasted hope equally prevalent there. Neither the moderation of our views, nor the justice of our pretensions, can ensure success. But "time and chance happen to all." Against the stream of events, both the worthy and the undeserving are obliged to struggle; and both are frequently overborne alike by the current.

7. Besides disappointment in pursuit, dissatisfaction in enjoyment is a farther vanity, to which the human state is subject. This is the severest of all mortifications; after having been successfu

in the pursuit, to be baffled in the enjoyment itself. Yet this is found to be an evil still more general than the former. Some may be so fortunate as to attain what they have pursued; but none are rendered completely happy by what they have attained.

8. Disappointed hope is misery; and yet successful hope is only imperfect bliss. Look through all the ranks of mankind. Examine the condition of those who appear most prosperous; and you will find that they are never just what they desire to be. If retired, they languish for action; if busy, they complain of fatigue. If in middle life, they are impatient for distinction; if in high stations, they sigh after freedom and ease. Something is still wanting to that plenitude of satisfaction, which they expected to acquire. Together with every wish that is gratified, a new demand arises. One void opens in the heart, as another is filled. On wishes, wishes grow; and to the end, it is rather the expectation of what they have not, than the enjoyment of what they have, which occupies and interests the most successful.

9. This dissatisfaction in the midst of human pleasure, springs partly from the nature of our enjoyments themselves, and partly from circumstances which corrupt them. No wordly enjoyments are adequate to the high desires and powers of an immortal spirit. Fancy paints them at a distance with splendid colours; but possession unveils the fallacy. The eagerness of passion bestows upon them, at first, a brisk and lively relish. But it is their fate always to pall by familiarity, and sometimes to pass from satiety into disgust.

10. Happy would the poor man think himself, if he could enter on all the treasures of the rich; and happy for a short time he might be: but before he had long contemplated and admired his state, his possessions would seem to lessen, and his cares would grow.

11. Add to the unsatisfying nature of our pleasures, the attending circumstances which never fail to corrupt them. For, such as they are, they are at no time possessed unmixed. To human lips it is not given to taste the cup of pure joy. When external circumstances show fairest to the world, the envied man groans in private under his own burden. Some vexation disquiets, some passion corrodes him; some distress, either felt or feared, gnaws like a worm, the root of his felicity. When there is nothing from without to disturb the prosperous, a secret poison operates within. For worldly happiness ever tends to destroy itself, by corrupting the heart. It fosters the loose and the violent passions. It engenders noxious habits; and taints the mind with false delicacy, which makes it feel a thousand unreal evils.

12. But put the case in the most favourable light. Lay aside from human pleasures both disappointment in pursuit, and deceitfulness in enjoyment; suppose them to be fully attainable, and completely satisfactory; still there remains to be considered the vanity of uncertain possession and short duration. Were there in worldly things any fixed point of security which we could gain, the mind would then have some basis on which to rest.

13. But our condition is such, that every thing wavers and totters around us. "Boast not thyself of to-morrow; for thou knowest not what a day may bring forth." It is much if, during its course, thou hearest not of somewhat to disquiet or alarm thee.

For life never proceeds long in a uniform train. It is continually varied by unexpected events.

14. The seeds of alteration are every where sown; and the sunshine of prosperity commonly accelerates their growth. If our enjoyments are numerous, we lie more open on different sides to be wounded. If we have possessed them long, we have greater cause to dread an approaching change. By slow degrees prosperity rises; but rapid is the progress of evil. It requires no preparation to bring it forward.

15. The edifice which it cost much time and labour to erect, one inauspicious event, one sudden blow, can level with the dust. Even supposing the accidents of life to leave us untouched, human bliss must still be transitory; for man changes of himself. No course of enjoyment can delight us long. What amused our youth, loses its charm in maturer age. As years advance, our powers are blunted, and our pleasurable feelings decline.

16. The silent lapse of time is ever carrying somewhat from us, till at length the period comes, when all must be swept away. The prospect of this termination of our labours and pursuits, is sufficient to mark our state with vanity. "Our days are a hand's breadth, and our age is as nothing." Within that little space is all our enterprise bounded. We crowd it with toils and cares, with contention and strife. We project great designs, entertain high hopes, and then leave our plans unfinished, and sink into oblivion.

17. This much let it suffice to have said concerning the vanity of the world. That too much has not been said, must appear to every one who considers how generally mankind lean to the opposite side; and how often, by undue attachment to the present state, they both feed the most sinful passions, and "pierce themselves through with many sorrows." BLAIR.

## SECTION XIX.

*What are the real and solid enjoyments of human life.*

1. It must be admitted, that unmixed and complete happiness is unknown on earth. No regulation of conduct can altogether prevent passions from disturbing our peace, and misfortunes from wounding our heart. But after this concession is made, will it follow, that there is no object on earth which deserves our pursuit, or that all enjoyment becomes contemptible which is not perfect? Let us survey our state with an impartial eye, and be just to the various gifts of Heaven.

2. How vain soever this life, considered in itself, may be, the comforts and hopes of religion are sufficient to give solidity to the enjoyments of the righteous. In the exercise of good affections, and the testimony of an approving conscience; in the sense of peace and reconciliation with God, through the great Redeemer of mankind; in the firm confidence of being conducted through all the trials of life, by infinite Wisdom and Goodness; and in the joyful prospect of arriving, in the end, at immortal felicity; they possess a happiness which, descending from a purer and more perfect region than this world, partakes not of its vanity.

3. Besides the enjoyments peculiar to religion, there are other pleasures of our present state, which, though of an inferior order, must not be overlooked in the estimate of human life. It is ne-

sessary to call attention to these, in order to check that repining and unthankful spirit to which man is always too prone.

4. Some degree of importance must be allowed to the comforts of health, to the innocent gratifications of sense, and to the entertainment afforded us by all the beautiful scenes of nature; some to the pursuits and harmless amusements of social life; and more to the internal enjoyments of thought and reflection, and to the pleasures of affectionate intercourse with those whom we love. These comforts are often held in too low estimation, merely because they are ordinary and common; although that is the circumstance which ought, in reason, to enhance their value. They lie open, in some degree, to all; extend through every rank of life; and fill up agreeably many of those spaces in our present existence, which are not occupied with higher objects, or with serious cares.

5. From this representation it appears that, notwithstanding the vanity of the world, a considerable degree of comfort is attainable in the present state. Let the recollection of this serve to reconcile us to our condition, and to repress the arrogance of complaints and murmurs.—What art thou, O son of man! who, having sprung but yesterday out of the dust, darest to lift up thy voice against thy Maker, and to arraign his providence, because all things are not ordered according to thy wish?

6. What title hast thou to find fault with the order of the universe, whose lot is so much beyond what thy virtue or merit gave thee ground to claim! Is it nothing to thee to have been introduced into this magnificent world; to have been admitted as a spectator of the Divine wisdom and works; and to have had access to all the comforts which nature, with a bountiful hand, has poured forth around thee? Are all the hours forgotten which thou hast passed in ease, in complacency, or joy?

7. Is it a small favour in thy eyes, that the hand of Divine Mercy has been stretched forth to aid thee; and, if thou reject not its proffered assistance, is ready to conduct thee to a happier state of existence? When thou comparest thy condition with thy desert, blush, and be ashamed of thy complaints. Be silent, be grateful, and adore. Receive with thankfulness the blessings which are allowed thee. Revere that government which at present refuses thee more. Rest in this conclusion, that though there are evils in the world, its Creator is wise and good, and has been bountiful to thee. BLAIR.

## SECTION XX.
*Scale of beings.*

1. Though there is a great deal of pleasure in contemplating the material world; by which I mean, that system of bodies, into which nature has so curiously wrought the mass of dead matter, with the several relations that those bodies bear to one another; there is still, methinks, something more wonderful and surprising, in contemplations on the world of life; by which I intend, all those animals with which every part of the universe is furnished. The material world is only the shell of the universe: the world of life are its inhabitants.

2. If we consider those parts of the material world, which lie the nearest to us, and are therefore subject to our observation, and in-

quiries, it is amazing to consider the infinity of animals with which they are stocked. Every part of matter is peopled; every green leaf swarms with inhabitants. There is scarcely a single humour in the body of a man, or of any other animal, in which our glasses do not discover myriads of living creatures. We find, even in the most solid bodies, as in marble itself, innumerable cells and cavities, which are crowded with imperceptible inhabitants, too little for the naked eye to discover.

3. On the other hand, if we look into the more bulky parts of nature, we see the seas, lakes, and rivers, teeming with numberless kinds of living creatures. We find every mountain and marsh, wilderness and wood, plentifully stocked with birds and beasts; and every part of matter affording proper necessaries and conveniences, for the livelihood of the multitudes which inhabit it.

4. The author of "the Plurality of Worlds," draws a very good argument from this consideration, for the peopling of every planet; as indeed it seems very probable, from the analogy of reason, that if no part of matter, with which we are acquainted, lies waste and useless, those great bodies, which are at such a distance from us, are not desert and unpeopled; but rather, that they are furnished with beings adapted to their respective situations.

5. Existence is a blessing to those beings only which are endowed with perception; and is in a manner thrown away upon dead matter, any farther than as it is subservient to beings which are conscious of their existence. Accordingly we find, from the bodies which lie under our observation, that matter is only made as the basis and support of animals; and that there is no more of the one than what is necessary for the existence of the other.

6. Infinite goodness is of so communicative a nature, that it seems to delight in conferring existence upon every degree of perceptive being. As this is a speculation, which I have often pursued with great pleasure to myself, I shall enlarge farther upon it, by considering that part of the scale of beings, which comes within our knowledge.

7. There are some living creatures, which are raised but just above dead matter. To mention only that species of shell-fish, which is formed in the fashion of a cone; that grows to the surface of several rocks; and immediately dies, on being severed from the place where it grew. There are many other creatures but one remove from these, which have no other sense than that of feeling and taste. Others have still an additional one of hearing; others of smell; and others, of sight.

8. It is wonderful to observe, by what a gradual progress the world of life advances, through a prodigious variety of species, before a creature is formed, that is complete in all its senses: and even among these, there is such a different degree of perfection, in the sense which one animal enjoys beyond what appears in another, that though the sense in different animals is distinguished by the same common denomination, it seems almost of a different nature.

9. If, after this, we look into the several inward perfections of cunning and sagacity, or what we generally call instinct, we find them rising, after the same manner, imperceptibly one above an-

other; and receiving additional improvements, according to the species in which they are implanted. This progress in nature is so very gradual, that the most perfect of an inferior species, comes very near to the most imperfect of that which is immediately above it.

10. The exuberant and overflowing goodness of the Supreme Being, whose mercy extends to all his works, is plainly seen, as I have before hinted, in his having made so very little matter, at least what falls within our knowledge, that does not swarm with life. Nor is his goodness less seen in the diversity, than in the multitude of living creatures. Had he made but one species of animals, none of the rest would have enjoyed the happiness of existence: he has therefore, *specified*, in his creation, every degree of life, every capacity of being.

11. The whole chasm of nature, from a plant to a man, is filled up with diverse kinds of creatures, rising one after another, by an ascent so gentle and easy, that the little transitions and deviations from one species to another, are almost insensible. This intermediate space is so well husbanded and managed, that there is scarcely a degree of perception, which does not appear in some one part of the world of life. Is the goodness, or the wisdom of the Divine Being, more manifested in this his proceeding?

12. There is a consequence, besides those I have already mentioned, which seems very naturally deducible from the foregoing considerations. If the scale of being rises by so regular a progress, so high as man, we may, by parity of reason, suppose, that it still proceeds gradually through those beings which are of a superior nature to him; since there is infinitely greater space and room for different degrees of perfection, between the Supreme Being and man, than between man and the most despicable insect.

13. In this great system of being, there is no creature so wonderful in its nature, and which so much deserves our particular attention, as man; who fills up the middle space between the animal and the intellectual nature, the visible and the invisible world; and who is that link in the chain of being, which forms the connexion between both. So that he who, in one respect, is associated with angels and archangels, and may look upon a being of infinite perfection as his father, and the highest order of spirits as his brethren, may, in another respect, say to "corruption, thou art my father, and to the worm, thou art my mother and my sister." ADDISON.

## SECTION XXI.
*Trust in the care of Providence recommended.*

1. MAN, considered in himself, is a very helpless, and a very wretched being. He is subject every moment to the greatest calamities and misfortunes. He is beset with dangers on all sides; and may become unhappy by numberless casualties, which he could not foresee, nor have prevented had he foreseen them.

2. It is our comfort, while we are obnoxious to so many accidents, that we are under the care of ONE who directs contingencies, and has in his hands the management of every thing that is capable of annoying or offending us; who knows the assistance we stand in need of, and is always ready to bestow it on those who ask it of him.

3. The natural homage, which such a creature owes to so infinitely wise and good a Being, is a firm reliance on him for the blessings and conveniences of life; and an habitual trust in him, for deliverance out of all such dangers and difficulties as may befall us.

4. The man who always lives in this disposition of mind, has not the same dark and melancholy views of human nature, as he who considers himself abstractedly from this relation to the Supreme Being. At the same time that he reflects upon his own weakness and imperfection, he comforts himself with the contemplation of those divine attributes, which are employed for his safety, and his welfare. He finds his want of foresight made up, by the omniscience of him who is his support. He is not sensible of his own want of strength, when he knows that his helper is almighty.

5. In short, the person who has a firm trust in the Supreme Being, is powerful in his power, wise by his wisdom, happy by his happiness. He reaps the benefit of every divine attribute; and loses his own insufficiency in the fulness of infinite perfection. To make our lives more easy to us, we are commanded to put our trust in him, who is thus able to relieve and succour us; the Divine Goodness having made such a reliance a duty, notwithstanding we should have been miserable, had it been forbidden us.

6. Among several motives, which might be made use of to recommend this duty to us, I shall only take notice of those that follow. The first and strongest is, that we are promised, he will not fail those who put their trust in him. But without considering the supernatural blessing, which accompanies this duty, we may observe, that it has a natural tendency to its own reward; or, in other words, that this firm trust and confidence in the great Disposer of all things, contribute very much to the getting clear of any affliction, or to the bearing of it manfully.

7. A person who believes he has his succour at hand, and that he acts in the sight of his friend, often exerts himself beyond his abilities; and does wonders, that are not to be matched by one who is not animated with such a confidence of success. Trust in the assistance of an Almighty Being, naturally produces patience, hope, cheerfulness, and all other dispositions of mind, which alleviate those calamities that we are not able to remove.

8. The practice of this virtue administers great comfort to the mind of man, in times of poverty and affliction; but most of all, in the hour of death. When the soul is hovering, in the last moments of its separation; when it is just entering on another state of existence, to converse with scenes, and objects, and companions, that are altogether now; what can support her under such tremblings of thought, such fear, such anxiety, such apprehensions, but the casting of all her cares upon HIM, who first gave her being; who has conducted her through one stage of it; and who will be always present, to guide and comfort her in her progress through eternity?

ADDISON.

## SECTION XXII.

### *Piety and gratitude enliven prosperity.*

1. PIETY, and gratitude to God, contribute, in a high degree, to enliven prosperity. Gratitude is a pleasing emotion. The sense of being distinguished by the kindness of another, gladdens the

heart, warms it with reciprocal affection, and gives to any possession which is agreeable in itself, a double relish, from its being the gift of a friend. Favours conferred by men, I acknowledge, may prove burdensome. For human virtue is never perfect; and sometimes unreasonable expectations on the one side, sometimes a mortifying sense of dependence on the other, corrode in secret the pleasures of benefits, and convert the obligations of friendship into grounds of jealousy.

2. But nothing of this kind can affect the intercourse of gratitude with Heaven. Its favours are wholly disinterested; and with a gratitude the most cordial and unsuspicious, a good man looks up to that Almighty Benefactor, who aims at no end but the happiness of those whom he blesses, and who desires no return from them, but a devout and thankful heart. While others can trace their prosperity to no higher source than a concurrence of worldly causes; and, often, of mean or trifling incidents, which occasionally favoured their designs; with what superior satifaction does the servant of God remark the hand of that gracious power which hath raised him up; which hath happily conducted him through the various steps of life, and crowned him with the most favourable distinction beyond his equals?

3. Let us farther consider, that not only gratitude for the past, but a cheering sense of divine favour at the present, enters into the pious emotion. They are only the virtuous, who in their prosperous days hear this voice addressed to them, "Go thy way, eat thy bread with joy, and drink thy wine with a cheerful heart; for God now accepteth thy works." He who is the author of their prosperity, gives them a title to enjoy, with complacency, his own gift.

4. While bad men snatch the pleasures of the world as by stealth, without countenance from the great Proprietor of the world, the righteous sit openly down to the feast of life, under the smile of approving heaven. No guilty fears damp their joys. The blessing of God rests upon all that they possess; his protection surrounds them; and hence, "in the habitations of the righteous, is found the voice of rejoicing and salvation." A lustre unknown to others, invests, in their sight, the whole face of nature.

5. Their piety reflects a sunshine from heaven upon the prosperity of the world; unites in one point of view, the smiling aspect, both of the powers above, and of the objects below. Not only have they as full a relish as others, for the innocent pleasures of life, but, moreover, in these they hold communion with their divine benefactor. In all that is good or fair, they trace his hand. From the beauties of nature, from the improvements of art, from the enjoyments of social life, they raise their affection to the source of all the happiness which surrounds them; and thus widen the sphere of their pleasures, by adding intellectual, and spiritual, to earthly joys.

6. For illustration of what I have said on this head, remark that cheerful enjoyment of a prosperous state, which king David had when he wrote the twenty-third psalm; and compare the highest pleasures of the riotous sinner, with the happy and satisfied spirit which breathes throughout that psalm.—In the midst of the splendour of royalty, with what amiable simplicity of gratitude does he

look up to the Lord as "his Shepherd;" happier in ascribing all his success to Divine favour, than to the policy of his councils, or to the force of his arms!

7. How many instances of divine goodness arose before him in pleasing remembrance, when, with such relish, he speaks of the "green pastures and still waters, beside which God had led him; of his cup which he had made to overflow; and of the table which he had prepared for him in the presence of his enemies!" With what perfect tranquillity does he look forward to the time of his passing through "the valley of the shadow of death;" unappalled by that spectre, whose most distant appearance blasts the prosperity of sinners! He fears no evil, as long as "the rod and the staff" of his Divine Shepherd are with him; and, through all the unknown periods of this and of future existence, commits himself to his guidance with secure and triumphant hope: "Surely goodness and mercy will follow me all the days of my life; and I shall dwell in the house of the Lord for ever."

8. What a purified, sentimental enjoyment of prosperity is here exhibited! How different from that gross relish of worldly pleasures, which belongs to those who behold only the terrestrial side of things; who raise their views to no higher objects than the succession of human contingencies, and the weak efforts of human ability; who have no protector or patron in the heavens, to enliven their prosperity, or to warm their hearts with gratitude and trust!  BLAIR.

## SECTION XXIII.

*Virtue, when deeply rooted, is not subject to the influence of fortune.*

1. THE city of Sidon having surrendered to Alexander, he ordered Hephestion to bestow the crown on him whom the Sidonians should think most worthy of that honour. Hephestion being at that time resident with two young men of distinction, offered them the kingdom; but they refused it, telling him that it was contrary to the laws of their country, to admit any one to that honour, who was not of the royal family.

2. He then, having expressed his admiration of their disinterested spirit, desired them to name one of the royal race, who might remember that he had received the crown through their hands. Overlooking many, who would have been ambitious of this high honour, they made choice of Abdolonymus, whose singular merit had rendered him conspicuous, even in the vale of obscurity. Though remotely related to the royal family, a series of misfortunes had reduced him to the necessity of cultivating a garden, for a small stipend, in the suburbs of the city.

3. While Abdolonymus was busily employed in weeding his garden, the two friends of Hephestion, bearing in their hands the ensigns of royalty, approached him, and saluted him king. They informed him that Alexander had appointed him to that office; and required him immediately to exchange his rustic garb, and utensils of husbandry, for the regal robe and sceptre. At the same time, they admonished him, when he should be seated on the throne, and have a nation in his power, not to forget the humble condition from which he had been raised.

4. All this, at the first, appeared to Abdolonymus as an illusion of the fancy, or an insult offered to his poverty. He requested them not to trouble him farther with their impertinent jests; and to find some other way of amusing themselves, which might leave him in the peaceable enjoyment of his obscure habitation.—At length, however, they convinced him, that they were serious in their proposal; and prevailed upon him to accept the regal office, and accompany them to the palace.

5. No sooner was he in possession of the government, than pride and envy created him enemies; who whispered their murmurs in every place, till at last they reached the ear of Alexander. He commanded the new-elected prince to be sent for; and inquired of him, with what temper of mind he had borne his poverty. "Would to Heaven," replied Abdolonymus, "that I may be able to bear my crown with equal moderation: for when I possessed little, I wanted nothing: these hands supplied me with whatever I desired." From this answer, Alexander formed so high an idea of his wisdom, that he confirmed the choice which had been made; and annexed a neighbouring province to the government of Sidon.

QUINTUS CURTIUS.

## SECTION XXIV.

*The Speech of* FABRICIUS, *a Roman ambassador, to king Pyrrhus, who attempted to bribe him to his interests, by the offer of a great sum of money.*

1. WITH regard to my poverty, the king has, indeed, been justly informed. My whole estate consists in a house of but mean appearance, and a little spot of ground; from which, by my own labour, I draw my support. But if, by any means, thou hast been persuaded to think that this poverty renders me of less consequence in my own country, or in any degree unhappy, thou art greatly deceived.

2. I have no reason to complain of fortune: she supplies me with all that nature requires; and if I am without superfluities, I am also free from the desire of them. With these, I confess I should be more able to succour the necessitous, the only advantage for which the wealthy are to be envied; but small as my possessions are, I can still contribute something to the support of the state, and the assistance of my friends.

3. With respect to honours, my country places me, poor as I am, upon a level with the richest: for Rome knows no qualifications for great employments, but virtue and ability. She appoints me to officiate in the most august ceremonies of religion; she in trusts me with the command of her armies; she confides to my care the most important negociations. My poverty does not lessen the weight and influence of my counsels in the senate.

4. The Roman people honour me for that very poverty, which king Pyrrhus considers as a disgrace. They know the many opportunities I have had to enrich myself, without censure; they are convinced of my disinterested zeal for their prosperity: and if I have any thing to complain of, in the return they make me, it is only the excess of their applause. What value, then, can I put upon thy gold and silver? What king can add any thing to my fortune? Always attentive to discharge the duties incumbent upon

me, I have a mind free from self-reproach; and I have an honest fame.

## SECTION XXV
### Character of JAMES I. king of England

1. No prince, so little enterprising and so inoffensive, was ever so much exposed to the opposite extremes of calumny and flattery, of satire and panegyric. And the factions which began in his time, being still continued, have made his character be as much disputed to this day, as is commonly that of princes who are our contemporaries.

2. Many virtues, however, it must be owned, he was possessed of; but not one of them pure, or free from the contagion of the neighbouring vices. His generosity bordered on profusion, his learning on pedantry, his pacific disposition on pusillanimity, his wisdom on cunning, his friendship on light fancy and boyish fondness.

3. While he imagined that he was only maintaining his own authority, he may perhaps be suspected in some of his actions, and still more of his pretensions, to have encroached on the liberties of his people. While he endeavoured, by an exact neutrality, to acquire the good will of all his neighbours, he was able to preserve fully the esteem and regard of none. His capacity was considerable, but fitter to discourse on general maxims, than to conduct any intricate business.

4. His intentions were just, but more adapted to the conduct of private life, than to the government of kingdoms. Awkward in his person, and ungainly in his manners, he was ill qualified to command respect: partial and undiscerning in his affections, he was little fitted to acquire general love. Of a feeble temper, more than of a frugal judgment; exposed to our ridicule from his vanity, but exempt from our hatred by his freedom from pride and arrogance.

5. And, upon the whole, it may be pronounced of his character, that all his qualities were sullied with weakness, and embellished by humanity. Political courage he was certainly devoid of; and from thence chiefly is derived the strong prejudice, which prevails against his personal bravery: an inference, however, which must be owned, from general experience, to be extremely fallacious. HUME.

## SECTION XXVI.
### CHARLES V. emperor of Germany, resigns his dominions, and retires from the world.

1. THIS great emperor, in the plenitude of his power, and in possession of all the honours which can flatter the heart of man, took the extraordinary resolution, to resign his kingdoms; and to withdraw entirely from any concern in business or the affairs of this world, in order that he might spend the remainder of his days in retirement and solitude.

2. Though it requires neither deep reflection, nor extraordinary discernment, to discover that the state of royalty is not exempt from cares and disappointments; though most of those who are exalted to a throne, find solicitude, and satiety, and disgust, to be their perpetual attendants, in that envied

descend voluntarily from the supreme to a subordinate station, and to relinquish the possession of power in order to attain the enjoyment of happiness, seems to be an effort too great for the human mind.

3. Several instances, indeed, occur in history, of monarchs who have quitted a throne, and have ended their days in retirement. But they were either weak princes, who took this resolution rashly, and repented of it as soon as it was taken; or unfortunate princes, from whose hands some strong rival had wrested their sceptre, and compelled them to descend with reluctance into a private station.

4. Dioclesian is, perhaps, the only prince capable of holding the reins of government, who ever resigned them from deliberate choice; and who continued, during many years, to enjoy the tranquillity of retirement, without fetching one penitent sigh, or casting back one look of desire, towards the power or dignity which he had abandoned.

5. No wonder, then, that Charles's resignation should fill all Europe with astonishment; and give rise, both among his contemporaries, and among the historians of that period, to various conjectures concerning the motives which determined a prince, whose ruling passion had been uniformly the love of power, at the age of fifty-six, when objects of ambition operate with full force on the mind, and are pursued with the greatest ardour, to take a resolution so singular and unexpected.

6. The emperor, in pursuance of his determination, having assembled the states of the Low Countries at Brussels, seated himself, for the last time, in the chair of state; on one side of which was placed his son, and on the other, his sister the queen of Hungary, regent of the Netherlands, with a splendid retinue of the grandees of Spain and princes of the empire standing behind him.

7. The president of the council of Flanders, by his command, explained, in a few words, his intention in calling this extraordinary meeting of the states. He then read the instrument of resignation, by which Charles surrendered to his son Philip all his territories, jurisdiction, and authority in the Low Countries; absolving his subjects there from their oath of allegiance to him, which he required them to transfer to Philip his lawful heir; and to serve him with the same loyalty and zeal that they had manifested, during so long a course of years, in support of his government.

8. Charles then rose from his seat, and leaning on the shoulder of the prince of Orange, because he was unable to stand without support, he addressed himself to the audience; and, from a paper which he held in his hand, in order to assist his memory, he recounted, with dignity, but without ostentation, all the great things which he had undertaken and performed, since the commencement of his administration.

9. He observed, that from the seventeenth year of his age, he had dedicated all his thoughts and attention to public objects, reserving no portion of his time for the indulgence of his ease, and very little for the enjoyment of private pleasure; that either in a pacific or hostile manner, he had visited Germany nine times, Spain six times, France four times, Italy seven times, the Low Countries

ten times, England twice, Africa as often, and had made eleven voyages by sea; that while his health permitted him to discharge his duty, and the vigour of his constitution was equal, in any degree, to the arduous office of governing dominions so extensive, he had never shunned labour, nor repined under fatigue; that now, when his health was broken, and his vigour exhausted by the rage of an incurable distemper, his growing infirmities admonished him to retire; nor was he so fond of reigning, as to retain the sceptre in an impotent hand, which was no longer able to protect his subjects, or to render them happy; that instead of a sovereign worn out with diseases, and scarcely half alive, he gave them one in the prime of life, accustomed already to govern, and who added to the vigour of youth all the attention and sagacity of maturer years; that if, during the course of a long administration, he had committed any material error in government, or if, under the pressure of so many and great affairs, and amidst the attention which he had been obliged to give to them, he had either neglected or injured any of his subjects, he now implored their forgiveness; that, for his part, he should ever retain a grateful sense of their fidelity and attachment, and would carry the remembrance of it along with him to the place of his retreat, as his sweetest consolation, as well as the best reward for all his services; and in his last prayers to Almighty God, would pour forth his ardent wishes for their welfare.

10. Then turning towards Philip, who fell on his knees and kissed his father's hand, "If," says he, "I had left you, by my death, this rich inheritance, to which I have made such large additions, some regard would have been justly due to my memory on that account; but now, when I voluntarily resign to you what I might have still retained, I may well expect the warmest expressions of thanks on your part. With these, however, I dispense; and shall consider your concern for the welfare of your subjects, and your love of them, as the best and most acceptable testimony of your gratitude to me. It is in your power, by a wise and virtuous administration, to justify the extraordinary proof which I give this day of my paternal affection, and to demonstrate that you are worthy of the confidence which I repose in you. Preserve an inviolable regard for religion; maintain the Catholic faith in its purity; let the laws of your country be sacred in your eyes; encroach not on the rights and privileges of your people; and if the time shall ever come, when you shall wish to enjoy the tranquillity of private life, may you have a son endowed with such qualities, that you can resign your sceptre to him, with as much satisfaction as I give up mine to you."

11. As soon as Charles had finished this long address to his subjects, and to their new sovereign, he sunk into the chair, exhausted and ready to faint with the fatigue of so extraordinary an effort. During his discourse, the whole audience melted into tears; some from admiration of his magnanimity; others softened by the expressions of tenderness towards his son, and of love to his people; and all were affected with the deepest sorrow, at losing a sovereign, who had distinguished the Netherlands, his native country, with particular marks of his regard and attachment.

## SECTION XXVII.
### *The same subject continued.*

1. A FEW weeks after the resignation of the Netherlands, Charles, in an assembly no less splendid, and with a ceremonial equally pompous, resigned to his son the crowns of Spain, with all the territories depending on them, both in the old and in the new world. Of all these vast possessions, he reserved nothing for himself, but an annual pension of a hundred thousand crowns, to defray the charges of his family, and to afford him a small sum for acts of beneficence and charity.

2. Nothing now remained to detain him from that retreat for which he languished. Every thing having been prepared some time for his voyage, he set out for Zuitburgh in Zealand, where the fleet had orders to rendezvous. In his way thither, he passed through Ghent: and after stopping there a few days, to indulge that tender and pleasing melancholy, which arises in the mind of every man in the decline of life, on visiting the place of his nativity, and viewing the scenes and objects familiar to him in his early youth, he pursued his journey, accompanied by his son Philip, his daughter the arch-duchess, his sisters the dowager queens of France and Hungary, Maximilian his son-in-law, and a numerous retinue of the Flemish nobility. Before he went on board, he dismissed them, with marks of his attention or regard; and taking leave of Philip with all the tenderness of a father who embraced his son for the last time, he set sail under convoy of a large fleet of Spanish, Flemish, and English ships.

3. His voyage was prosperous and agreeable; and he arrived at Laredo in Biscay, on the eleventh day after he left Zealand. As soon as he landed, he fell prostrate on the ground; and considering himself now as dead to the world, he kissed the earth, and said, "Naked came I out of my mother's womb, and naked I now return to thee, thou common mother of mankind." From Laredo he proceeded to Valladolid. There he took a last and tender leave of his two sisters; whom he would not permit to accompany him to his solitude, though they entreated it with tears: not only that they might have the consolation of contributing, by their attendance and care, to mitigate or to sooth his sufferings, but that they might reap instruction and benefit, by joining with him in those pious exercises, to which he had consecrated the remainder of his days.

4. From Valladolid, he continued his journey to Plazencia in Estremadura. He had passed through that city a great many years before; and having been struck at that time with the delightful situation of the monastery of St. Justus, belonging to the order of St. Jerome, not many miles distant from that place, he had then observed to some of his attendants, that this was a spot to which Dioclesian might have retired with pleasure. The impression had remained so strong on his mind, that he pitched upon it as the place of his retreat.

5. It was seated in a vale of no great extent, watered by a small brook, and surrounded by rising grounds, covered with lofty trees. From the nature of the soil, as well as the temperature of the

climate, it was esteemed the most healthful and delicious situation in Spain.

6. Some months before his resignation, he had sent an architect thither, to add a new apartment to the monastery, for his accommodation; but he gave strict orders that the style of the building should be such as suited his present station, rather than his former dignity. It consisted only of six rooms, four of them in the form of friars' cells, with naked walls; the other two, each twenty feet square, were hung with brown cloth, and furnished in the most simple manner. They were all on a level with the ground; with a door on one side into a garden, of which Charles himself had given the plan, and had filled it with various plants, which he proposed to cultivate with his own hands. On the other side, they communicated with the chapel of the monastery, in which he was to perform his devotions.

7. Into this humble retreat, hardly sufficient for the comfortable accommodation of a private gentleman, did Charles enter, with twelve domestics only. He buried there, in solitude and silence, his grandeur, his ambition, together with all those vast projects, which, during half a century, had alarmed and agitated Europe; filling every kingdom in it, by turns, with the terror of his arms, and the dread of being subjected to his power.

8. In this retirement, Charles formed such a plan of life for himself, as would have suited the condition of a private person of a moderate fortune. His table was neat but plain; his domestics few; his intercourse with them familiar; all the cumbersome and ceremonious forms of attendance on his person were entirely abolished, as destructive of that social ease and tranquillity, which he courted, in order to sooth the remainder of his days. As the mildness of the climate, together with his deliverance from the burdens and cares of government, procured him, at first, a considerable remission from the acute pains with which he had been long tormented, he enjoyed, perhaps, more complete satisfaction in this humble solitude, than all his grandeur had ever yielded him.

9. The ambitious thoughts and projects which had so long engrossed and disquieted him, were quite effaced from his mind. Far from taking any part in the political transactions of the princes of Europe, he restrained his curiosity even from any inquiry concerning them; and he seemed to view the busy scene which he had abandoned, with all the contempt and indifference arising from his thorough experience of its vanity, as well as from the pleasing reflection of having disentangled himself from its cares.

DR. ROBERTSON.

# PART II.

## *PIECES IN POETRY.*

### CHAPTER I.

SELECT SENTENCES AND PARAGRAPHS.

#### SECTION I.

SHORT AND EASY SENTENCES.

*Education.*
'Tis education forms the common mind;
Just as the twig is bent, the tree's inclin'd.

*Candour.*
With pleasure let us own our errors past :'
And make each day a critic on the last.

*Reflection.*
A soul without reflection, like a pile
Without inhabitant, to ruin runs.

*Secret Virtue.*
The private path, the secret acts of men,
If noble, far the noblest of their lives.

*Necessary knowledge easily attained.*
Our needful knowledge, like our needful food,
Unhedg'd, lies open in life's common field;
And bids all welcome to the vital feast.

*Disappointment.*
Disappointment lurks in many a prize,
As bees in flow'rs; and stings us with success.

*Virtuous elevation.*
The mind that would be happy, must be great;
Great in its wishes; great in its surveys.
Extended views a narrow mind extend.

*Natural and fanciful life.*
Who lives to nature, rarely can be poor;
Who lives to fancy, never can be rich;

*Charity.*
In faith and hope the world will disagree;
But all mankind's concern is charity.

*The prize of virtue.*
What nothing earthly gives, or can destroy,
The soul's calm sunshine, and the heart-felt joy,
Is virtue's prize.

*Sense and modesty connected.*
Distrustful sense with modest caution speaks;
It still looks home, and short excursions makes;
But rattling nonsense in full volleys breaks.

*NOTE.*—In the first chapter, the Compiler has exhibited a considerable variety of poetical construction, for the young reader's preparatory exercise.

### *Moral discipline salutary.*

Heav'n gives us friends to bless the present scene;
Resumes them to prepare us for the next.
All evils natural are moral goods;
All discipline, indulgence, on the whole.

### *Present blessings undervalued.*

Like birds, whose beauties languish, half conceal'd,
Till, mounted on the wing, their glossy plumes
Expanded shine with azure, green, and gold,
How blessings brighten as they take their flight!

### *Hope.*

Hope, of all passions most befriends us here;
Passions of prouder name befriend us less.
Joy has her tears, and transport has her death;
Hope, like a cordial, innocent, though strong,
Man's heart, at once, inspirits and serenes.

### *Happiness modest and tranquil.*

——————Never man was truly blest,
But it compos'd, and gave him such a cast
As folly might mistake for want of joy:
A cast unlike the triumph of the proud;
A modest aspect, and a smile at heart.

### *True greatness.*

Who noble ends by noble means obtains,
Or failing, smiles in exile or in chains,
Like good Aurelius let him reign, or bleed
Like Socrates, that man is great indeed.

### *The tear of sympathy.*

No radiant pearl, which crested fortune wears,
No gem, that twinkling hangs from beauty's ears,
Nor the bright stars, which night's blue arch adorn,
Nor rising suns that gild the vernal morn,
Shine with such lustre, as the tear that breaks,
For others' wo, down Virtue's manly cheeks.

## SECTION II.

**VERSES IN WHICH THE LINES ARE OF DIFFERENT LENGTH.**

### *Bliss of celestial origin.*

RESTLESS mortals toil for nought;
Bliss in vain from earth is sought;
Bliss, a native of the sky,
Never wanders. Mortals, try;
There you cannot seek in vain;
For to seek her is to gain.

### *The passions.*

The passions are a num'rous crowd,
Imperious, positive, and loud.
Curb these licentious sons of strife;
Hence chiefly rise the storms of life:
If they grow mutinous, and rave,
They are thy masters, thou their slave.

### *Trust in Providence recommended.*

'Tis Providence alone secures,
In ev'ry change, both mine and yours.

Safety consists not in escape
From dangers of a frightful shape:
An earthquake may be bid to spare
The man that's strangled by a hair.
Fate steals along with silent tread,
Found oft'nest in what least we dread;
Frowns in the storm with angry brow,
But in the sunshine strikes the blow.

*Epitaph.*
How lov'd, how valu'd once, avails thee not,
To whom related, or by whom begot:
A heap of dust alone remains of thee;
'Tis all thou art, and all the proud shall be.

*Fame.*
All fame is foreign, but of true desert;
Plays round the head, but comes not to the heart.
One self-approving hour, whole years outweighs
Of stupid starers, and of loud huzzas;
And more true joy Marcellus exil'd feels,
Than Cæsar with a senate at his heels.

*Virtue the guardian of youth.*
Down the smooth stream of life the stripling darts,
Gay as the morn; bright glows the vernal sky,
Hope swells his sails, and Passion steers his course.
Safe glides his little bark along the shore,
Where Virtue takes her stand: but if too far
He launches forth beyond discretion's mark,
Sudden the tempest scowls, the surges roar,
Blot his fair day, and plunge him in the deep.

*Sunrise.*
But yonder comes the powerful king of day,
Rejoicing in the east. The less'ning cloud,
The kindling azure, and the mountain's brow,
Illum'd with fluid gold, his near approach
Betoken glad. Lo, now, apparent all
Aslant the dew-bright earth, and colour'd air,
He looks in boundless majesty abroad;
And sheds the shining day, that burnish'd plays
On rocks, and hills, and tow'rs, and wand'ring streams,
High gleaming from afar.

*Self-government.*
May I govern my passions with absolute sway;
And grow wiser and better as life wears away.

*Shepherd.*
On a mountain, stretch'd beneath a hoary willow,
Lay a shepherd swain, and view'd the rolling billow.

## THE ENGLISH READER.
### SECTION III.
VERSES CONTAINING EXCLAMATIONS, INTERROGATIONS, AND PARENTHESES.

*Competence.*
A COMPETENCE is all we can enjoy:
Oh! be content, where Heav'n can give no more!

*Reflection essential to happiness.*
Much joy not only speaks small happiness,
But happiness that shortly must expire.
Can joy unbottom'd in reflection, stand?
And, in a tempest, can reflection live?

*Friendship.*
Can gold gain friendship? Impudence of hope!
As well mere man an angel might beget.
Love, and love only, is the loan for love.
Lorenzo! pride repress; nor hope to find
A friend, but what has found a friend in thee.
All like the purchase; few the price will pay:
And this makes friends such miracles below.

*Patience.*
Beware of desp'rate steps. The darkest day
(Live till to-morrow) will have pass'd away.

*Luxury.*
——————————O luxury!
Bane of elated life, of affluent states,
What dreary change, what ruin is not thine!
How doth thy bowl intoxicate the mind!
To the soft entrance of thy rosy cave,
How dost thou lure the fortunate and great!
Dreadful attraction!

*Virtuous activity.*
Seize, mortals! seize the transient hour;
Improve each moment as it flies:
Life's a short summer—man a flow'r;
He dies—Alas!—how soon he dies!

*The source of happiness.*
Reason's whole pleasure, all the joys of sense,
Lie in three words, health, peace, and competence:
But health consists with temperance alone;
And peace, O virtue! peace is all thy own.

*Placid emotion.*
Who can forbear to smile with nature? Can
The stormy passions in the bosom roll,
While ev'ry gale is peace, and ev'ry grove
Is melody?

*Solitude.\**
O sacred solitude; divine retreat!
Choice of the prudent! envy of the great!
By thy pure stream, or in thy waving shade,
We court fair wisdom, that celestial maid:

\* By solitude here is meant, a temporary seclusion from the world.

The genuine offspring of her lov'd embrace,
(Strangers on earth,) are innocence and peace.
There from the ways of men laid safe ashore,
We smile to hear the distant tempest roar;
There, bless'd with health, with bus'ness unperplex'd,
This life we relish, and ensure the next.

*Presume not on to-morrow.*

In human hearts what bolder thoughts can rise,
Than man's presumption on to-morrow's dawn?
Where is to-morrow? In another world.
For numbers this is certain; the reverse
Is sure to none.

*Dum vivimus vivamus.—Whilst we live, let us live.*

"Live, while you live," the epicure would say,
"And seize the pleasures of the present day."
"Live, while you live," the sacred preacher cries;
"And give to God each moment as it flies."
Lord! in my views, let both united be;
I live in pleasure, when I live to thee!    DODDRIDGE

## SECTION IV.

### VERSES IN VARIOUS FORMS.

*The security of Virtue.*

LET coward guilt, with pallid fear,
  To shelt'ring caverns fly,
And justly dread the vengeful fate,
  That thunders through the sky.
Protected by that hand, whose law,
  The threat'ning storms obey,
Intrepid virtue smiles secure,
  As in the blaze of day.

*Resignation.*

And Oh! by error's force subdu'd,
  Since oft my stubborn will
Prepost'rous shuns the latent good,
  And grasps the specious ill,
Not to my wish, but to my want,
  Do thou thy gifts apply;
Unask'd, what good thou knowest grant;
  What ill, though ask'd, deny.

*Compassion.*

I have found out a gift for my fair;
  I have found where the wood-pigeons breed:
But let me that plunder forbear!
  She will say 'tis a barbarous deed.
For he ne'er can be true, she averr'd,
  Who can rob a poor bird of its young:
And I lov'd her the more, when I heard
  Such tenderness fall from her tongue.

### Epitaph.

Here rests his head upon the lap of earth,
 A youth to fortune and to fame unknown;
Fair science frown'd not on his humble birth,
 And melancholy mark'd him for her own.
Large was his bounty, and his soul sincere;
 Heav'n did a recompense as largely send:
He gave to mis'ry all he had—a tear;
 He gain'd from Heav'n ('twas all he wish'd) a friend.
No further seek his merits to disclose,
 Or draw his frailties from their dread abode,
(There they alike in trembling hope repose,)
 The bosom of his Father and his God.

### Joy and sorrow connected.

Still, where rosy pleasure leads,
See a kindred grief pursue;
Behind the steps that mis'ry treads,
Approaching comforts view.
The hues of bliss more brightly glow,
Chastis'd by sable tints of wo;
And blended form, with artful strife,
The strength and harmony of life.

### The golden mean.

He that holds fast the golden mean,
And lives contentedly between
 The little and the great,
Feels not the wants that pinch the poor,
Nor plagues that haunt the rich man's door,
 Imbitt'ring all his state.
The tallest pines feel most the pow'r
Of wint'ry blast; the loftiest tow'r
 Comes heaviest to the ground.
The bolts that spare the mountain's side,
His cloud-capt eminence divide;
 And spread the ruin round.

### Moderate views and aims recommended.

With passions unruffled, untainted with pride,
 By reason my life let me square;
The wants of my nature are cheaply supplied;
 And the rest are but folly and care.
How vainly, through infinite trouble and strife,
 The many their labours employ!
Since all that is truly delightful in life,
 Is what all, if they please, may enjoy.

### Attachment to life.

The tree of deepest root is found,
 Least willing still to quit the ground:
'Twas therefore said, by ancient sages,
 That love of life increas'd with years,
So much, that in our later stages,
 When pains grow sharp, and sickness rages,
The greatest love of life appears.

### Virtue's address to pleasure.*

Vast happiness enjoy thy gay allies!
  A youth of follies, an old age of cares;
Young yet enervate, old yet never wise,
  Vice wastes their vigour, and their mind impairs.
Vain, idle, delicate, in thoughtless ease,
  Reserving woes for age, their prime they spend;
All wretched, hopeless, in the evil days,
  With sorrow to the verge of life they tend.
Griev'd with the present, of the past asham'd,
They live and are despis'd; they die, no more are nam'd.

## SECTION V.

**VERSES IN WHICH SOUND CORRESPONDS TO SIGNIFICATION**

### Smooth and rough verse.

SOFT is the strain when zephyr gently blows,
And the smooth stream in smoother numbers flows.
But when loud surges lash the sounding shore,
The hoarse rough verse should like the torrent roar.

### Slow motion imitated.

When Ajax strives some rock's vast weight to throw,
The line too labours, and the words move slow.

### Swift and easy motion.

Not so when swift Camilla scours the plain,
Flies o'er th' unbending corn, and skims along the main.

### Felling trees in a wood.

Loud sounds the axe, redoubling strokes on strokes;
On all sides round the forest hurls her oaks
Headlong. Deep echoing groan the thickets brown:
Then rustling, crackling, crashing, thunder down.

### Sound of a bow-string.

——————————The string let fly
Twang'd short and sharp, like the shrill swallow's cry

### The pheasant.

See! from the brake the whirring pheasant springs,
And mounts exulting on triumphant wings.

### Scylla and Charybdis.

Dire Scylla there a scene of horror forms,
And here Charybdis fills the deep with storms.
When the tide rushes from her rumbling caves,
The rough rock roars; tumultuous boil the waves.

### Boisterous and gentle sounds.

Two craggy rocks projecting to the main,
The roaring winds tempestuous rage restrain:
Within, the waves in softer murmurs glide;
And ships secure without their halsers ride.

* Sensual pleasure.

*Laborious and impetuous motion.*
With many a weary step, and many a groan,
Up the high hill he heaves a huge round stone:
The huge round stone resulting with a bound,
Thunders impetuous down, and smokes along the ground.

*Regular and slow movement.*
First march the heavy mules securely slow
O'er hills, o'er dales, o'er crags, o'er rocks they go.

*Motion slow and difficult.*
A needless Alexandrine ends the song,
That, like a wounded snake, drags its slow length along.

*A rock torn from the brow of a mountain.*
Still gath'ring force, it smokes, and urg'd amain,
Whirls, leaps, and thunders down, impetuous to the plain.

*Extent and violence of the waves.*
The waves behind impel the waves before,
Wide-rolling, foaming high, and tumbling to the shore.

*Pensive numbers.*
In these deep solitudes and awful cells,
Where heav'nly pensive contemplation dwells,
And ever-musing melancholy reigns.

*Battle.*
——————Arms on armour, clashing, bray'd
Horrible discord; and the madding wheels
Of brazen fury rag'd.

*Sound imitating reluctance.*
For who, to dumb forgetfulness a prey,
  This pleasing anxious being e'er resign'd;
Left the warm precincts of the cheerful day,
  Nor cast one longing, ling'ring look behind?

## SECTION VI.

#### PARAGRAPHS OF GREATER LENGTH.

*Connubial affection.*

THE love that cheers life's latest stage,
Proof against sickness and old age,
Preserv'd by virtue from declension,
Becomes not weary of attention:
But lives, when that exterior grace,
Which first inspir'd the flame, decays.
'Tis gentle, delicate, and kind,
To faults compassionate, or blind;
And will with sympathy endure
Those evils it would gladly cure.
But angry, coarse, and harsh expression,
Shows love to be a mere profession;
Proves that the heart is none of his,
Or soon expels him if it is.

### Swarms of flying insects.

Thick in yon stream of light a thousand ways,
Upward and downward, thwarting and convolv'd,
The quiv'ring nations sport; till tempest-wing'd,
Fierce winter sweeps them from the face of day.
Ev'n so, luxurious men, unheeding, pass
An idle summer life, in fortune's shine,
A season's glitter! Thus they flutter on,
From toy to toy, from vanity to vice;
Till, blown away by death, oblivion comes
Behind, and strikes them from the book of life.

### Beneficence its own reward.

My fortune (for I'll mention all,
And more than you dare tell) is small;
Yet ev'ry friend partakes my store,
And want goes smiling from my door.
Will forty shillings warm the breast
Of worth or industry distress'd!
This sum I cheerfully impart;
'Tis fourscore pleasures to my heart.
And you may make, by means like these,
Five talents ten, whene'er you please.
'Tis true, my little purse grows light;
But then I sleep so sweet at night!
This grand specific will prevail,
When all the doctor's opiates fail.

### Virtue the best treasure.

Virtue, the strength and beauty of the soul,
Is the best gift of Heav'n: a happiness
That, even above the smiles and frowns of fate,
Exalts great nature's favourites: a wealth
That ne'er encumbers; nor to baser hands
Can be transferr'd. It is the only good
Man justly boasts of, or can call his own.
Riches are oft by guilt and baseness earn'd.
But for one end, one much-neglected use,
Are riches worth our care; (for nature's wants
Are few, and without opulence supplied;)
This noble end is to produce the soul;
To show the virtues in their fairest light;
And make humanity the minister
Of bounteous Providence.

### Contemplation.

As yet 'tis midnight deep. The weary clouds,
Slow meeting, mingle into solid gloom.
Now, while the drowsy world lies lost in sleep,
Let me associate with the serious night,
And contemplation her sedate compeer;
Let me shake off th' intrusive cares of day,
And lay the meddling senses all aside.
  Where now, ye lying vanities of life!
Ye ever tempting, ever cheating train!

Where are you now? and what is your amount?
Vexation, disappointment, and remorse.
Sad, sick'ning thought! And yet, deluded man,
A scene of crude disjointed visions past,
And broken slumbers, rises still resolv'd,
With new flush'd hopes, to run the giddy round.

*Pleasure of piety.*

A Deity believ'd, is joy begun;
A Deity ador'd, is joy advanc'd;
A Deity belov'd, is joy matur'd.
Each branch of piety delight inspires:
Faith builds a bridge from this world to the next,
O'er death's dark gulf, and all its horror hides;
Praise, the sweet exhalation of our joy,
That joy exalts, and makes it sweeter still;
Pray'r ardent opens heav'n, lets down a stream
Of glory, on the consecrated hour
Of man in audience with the Deity.

## CHAPTER II.

### NARRATIVE PIECES.

### SECTION I.

*The bears and the bees.*

1. As two young bears, in wanton mood,
   Forth issuing from a neighbouring wood,
   Came where th' industrious bees had stor'd,
   In artful cells, their luscious hoard;
   O'erjoy'd they seiz'd, with eager haste,
   Luxurious on the rich repast.
   Alarm'd at this, the little crew
   About their ears vindictive flew.

2. The beasts, unable to sustain
   Th' unequal combat, quit the plain;
   Half-blind with rage, and mad with pain,
   Their native shelter they regain;
   There sit, and now, discreeter grown,
   Too late their rashness they bemoan;
   And this by dear experience gain,
   That pleasure's ever bought with pain.

3. So when the gilded baits of vice
   Are plac'd before our longing eyes,
   With greedy haste we snatch our fill,
   And swallow down the latent ill:
   But when experience opes our eyes,
   Away the fancied pleasure flies.
   It flies, but oh! too late we find,
   It leaves a real sting behind.      MERRICK.

## SECTION II.

*The nightingale and the glow-worm.*

1. A NIGHTINGALE, that all day long
   Had cheer'd the village with his song,
   Nor yet at eve his note suspended,
   Nor yet when eventide was ended,
   Began to feel, as well he might,
   The keen demands of appetite;
   When, looking eagerly around,
   He spied far off, upon the ground,
   A something shining in the dark,
   And knew the glow-worm by his spark.
   So, stooping down from hawthorn top,
   He thought to put him in his crop.

2. The worm, aware of his intent,
   Harangued him thus, right eloquent—
   'Did you admire my lamp,' quoth he,
   'As much as I your minstrelsy,
   You would abhor to do me wrong,
   As much as I to spoil your song;
   For 'twas the self-same pow'r divine,
   Taught you to sing, and me to shine;
   That you with music, I with light,
   Might beautify and cheer the night.'

3. The songster heard his short oration,
   And, warbling out his approbation,
   Releas'd him, as my story tells,
   And found a supper somewhere else.
   Hence, jarring sectaries may learn
   Their real int'rest to discern;
   That brother should not war with brother,
   And worry and devour each other:
   But sing and shine by sweet consent,
   Till life's poor transient night is spent;
   Respecting, in each other's case,
   The gifts of nature and of grace.

4. Those Christians best deserve the name,
   Who studiously make peace their aim:
   Peace, both the duty and the prize
   Of him that creeps, and him that flies. COWPER.

## SECTION III.

*The trials of virtue.*

1. PLAC'D on the verge of youth, my mind
   Life's op'ning scene survey'd:
   I view'd its ills of various kind,
   Afflicted and afraid.

2. But chief my fear the dangers mov'd,
   That virtue's path enclose:
   My heart the wise pursuit approv'd;
   But O, what toils oppose!

3. For see, ah see! while yet her ways
   With doubtful step I tread,
   A hostile world its terrors raise,
   Its snares delusive spread.

4. O how shall I, with heart prepar'd,
   Those terrors learn to meet?
   How, from the thousand snares to guard
   My unexperienc'd feet?

5. As thus I mus'd, oppressive sleep
   Soft o'er my temples drew
   Oblivion's veil.—The wat'ry deep,
   An object strange and new,

6. Before me rose: on the wide shore
   Observant as I stood,
   The gathering storms around me roar
   And heave the boiling flood.

7. Near and more near the billows rise;
   Ev'n now my steps they lave;
   And death to my affrighted eyes
   Approach'd in every wave.

8. What hope, or whither to retreat!
   Each nerve at once unstrung;
   Chill fear had fetter'd fast my feet,
   And chain'd my speechless tongue.

9. I felt my heart within me die;
   When sudden to mine ear
   A voice, descending from on high,
   Reprov'd my erring fear.

10. "What tho' the swelling surge thou see
    Impatient to devour;
    Rest, mortal, rest on God's decree,
    And thankful own his pow'r.

11. Know, when he bade the deep appear,
    'Thus far,' th' Almighty said,
    'Thus far, no farther, rage; and here
    'Let thy proud waves be stay'd.'"

12. I heard; and lo! at once controll'd,
    The waves, in wild retreat,
    Back on themselves reluctant roll'd,
    And murm'ring left my feet.

13. Deeps to assembling deeps in vain
    Once more the signal gave:
    The shores the rushing weight sustain,
    And check th' usurping wave.

14. Convinc'd, in nature's volume wise,
    The imag'd truth I read;
    And sudden from my waking eyes
    Th' instructive vision fled.

15. Then why thus heavy, O my soul!
    Say why, distrustful still,

Thy thoughts with vain impatience roll
O'er scenes of future ill?

16. Let faith suppress each rising fear,
Each anxious doubt exclude:
Thy Maker's will has plac'd thee here,
A Maker wise and good!

17. He to thy ev'ry trial knows
Its just restraint to give;
Attentive to behold thy woes,
And faithful to relieve.

18. Then why thus heavy, O my soul!
Say why, distrustful still,
Thy thoughts with vain impatience roll
O'er scenes of future ill?

19. Tho' griefs unnumber'd throng thee round,
Still in thy God confide,
Whose finger marks the seas their bound,
And curbs the headlong tide.     MERRICK.

## SECTION IV.

### *The youth and the philosopher.*

1. A GRECIAN youth of talents rare,
Whom Plato's philosophic care
Had form'd for virtue's nobler view,
By precept and example too,
Would often boast his matchless skill,
To curb the steed, and guide the wheel;
And as he pass'd the gazing throng,
With graceful ease, and smack'd the thong,
The idiot wonder they express'd,
Was praise and transport to his breast.

2. At length, quite vain, he needs would show
His master what his art could do;
And bade his slaves the chariot lead
To Academus' sacred shade.
The trembling grove confess'd its fright,
The wood-nymphs started at the sight;
The muses drop the learned lyre,
And to their inmost shades retire.

3. Howe'er, the youth, with forward air;
Bows to the sage, and mounts the car.
The lash resounds, the coursers spring,
The chariot marks the rolling ring;
And gath'ring crowds, with eager eyes,
And shouts, pursue him as he flies.

4. Triumphant to the goal return'd,
With nobler thirst his bosom burn'd;
And now along th' indented plain
The self-same track he marks again,
Pursues with care the nice design,
Nor ever deviates from the line.

Amazement seiz'd the circling crowd;
The youths with emulation glow'd;
Ev'n bearded sages hail'd the boy;
And all but Plato gaz'd with joy.

5. For he, deep-judging sage, beheld
With pain the triumphs of the field:
And when the charioteer drew nigh,
And, flush'd with hope, had caught his eye,
"Alas! unhappy youth," he cry'd,
"Expect no praise from me," (and sigh'd.)

6. "With indignation I survey
Such skill and judgment thrown away:
The time profusely squander'd there,
On vulgar arts beneath thy care,
If well employ'd, at less expense,
Had taught thee honour, virtue, sense;
And rais'd thee from a coachman's fate
To govern men, and guide the state." WHITEHEAD.

## SECTION V.

*Discourse between Adam and Eve, retiring to rest.*

1. Now came still ev'ning on, and twilight gray
Had in her sober liv'ry all things clad.
Silence accompanied; for beast and bird,
They to their grassy couch, these to their nests
Were slunk; all but the wakeful nightingale.
She all night long her am'rous descant sung:
Silence was pleas'd. Now glow'd the firmament
With living sapphires: Hesperus, that led
The starry host, rode brightest, till the moon,
Rising in clouded majesty, at length,
Apparent queen unveil'd her peerless light,
And o'er the dark her silver mantle threw.

2. When Adam thus to Eve: "Fair consort, th' hour
Of night, and all things now retir'd to rest,
Mind us of like repose; since God hath set
Labour and rest, as day and night, to men
Successive; and the timely dew of sleep,
Now falling with soft slumb'rous weight, inclines
Our eye-lids. Other creatures all day long
Rove idle unemploy'd, and less need rest:
Man hath his daily work of body or mind
Appointed, which declares his dignity,
And the regard of Heav'n on all his ways;
While other animals unactive range,
And of their doings God takes no account.

3. To-morrow, ere fresh morning streak the east
With first approach of light, we must be risen,
And at our pleasant labour; to reform
Yon flow'ry arbours, yonder alleys green,
Our walk at noon, with branches overgrown,
That mock our scant manuring, and require
More hands than ours to lop their wanton growth.

## NARRATIVE PIECES.

Those blossoms also, and those dropping gums,
That lie bestrown, unsightly and unsmooth,
Ask riddance, if we mean to tread with ease.
Mean while, as nature wills, night bids us rest."

4. To whom thus Eve, with perfect beauty adorn'd:
"My author and disposer, what thou bidst,
Unargu'd I obey; so God ordains.
With thee conversing I forget all time;
All seasons and their change, all please alike.
Sweet is the breath of morn, her rising sweet,
With charm of earliest birds; pleasant the sun
When first on this delightful land he spreads
His orient beams, on herb, tree, fruit, and flow'r,
Glist'ring with dew; fragrant the fertile earth
After soft show'rs; and sweet the coming on
Of grateful evening mild; then silent night,
With this her solemn bird, and this fair moon,
And these the gems of heav'n, her starry train:

5. But neither breath of morn, when she ascends
With charm of earliest birds; nor rising sun
On this delightful land; nor herb, fruit, flow'r,
Glist'ring with dew; nor fragrance after show'rs:
Nor grateful evening mild; nor silent night
With this her solemn bird; nor walk by moon,
Or glitt'ring star-light,—without thee is sweet.
But wherefore all night long shine these? for whom
This glorious sight, when sleep hath shut all eyes?"

6. To whom our gen'ral ancestor reply'd:
"Daughter of God and man, accomplish'd Eve,
These have their course to finish round the earth,
By morrow ev'ning; and from land to land,
In order, though to nations yet unborn,
Minist'ring light prepar'd, they set and rise;
Lest total darkness should by night regain
Her old possession, and extinguish life
In nature and all things; which these soft fires
Not only enlighten, but, with kindly heat
Of various influence, foment and warm,
Temper or nourish; or in part shed down
Their stellar virtue on all kinds that grow
On earth, made hereby apter to receive
Perfection from the sun's more potent ray.

7. These then, though unbeheld in deep of night,
Shine not in vain; nor think, though men were none,
That heav'n would want spectators, God want praise;
Millions of spiritual creatures walk the earth
Unseen, both when we wake, and when we sleep.
All these with ceaseless praise his works behold,
Both day and night. How often, from the steep
Of echoing hill or thicket have we heard
Celestial voices to the midnight air,
Sole, or responsive each to others' note,
Singing their great Creator? Oft in bands,

While they keep watch, or nightly rounding walk
With heav'nly touch of instrumental sounds,
In all harmonic number join'd, their songs
Divide the night, and lift our thoughts to heav'n."

8. Thus talking hand in hand alone they pass'd
On to their blissful bow'r.———————————
————————————There arriv'd, both stood,
Both turn'd; and under open sky ador'd
The God that made both sky, air, earth, and heav'n,
Which they beheld, the moon's resplendent globe,
And starry pole. "Thou also mads't the night,
Maker Omnipotent, and thou the day,
Which we, in our appointed work employ'd,
Have finish'd, happy in our mutual help,
And mutual love, the crown of all our bliss
Ordain'd by thee; and this delicious place
For us too large, where thy abundance wants
Partakers, and uncropt falls to the ground.
But thou hast promis'd from us two a race,
To fill the earth, who shall with us extol
Thy goodness infinite, both when we wake,
And when we seek, as now, thy gift of sleep." MILTON.

## SECTION VI.

### *Religion and Death.*

1. Lo! a form divinely bright
Descends, and bursts upon my sight;
A seraph of illustrious birth!
(Religion was her name on earth;)
Supremely sweet her radiant face,
And blooming with celestial grace!
Three shining cherubs form'd her train,
Wav'd their light wings, and reach'd the plain:
Faith, with sublime and piercing eye,
And pinions flutt'ring for the sky;
Here Hope, that smiling angel stands,
And golden anchors grace her hands;
There Charity in robes of white,
Fairest and fav'rite maid of light.

2. The seraph spoke—"'Tis reason's part
To govern and to guard the heart;
To lull the wayward soul to rest,
When hopes and fears distract the breast.
Reason may calm this doubtful strife,
And steer thy bark through various life:
But when the storms of death are nigh,
And midnight darkness veils the sky,
Shall Reason then direct thy sail,
Disperse the clouds, or sink the gale?
Stranger, this skill alone is mine,
Skill that transcends his scanty line."

3. "Revere thyself—thou'rt near allied
To angels on thy better side.
How various e'er their ranks or kinds,
Angels are but unbodied minds:
When the partition-walls decay,
Men emerge angels from their clay.
Yes, when the frailer body dies,
The soul asserts her kindred skies.
But minds, though sprung from heav'nly race,
Must first be tutor'd for the place:
The joys above are understood,
And relish'd only by the good.
Who shall assume this guardian care;
Who shall secure their birth-right there?
Souls are my charge—to me 'tis giv'n
To train them for their native heav'n."

4. "Know then—who bow the early knee,
And give the willing heart to me;
Who wisely, when Temptation waits,
Elude her frauds, and spurn her baits;
Who dare to own my injur'd cause,
Though fools deride my sacred laws;
Or scorn to deviate to the wrong,
Though persecution lifts her thong;
Though all the sons of hell conspire
To raise the stake and light the fire;
Know, that for such superior souls,
There lies a bliss beyond the poles:
Where spirits shine with purer ray,
And brighten to meridian day;
Where love, where boundless friendship rules;
(No friends that change, no love that cools;)
Where rising floods of knowledge roll,
And pour, and pour upon the soul!"

5. "But where's the passage to the skies?—
The road through death's black valley lies.
Nay, do not shudder at my tale;
Tho' dark the shades, yet safe the vale.
This path the best of men have trod;
And who'd decline the road to God?
Oh! 'tis a glorious boon to die!
This favour can't be priz'd too high."

6. While thus she spoke, my looks express'd
The raptures kindling in my breast;
My soul a fix'd attention gave;
When the stern monarch of the grave,
With haughty strides approach'd:—amaz'd
I stood, and trembled as I gaz'd.
The seraph calm'd each anxious fear,
And kindly wip'd the falling tear;
Then hasten'd with expanded wing
To meet the pale, terrific king.

7. But now what milder scenes arise!
　　The tyrant drops his hostile guise;
　　He seems a youth divinely fair,
　　In graceful ringlets waves his hair;
　　His wings their whit'ning plumes display,
　　His burnish'd plumes reflect the day;
　　Light flows his shining azure vest,
　　And all the angel stands confess'd.
　　I view'd the change with sweet surprise;
　　And, Oh! I panted for the skies:
　　Thank'd heav'n, that e'er I drew my breath;
　　And triumph'd in the thoughts of death.　COTTON.

## CHAPTER III.
### DIDACTIC PIECES.
### SECTION I.

*The vanity of wealth.*

1. No more thus brooding o'er yon heap,
　　With av'rice painful vigils keep;
　　Still unenjoy'd the present store,
　　Still endless sighs are breath'd for more.
　　Oh! quit the shadow, catch the prize,
　　Which not all India's treasure buys!
　　To purchase heav'n has gold the pow'r?
　　Can gold remove the mortal hour?
　　In life can love be bought with gold?
　　Are friendship's pleasures to be sold?
　　No—all that's worth a wish—a thought,
　　Fair virtue gives unbrib'd, unbought.
　　Cease then on trash thy hopes to bind;
　　Let nobler views engage thy mind.　DR. JOHNSON.

### SECTION II.

*Nothing formed in vain.*

1. LET no presuming impious railer tax
　　Creative wisdom; as if aught was form'd
　　In vain, or not for admirable ends.
　　Shall little haughty ignorance pronounce
　　His works unwise, of which the smallest part
　　Exceeds the narrow vision of her mind?
　　As if, upon a full-proportion'd dome,
　　On swelling columns heav'd, the pride of art!
　　A critic-fly, whose feeble ray scarce spreads
　　An inch around, with blind presumption bold,
　　Should dare to tax the structure of the whole.

2. And lives the man, whose universal eye
　　Has swept at once th' unbounded scheme of things;
　　Mark'd their dependence so, and firm accord
　　As with unfalt'ring accent to conclude,
　　That this availeth nought? Has any seen

The mighty chain of beings, less'ning down
From infinite perfection, to the brink
Of dreary nothing, desolate abyss!
From which astonish'd, thought, recoiling, turns?
Till then alone let zealous praise ascend,
And hymns of holy wonder, to that POWER,
Whose wisdom shines as lovely in our minds,
As on our smiling eyes his servant sun.  THOMSON.

### SECTION III.
*On pride.*

1. OF all the causes, which conspire to blind
Man's erring judgment, and misguide the mind,
What the weak head with strongest bias rules,
Is pride, the never-failing vice of fools.
Whatever nature has in worth deny'd,
She gives in large recruits of needful pride!
For, as in bodies, thus in souls, we find
What wants in blood and spirits, swell'd with wind.
Pride, where wit fails, steps in to our defence,
And fills up all the mighty void of sense.

2. If once right reason drives that cloud away,
Truth breaks upon us with resistless day.
Trust not yourself; but, your defects to know,
Make use of ev'ry friend—and ev'ry foe.
A little learning is a dangerous thing;
Drink deep, or taste not the Pierian spring.
There shallow draughts intoxicate the brain;
And drinking largely sobers us again.

3. Fir'd at first sight with what the muse imparts,
In fearless youth we tempt the heights of arts,
While, from the bounded level of our mind,
Short views we take, nor see the lengths behind;
But more advanc'd, behold, with strange surprise,
New distant scenes of endless science rise!
So, pleas'd at first the tow'ring Alps we try,
Mount o'er the vales, and seem to tread the sky;
Th' eternal snows appear already past,
And the first clouds and mountains seem the last:
But, those attain'd, we tremble to survey
The growing labours of the lengthen'd way;
Th' increasing prospect tires our wand'ring eyes;
Hills peep o'er hills, and Alps on Alps arise.  POPE.

### SECTION IV.
*Cruelty to brutes censured.*

1. I WOULD not enter on my list of friends,
(Though grac'd with polish'd manners and fine sense,
Yet wanting sensibility,) the man
Who needlessly sets foot upon a worm.
An inadvertent step may crush the snail,
That crawls at evening in the public path;
But he that has humanity, forewarn'd,
Will tread aside, and let the reptile live.

2. The creeping vermin, loathsome to the sight,
And charg'd perhaps with venom, that intrudes
A visitor unwelcome into scenes
Sacred to neatness and repose, th' alcove,
The chamber, or refectory, may die.
A necessary act incurs no blame.
Not so, when held within their proper bounds,
And guiltless of offence they range the air,
Or take their pastime in the spacious field:
There they are privileg'd. And he that hunts
Or harms them there, is guilty of a wrong;
Disturbs th' economy of nature's realm,
Who when she form'd, design'd them an abode.

3. The sum is this: if man's convenience, health,
Or safety, interefere, his rights and claims,
Are paramount, and must extinguish theirs.
Else they are all—the meanest things that are,
As free to live and to enjoy that life,
As God was free to form them at the first,
Who, in his sovereign wisdom, made them all.

4. Ye, therefore, who love mercy, teach your sons
To love it too. The spring time of our years
Is soon dishonour'd and defil'd, in most,
By budding ills, that ask a prudent hand
To check them. But, alas! none sooner shoots,
If unrestrain'd, into luxuriant growth,
Than cruelty, most dev'lish of them all.

5. Mercy to him that shows it, is the rule
And righteous limitation of its act,
By which Heav'n moves in pard'ning guilty man:
And he that shows none, being ripe in years,
And conscious of the outrage he commits,
Shall seek it, and not find it in his turn.   COWPER

## SECTION V.

*A paraphrase on the latter part of the 6th chapter of St. Matthew*

1. WHEN my breast labours with oppressive care,
And o'er my cheek descends the falling tear;
While all my warring passions are at strife,
Oh! let me listen to the words of life!
Raptures deep-felt his doctrine did impart,
And thus he rais'd from earth the drooping heart.

2. "Think not, when all your scanty stores afford,
Is spread at once upon the sparing board;
Think not, when worn the homely robe appears,
While on the roof the howling tempest bears;
What farther shall this feeble life sustain,
And what shall clothe these shiv'ring limbs again.

3. Say, does not life its nourishment exceed?
And the fair body its investing weed?
Behold! and look away your low despair—
See the light tenants of the barren air:

# Chap. 3. DIDACTIC PIECES.

4. To them, nor stores, nor granaries, belong;
Nought, but the woodland, and the pleasing song;
Yet, your kind heav'nly Father bends his eye
On the least wing that flits along the sky
To him they sing when spring renews the plain;
To him they cry, in winter's pinching reign;
Nor is their music, nor their plaint in vain:
He hears the gay, and the distressful call;
And with unsparing bounty fills them all."

5. "Observe the rising lily's snowy grace;
Observe the various vegetable race:
They neither toil, nor spin, but careless grow;
Yet see how warm they blush! how bright they glow!
What regal vestments can with them compare!
What king so shining! or what queen so fair!"

6. "If ceaseless, thus, the fowls of heav'n he feeds;
If o'er the fields such lucid robes he spreads;
Will he not care for you, ye faithless, say?
Is he unwise? or, are ye less than they?"  THOMSON.

## SECTION VI.
*The death of a good man a strong incentive to virtue.*

1. THE chamber where the good man meets his fate,
Is privileg'd beyond the common walk
Of virtuous life, quite in the verge of heav'n.
Fly, ye profane! if not, draw near with awe,
Receive the blessing, and adore the chance,
That threw in this Bethesda your disease:
If unrestor'd by this, despair your cure.

2. For, here, resistless demonstration dwells;
A death-bed's a detector of the heart.
Here tir'd dissimulation drops her mask,
Thro' life's grimace, that mistress of the scene!
Here real, and apparent, are the same.
You see the man; you see his hold on heav'n,
If sound his virtue, as Philander's sound.

3. Heav'n waits not the last moment; owns her friends
On this side death; and points them out to men;
A lecture, silent, but of sov'reign pow'r!
To vice, confusion: and to virtue, peace.
Whatever farce the boastful hero plays,
Virtue alone has majesty in death;
And greater still, the more the tyrant frowns.  YOUNG.

## SECTION VII.
*Reflections on a future state, from a review of winter.*

1. 'TIS done! dread winter spreads his latest glooms,
And reigns tremendous o'er the conquer'd year.
How dead the vegetable kingdom lies!
How dumb the tuneful! Horror wide extends
His desolate domain. Behold, fond man!
See here thy pictur'd life: pass some few years,
Thy flow'ring spring, thy summer's ardent strength,

Thy sober autumn fading into age,
And pale concluding winter comes at last,
And shuts the scene.

2. Ah! whither now are fled
Those dreams of greatness? those unsolid hopes
Of happiness? those longings after fame?
Those restless cares? those busy bustling days?
Those gay-spent, festive nights? those veering thoughts,
Lost between good and ill, that shar'd thy life?

3. All now are vanish'd! Virtue sole survives,
Immortal, never-failing friend of man,
His guide to happiness on high. And see!
'Tis come, the glorious morn! the second birth
Of heav'n and earth! awak'ning nature hears
The new-creating word; and starts to life,
In ev'ry heighten'd form, from pain and death
For ever free. The great eternal scheme,
Involving all, and in a perfect whole
Uniting as the prospect wider spreads,
To reason's eye refin'd clears up apace.

4. Ye vainly wise! Ye blind presumptuous! now,
Confounded in the dust, adore that Power,
And Wisdom oft arraign'd: see now the cause
Why unassuming worth in secret liv'd,
And died neglected: why the good man's share
In life was gall, and bitterness of soul:
Why the lone widow and her orphans pin'd
In starving solitude; while luxury,
In palaces lay straining her low thought,
To form unreal wants: why heav'n-born truth,
And moderation fair, wore the red marks
Of superstition's scourge: why licens'd pain,
That cruel spoiler, that embosom'd foe,
Imbitter'd all our bliss.

5. Ye good distress'd!
Ye noble few! who here unbending stand
Beneath life's pressure, yet bear up awhile,
And what your bounded view which only saw
A little part, deem'd evil, is no more:
The storms of wint'ry time will quickly pass,
And one unbounded spring encircle all. THOMSON

## SECTION VIII.

*Adam's advice to Eve, to avoid temptation.*

1. "O WOMAN, best are all things as the will
Of God ordain'd them; his creating hand
Nothing imperfect or deficient left
Of all that he created, much less man,
Or aught that might his happy state secure,
Secure from outward force." Within himself
The danger lies, yet lies within his pow'r:
Against his will he can receive no harm.

2. But God left free the will; for what obeys
Reason, is free, and reason he made right;

## DIDACTIC PIECES.

But bid her well beware, and still erect,
Lest, by some fair appearing good surpris'd,
She dictate false, and misinform the will
To do what God expressly hath forbid.
Not then mistrust, but tender love, enjoins
That I should mind thee oft: and mind thou me.
3. Firm we subsist, yet possible to swerve,
Since reason not impossibly may meet
Some specious object by the foe suborn'd,
And fall into deception unaware,
Not keeping strictest watch, as she was warn'd.
Seek not temptation then, which to avoid
Were better, and most likely if from me
Thou sever not; trial will come unsought.
4. Wouldst thou approve thy constancy? approve
First thy obedience; th' other who can know,
Not seeing thee attempted, who attest?
But if thou think, trial unsought may find
Us both securer than thus warn'd thou seem'st,
Go; for thy stay, not free, absents thee more:
Go in thy native innocence; rely
On what thou hast of virtue, summon all;
For God towards thee hath done his part; do thine."
MILTON.

### SECTION IX.
*On procrastination.*

1. BE wise to-day; 'tis madness to defer:
Next day the fatal precedent will plead;
Thus on, till wisdom is push'd out of life.
Procrastination is the thief of time.
Year after year it steals, till all are fled;
And, to the mercies of a moment leaves
The vast concerns of an eternal scene.
2. Of man's miraculous mistakes, this bears
The palm, "That all men are about to live:"
For ever on the brink of being born.
All pay themselves the compliment to think,
They, one day, shall not drivel; and their pride
On this reversion takes up ready praise;
At least, their own; their future selves applauds;
How excellent that life they ne'er will lead!
Time lodg'd in their own hands is folly's vails;
That lodg'd in fate's, to wisdom they consign;
The thing they can't but purpose, they postpone.
'Tis not in folly, not to scorn a fool;
And scarce in human wisdom to do more.
3. All promise is poor dilatory man;
And that thro' ev'ry stage. When young, indeed,
In full content, we sometimes nobly rest,
Unanxious for ourselves; and only wish,
As duteous sons, our fathers were more wise.
At thirty, man suspects himself a fool;
Knows it at forty, and reforms his plan;
At fifty, chides his infamous delay;

Pushes his prudent purpose to resolve;
In all the magnanimity of thought,
Resolves, and re-resolves, then dies the same.

4. And why? Because he thinks himself immortal.
All men think all men mortal, but themselves;
Themselves, when some alarming shock of fate
Strikes thro' their wounded hearts the sudden dread;
But their hearts wounded, like the wounded air,
Soon close; where, past the shaft, no trace is found.
As from the wing no scar the sky retains;
The parted wave no furrow from the keel;
So dies in human hearts the thought of death.
Ev'n with the tender tear which Nature sheds
O'er those we love, we drop it in their grave.   YOUNG.

## SECTION X.

*That philosophy, which stops at secondary causes, reproved.*

1. HAPPY the man who sees a God employ'd
In all the good and ill that checker life!
Resolving all events, with their effects
And manifold results, into the will
And arbitration wise of the Supreme.
Did not his eye rule all things, and intend
The least of our concerns; (since from the least
The greatest oft originate;) could chance
Find place in his dominion, or dispose
One lawless particle to thwart his plan;
Then God might be surpris'd, and unforeseen
Contingence might alarm him, and disturb
The smooth and equal course of his affairs.

2. This truth, philosophy, though eagle-ey'd
In nature's tendencies, oft o'erlooks;
And having found his instrument, forgets
Or disregards, or, more presumptuous still,
Denies the pow'r that wields it.   God proclaims
His hot displeasure against foolish men
That live an atheist life; involves the heav'n
In tempests; quits his grasp upon the winds,
And gives them all their fury; bids a plague
Kindle a fiery boil upon the skin,
And putrefy the breath of blooming health;

3. He calls for famine, and the meagre fiend
Blows mildew from between his shrivel'd lips,
And taints the golden ear; he springs his mines
And desolates a nation at a blast:
Forth steps the spruce philosopher, and tells
Of homogeneal and discordant springs
And principles; of causes, how they work
By necessary laws their sure effects,
Of action and re-action.

4.                              He has found
The source of the disease that nature feels;
And bids the world take heart and banish fear.
Thou fool! will thy discov'ry of the cause

Suspend th' effect, or heal it? Has not God
Still wrought by means since first he made the world?
And did he not of old employ his means
To drown it? What is his creation less
Than a capacious reservoir of means,
Form'd for his use, and ready at his will?
Go, dress thine eyes with eye-salve; ask of him,
Or ask of whomsoever he has taught;
And learn, though late, the genuine cause of all. COWPER.

## SECTION XI.

*Indignant sentiments on national prejudices and hatred; and on slavery.*

1. OH, for a lodge in some vast wilderness,
Some boundless contiguity of shade,
Where rumour of oppression and deceit,
Of unsuccessful or successful war,
Might never reach me more! My ear is pain'd,
My soul is sick with ev'ry day's report
Of wrong and outrage with which earth is fill'd.
There is no flesh in man's obdurate heart;
It does not feel for man. The nat'ral bond
Of brotherhood is sever'd, as the flax
That falls asunder at the touch of fire.

2. He finds his fellow guilty of a skin
Not colour'd like his own; and having pow'r
T' enforce the wrong, for such a worthy cause
Dooms and devotes him as his lawful prey.
Lands intersected by a narrow frith
Abhor each other. Mountains interpos'd,
Make enemies of nations, who had else,
Like kindred drops, been mingled into one.

3. Thus man devotes his brother, and destroys;
And worse than all, and most to be deplor'd,
As human nature's broadest, foulest blot,
Chains him, and tasks him, and exacts his sweat
With stripes, that mercy, with a bleeding heart,
Weeps when she sees inflicted on a beast.

4. Then what is man! And what man seeing this,
And having human feelings, does not blush
And hang his head, to think himself a man.
I would not have a slave to till my ground,
To carry me, to fan me while I sleep,
And tremble when I wake, for all the wealth
That sinews bought and sold have ever earn'd.

5. No: dear as freedom is, and in my heart's
Just estimation priz'd above all price;
I had much rather be myself the slave,
And wear the bonds, than fasten them on him.
We have no slaves at home—then why abroad
And they themselves once ferried o'er the wave
That parts us, are emancipate and loos'd.

6. Slaves cannot breath in England: if their lungs
Receive our air, that moment they are free;

They touch our country, and their shackles fall.
That's noble, and bespeaks a nation proud
And jealous of the blessing. Spread it then,
And let it circulate through ev'ry vein
Of all your empire; that where Britain's power
Is felt, mankind may feel her mercy too. COWPER

## CHAPTER IV.
### DESCRIPTIVE PIECES.
### SECTION I.
*The morning in summer.*

1. THE meek-ey'd morn appears, mother of dews,
At first faint gleaming in the dappled east;
Till far o'er ether spreads the wid'ning glow;
And from before the lustre of her face
White break the clouds away. With quicken'd step
Brown night retires: young day pours in apace,
And opens all the lawny prospect wide.

2. The dripping rock, the mountain's misty top,
Swell on the sight, and brighten with the dawn.
Blue, thro' the dusk, the smoking currents shine;
And from the bladed field the fearful hare
Limps, awkward: while along the forest-glade
The wild deer trip, and often turning gaze
At early passenger. Music awakes
The native voice of undissembled joy;
And thick around the woodland hymns arise.

3. Rous'd by the cock, the soon-clad shepherd leaves
His mossy cottage, where with peace he dwells;
And from the crowded fold, in order, drives
His flock to taste the verdure of the morn.
Falsely luxurious, will not man awake;
And, springing from the bed of sloth, enjoy
The cool, the fragrant, and the silent hour,
To meditation due and sacred song?

4. For is there aught in sleep can charm the wise?
To lie in dead oblivion, losing half
The fleeting moments of too short a life;
Total extinction of th' enlighten'd soul!
Or else to feverish vanity alive,
Wilder'd, and tossing thro' distemper'd dreams?
Who would, in such a gloomy state, remain
Longer than nature craves; when ev'ry muse
And every blooming pleasure waits without,
To bless the wildly devious morning walk? THOMSON.

### SECTION II.
*Rural sounds, as well as rural sights, delightful.*

1. NOR rural sights alone, but rural sounds
Exhilarate the spirit, and restore
The tone of languid nature. Mighty winds,

That sweep the skirt of some far-spreading wood
Of ancient growth, make music, not unlike
The dash of ocean on his winding shore,
And lull the spirit while they fill the mind,
Unnumber'd branches waving in the blast,
And all their leaves fast flutt'ring all at once.
2. Nor less composure waits upon the roar
Of distant floods; or on the softer voice
Of neighb'ring fountain; or of rills that slip
Through the cleft rock, and, chiming as they fall
Upon loose pebbles, lose themselves at length
In matted grass, that, with a livelier green,
Betrays the secret of their silent course.
Nature inanimate employs sweet sounds;
But animated nature sweeter still,
To sooth and satisfy the human ear.
3. Ten thousand warblers cheer the day, and one
The live-long night. Nor these alone, whose notes
Nice finger'd art must emulate in vain;
But cawing rooks, and kites that swim sublime,
In still repeated circles, screaming loud,
The jay, the pye, and ev'n the boding owl
That hails the rising moon, have charms for me.
Sounds inharmonious in themselves, and harsh,
Yet heard in scenes where peace for ever reigns,
And only there, please highly for their sake. COWPER.

## SECTION III
### *The rose.*

1. The rose had been wash'd, just wash'd in a shower,
Which Mary to Anna convey'd;
The plentiful moisture encumber'd the flower,
And weigh'd down its beautiful head.
2. The cup was all fill'd, and the leaves were all wet,
And it seem'd to a fanciful view,
To weep for the buds it had left with regret,
On the flourishing bush where it grew.
3. I hastily seiz'd it, unfit as it was
For a nosegay, so dripping and drown'd;
And swinging it rudely, too rudely, alas!
I snapp'd it—it fell to the ground.
4. And such, I exclaim'd, is the pitiless part,
Some act by the delicate mind,
Regardless of wringing and breaking a heart,
Already to sorrow resign'd.
5. This elegant rose, had I shaken it less,
Might have bloom'd with its owner awhile:
And the tear that is wip'd with a little address,
May be follow'd perhaps by a smile. COWPER.

## SECTION IV.
### *Care of birds for their young.*

1. As thus the patient dam assiduous sits,
Not to be tempted from her tender task,

Or by sharp hunger, or by smooth delight,
Tho' the whole loosen'd spring around her blows,
Her sympathising partner takes his stand
High on th' opponent bank, and ceaseless sings
The tedious time away; or else supplies
Her place a moment, while she sudden flits
To pick the scanty meal.

2. Th' appointed time
With pious toil fulfill'd, the callow young,
Warm'd and expanded into perfect life,
Their brittle bondage break, and come to light,
A helpless family, demanding food
With constant clamour. O what passions then,
What melting sentiments of kindly care,
On the new parents seize!

3. Away they fly
Affectionate, and undesiring bear
The most delicious morsel to their young;
Which equally distributed, again
The search begins. Even so a gentle pair,
By fortune sunk, but form'd of gen'rous mould,
And charm'd with cares beyond the vulgar breast,
In some lone cot amid the distant woods,
Sustain'd alone by providential Heav'n,
Oft, as they weeping eye their infant train,
Check their own appetites, and give them all. THOMSON.

## SECTION V.

*Liberty and slavery contrasted. Part of a letter written from Italy by Addison.*

1. How has kind Heav'n adorn'd the happy land,
And scatter'd blessings with a wasteful hand!
But what avail her unexhausted stores,
Her blooming mountains, and her sunny shores,
With all the gifts that heav'n and earth impart,
The smiles of nature, and the charms of art,
While proud oppression in her valleys reigns,
And tyranny usurps her happy plains?
The poor inhabitant beholds in vain
The redd'ning orange, and the swelling grain;
Joyless he sees the growing oils and wines,
And in the myrtle's fragrant shade repines.

2. Oh, Liberty, thou pow'r supremely bright,
Profuse of bliss, and pregnant with delight!
Perpetual pleasures in thy presence reign;
And smiling plenty leads thy wanton train.
Eas'd of her load, subjection grows more light;
And poverty looks cheerful in thy sight.
Thou mak'st the gloomy face of nature gay;
Giv'st beauty to the sun, and pleasure to the day.
On foreign mountains, may the sun refine
The grape's soft juice, and mellow it to wine;
With citron groves adorn a distant soil,
And the fat olive swell with floods of oil

## DESCRIPTIVE PIECES.

We envy not the warmer clime, that lies
In ten degrees of more indulgent skies;
Nor at the coarseness of our heav'n repine,
Tho' o'er our heads the frozen Pleiads shine:
'Tis Liberty that crowns Britannia's isle,
And makes her barren rocks, and her bleak mountains smile.

### SECTION VI.

*Charity. A paraphrase on the 13th chapter of the first epistle to the Corinthians.*

1. Did sweeter sounds adorn my flowing tongue,
Than ever man pronounc'd or angel sung;
Had I all knowledge, human and divine,
That thought can reach, or science can define;
And had I pow'r to give that knowledge birth,
In all the speeches of the babbling earth;
Did Shadrach's zeal my glowing breast inspire,
To weary tortures, and rejoice in fire;
Or had I faith like that which Israel saw,
When Moses gave them miracles, and law:
Yet, gracious charity, indulgent guest,
Were not thy pow'r exerted in my breast;
Those speeches would send up unheeded pray'r;
That scorn of life would be but wild despair;
A cymbal's sound were better than my voice;
My faith were form; my eloquence were noise.

2. Charity, decent, modest, easy, kind,
Softens the high, and rears the abject mind;
Knows with just reins, and gentle hand, to guide
Betwixt vile shame, and arbitrary pride.
Not soon provok'd, she easily forgives;
And much she suffers, as she much believes.
Soft peace she brings wherever she arrives;
She builds our quiet, as she forms our lives;
Lays the rough paths of peevish nature even;
And opens in each heart a little heav'n.

3. Each other gift, which God on man bestows,
Its proper bounds, and due restriction knows;
To one fix'd purpose dedicates its pow'r;
And finishing its act, exists no more.
Thus, in obedience to what Heav'n decrees,
Knowledge shall fail, and prophecy shall cease;
But lasting charity's more ample sway,
Nor bound by time, nor subject to decay,
In happy triumph shall for ever live;
And endless good diffuse, and endless praise receive.

4. As through the artist's intervening glass,
Our eye observes the distant planets pass;
A little we discover; but allow,
That more remains unseen, than art can show;
So whilst our mind its knowledge would improve,
(Its feeble eye intent on things above,)
High as we may, we lift our reason up,
By faith directed, and confirm'd by hope;

Yet are we able only to survey,
Dawnings of beams, and promises of day;
Heav'n's fuller affluence mocks our dazzled sight;
Too great its swiftness, and too strong its light.
5. But soon the mediate clouds shall be dispell'd;
The sun shall soon be face to face beheld,
In all his robes, with all his glory on,
Seated sublime on his meridian throne.
Then constant faith, and holy hope shall die,
One lost in certainty, and one in joy:
Whilst thou, more happy pow'r, fair charity,
Triumphant sister, greatest of the three,
Thy office, and thy nature still the same,
Lasting thy lamp, and unconsum'd thy flame,
Shalt still survive—
Shalt stand before the host of heav'n confest,
For ever blessing, and for ever blest.

## SECTION VII.
*Picture of a good man.*

1. SOME angel guide my pencil, while I draw,
What nothing else than angel can exceed,
A man on earth devoted to the skies;
Like ships at sea, while in, above the world.
With aspect mild, and elevated eye,
Behold him seated on a mount serene,
Above the fogs of sense, and passion's storm:
All the black cares, and tumults of this life,
Like harmless thunders, breaking at his feet,
Excite his pity, not impair his peace.
2. Earth's genuine sons, the sceptred, and the slave,
A mingled mob! a wand'ring herd! he sees,
Bewilder'd in the vale; in all unlike!
His full reverse in all! What higher praise?
What stronger demonstration of the right?
The present all their care; the future his.
When public welfare calls, or private want,
They give to fame; his bounty he conceals.
Their virtues varnish nature; his exalt.
Mankind's esteem they court; and he his own.
3. Theirs the wild chase of false felicities;
His, the compos'd possession of the true.
Alike throughout is his consistent piece,
All of one colour, and an even thread;
While party-colour'd shades of happiness,
With hideous gaps between, patch up for them
A madman's robe; each puff of fortune blows
The tatters by, and shows their nakedness.
4. He sees with other eyes than theirs: where they
Behold a sun, he spies a Deity;
What makes them only smile, makes him adore.
Where they see mountains, he but atoms sees;
An empire in his balance, weighs a grain.
They things terrestrial worship as divine:

  His hopes immortal blow them by, as dust,
  That dims his sight and shortens his survey,
  Which longs, in infinite, to lose all bound.
5. Titles and honours (if they prove his fate)
  He lays aside to find his dignity;
  No dignity they find in aught besides.
  They triumph in externals, (which conceal
  Man's real glory,) proud of an eclipse:
  Himself too much he prizes to be proud;
  And nothing thinks so great in man, as man.
  Too dear he holds his int'rest, to neglect
  Another's welfare, or his right invade;
  Their int'rest, like a lion, lives on prey.
6. They kindle at the shadow of a wrong;
  Wrong he sustains with temper, looks on heav'n,
  Nor stoops to think his injurer his foe:
  Nought, but what wounds his virtue, wounds his peace.
  A cover'd heart their character defends;
  A cover'd heart denies him half his praise.
7. With nakedness his innocence agrees!
  While their broad foliage testifies their fall!
  Their no-joys end, where his full feast begins:
  His joys create, theirs murder, future bliss.
  To triumph in existence, his alone;
  And his alone triumphantly to think
  His true existence is not yet begun.
  His glorious course was, yesterday, complete:
  Death, then, was welcome; yet life still is sweet. YOUNG

## SECTION VIII.
### *The pleasures of retirement.*

1. O KNEW he but his happiness, of men
  The happiest he! who, far from public rage,
  Deep in the vale, with a choice few retir'd,
  Drinks the pure pleasures of the rural life.
2. What tho' the dome be wanting, whose proud gate,
  Each morning, vomits out the sneaking crowd
  Of flatterers false, and in their turn abus'd?
  Vile intercourse! What though the glitt'ring robe,
  Of ev'ry hue reflected light can give,
  Or floated loose, or stiff with mazy gold,
  The pride and gaze of fools, oppress him not?
  What tho', from utmost land and sea purvey'd,
  For him each rarer tributary life
  Bleeds not, and his insatiate table heaps
  With luxury and death? What tho' his bowl
  Flames not with costly juice; nor sunk in beds
  Oft of gay care, he tosses out the night,
  Or melts the thoughtless hours in idle state?
  What tho' he knows not those fantastic joys,
  That still amuse the wanton, still deceive;
  A face of pleasure, but a heart of pain;
  Their hollow moments undelighted all?
  Sure peace is his; a solid life estrang'd

To disappointment, and fallacious hope.
3. Rich in content, in nature's bounty rich,
In herbs and fruits; whatever greens the spring,
When heaven descends in showers; or bends the bough
When summer reddens, and when autumn beams;
Or in the wintry glebe whatever lies
Conceal'd, and fattens with the richest sap:
These are not wanting; nor the milky drove,
Luxuriant, spread o'er all the lowing vale;
Nor bleating mountains; nor the chide of streams,
And hum of bees, inviting sleep sincere
Into the guiltless breast, beneath the shade,
Or thrown at large amid the fragrant hay;
Nor aught besides of prospect, grove, or song,
Dim grottos, gleaming lakes, and fountains clear.
4. Here too dwells simple truth; plain innocence;
Unsullied beauty; sound unbroken youth,
Patient of labour, with a little pleas'd;
Health ever blooming; unambitious toil;
Calm contemplation, and poetic ease.         THOMSON.

## SECTION IX.

*The pleasure and benefit of an improved and well-directed imagination.*

1. OH! blest of Heaven, who not the languid songs
Of luxury, the siren! not the bribes
Of sordid wealth, nor all the gaudy spoils
Of pageant Honour, can seduce to leave
Those ever blooming sweets, which, from the store
Of nature, fair imagination culls,
To charm th' enliven'd soul! What tho' not all
Of mortal offspring can attain the height
Of envy'd life; tho' only few possess
Patrician treasures, or imperial state;
Yet nature's care, to all her children just,
With richer treasures, and an ampler state,
Endows at large whatever happy man
Will deign to use them.
2.                             His the city's pomp,
The rural honours his. Whate'er adorns
The princely dome, the column, and the arch,
The breathing marble and the sculptur'd gold,
Beyond the proud possessor's narrow claim,
His tuneful breast enjoys. For him, the spring
Distils her dews, and from the silken gem
Its lucid leaves unfolds: for him, the hand
Of autumn tinges every fertile branch
With blooming gold, and blushes like the morn.
Each passing hour sheds tribute from her wings,
And still new beauties meet his lonely walk,
And loves unfelt attract him. Not a breeze
Flies o'er the meadow; not a cloud imbibes
The setting sun's effulgence; not a strain
From all the tenants of the warbling shade

Ascends; but whence his bosom can partake
Fresh pleasure, unreprov'd.
3.                              Nor thence partakes
Fresh pleasure only; for th' attentive mind,
By this harmonious action on her powers,
Becomes herself harmonious: wont so oft
In outward things to meditate the charm
Of sacred order, soon she seeks at home,
To find a kindred order; to exert,
Within herself this elegance of love,
This fair inspir'd delight: her temper'd pow'rs
Refine at length, and every passion wears
A chaster, milder, more attractive mien.
4. But if to ampler prospects, if to gaze
On nature's form, where, negligent of all
These lesser graces, she assumes the port
Of that Eternal Majesty that weigh'd
The world's foundations, if to these the mind
Exalts her daring eye; then mightier far
Will be the change, and nobler. Would the forms
Of servile custom cramp her gen'rous pow'rs?
Would sordid policies, the barb'rous growth
Of ignorance and rapine, bow her down
To tame pursuits, to indolence and fear;
5. Lo! she appeals to nature, to the winds
And rolling waves, the sun's unwearied course,
The elements and seasons: all declare
For what th' eternal MAKER has ordain'd
The pow'rs of man: we feel within ourselves
His energy divine: he tells the heart,
He meant, he made us to behold and love
What he beholds and loves, the general orb
Of life and being; to be great like Him,
Beneficent and active. Thus the men
Whom nature's works instruct, with GOD himself
Hold converse; grow familiar, day by day,
With his conceptions; act upon his plan;
And form to his, the relish of their souls.    AKENSIDE.

---

## CHAPTER V.

### PATHETIC PIECES.

#### SECTION I.

*The hermit.*

1. AT the close of the day, when the hamlet is still,
   And mortals the sweets of forgetfulness prove;
When nought but the torrent is heard on the hill,
   And nought but the nightingale's song in the grove.
'Twas thus by the cave of the mountain afar,
   While his harp rung symphonious, a hermit began.
No more with himself or with nature at war,
   He thought as a sage, tho' he felt as a man.

2. "Ah! why, all abandon'd to darkness and wo;
  Why, lone Philomela, that languishing fall?
 For spring shall return, and a lover bestow,
  And sorrow no longer thy bosom inthral.
 But, if pity inspire thee, renew the sad lay,
  Mourn, sweetest complainer, man calls thee to mourn.
 O sooth him whose pleasures like thine pass away:
  Full quickly they pass—but they never return.

3. "Now gliding remote, on the verge of the sky,
  The moon half extinguish'd her crescent displays:
 But lately I mark'd, when majestic on high
  She shone, and the planets were lost in her blaze.
 Roll on, thou fair orb, and with gladness pursue
  The path that conducts thee to splendour again:
 But man's faded glory what change shall renew!
  Ah fool! to exult in a glory so vain!

4. "'Tis night, and the landscape is lovely no more:
  I mourn; but, ye woodlands, I mourn not for you;
 For morn is approaching, your charms to restore,
  Perfum'd with fresh fragrance, and glitt'ring with dew.
 Nor yet for the ravage of winter I mourn;
  Kind nature the embryo blossom will save:
 But when shall spring visit the mouldering urn!
  O when shall day dawn on the night of the grave!

5. "'Twas thus by the glare of false science betray'd,
  That leads, to bewilder; and dazzles, to blind;
 My thoughts wont to roam, from shade onward to shade,
  Destruction before me, and sorrow behind.
 O pity, great Father of light, then I cried,
  Thy creature who fain would not wander from thee!
 Lo, humbled in dust, I relinquish my pride:
  From doubt and from darkness thou only canst free.

6. "And darkness and doubt are now flying away;
  No longer I roam in conjecture forlorn:
 So breaks on the traveller, faint and astray,
  The bright and the balmy effulgence of morn.
 See truth, love, and mercy, in triumph descending,
  And nature all glowing in Eden's first bloom!
 On the cold cheek of death smiles and roses are blending,
  And beauty immortal awakes from the tomb."
                                             BEATTIE.

## SECTION II.

### *The beggar's petition.*

1. PITY the sorrows of a poor old man,
  Whose trembling limbs have borne him to your door;
 Whose days are dwindled to the shortest span;
  Oh! give relief, and Heaven will bless your store.

2. These tatter'd clothes my poverty bespeak,
  These hoary locks proclaim my lengthen'd years;
 And many a furrow in my grief-worn cheek,
  Has been the channel to a flood of tears.

3. Yon house, erected on the rising ground,
　　With tempting aspect drew me from my road;
　For plenty there a residence has found,
　　And grandeur a magnificent abode.
4. Hard is the fate of the infirm and poor!
　　Here, as I crav'd a morsel of their bread,
　A pamper'd menial drove me from the door,
　　To seek a shelter in an humbler shed.
5. Oh! take me to your hospitable dome;
　　Keen blows the wind, and piercing is the cold;
　Short is my passage to the friendly tomb;
　　For I am poor, and miserably old.
6. Should I reveal the sources of my grief,
　　If soft humanity e'er touch'd your breast,
　Your hands would not withhold the kind relief,
　　And tears of pity would not be represt.
7. Heav'n sends misfortunes; why should we repine?
　　'Tis Heav'n has brought me to the state you see;
　And your condition may be soon like mine,
　　The child of sorrow and of misery.
8. A little farm was my paternal lot;
　　Then like the lark I sprightly hail'd the morn;
　But ah! oppression forc'd me from my cot,
　　My cattle died, and blighted was my corn.
9. My daughter, once the comfort of my age,
　　Lur'd by a villain from her native home,
　Is cast abandon'd on the world's wide stage,
　　And doom'd in scanty poverty to roam.
10. My tender wife, sweet soother of my care!
　　Struck with sad anguish at the stern decree,
　Fell, ling'ring fell, a victim to despair;
　　And left the world to wretchedness and me.
11. Pity the sorrows of a poor old man,
　　Whose trembling limbs have borne him to your door,
　Whose days are dwindled to the shortest span:
　　Oh! give relief, and Heav'n will bless your store.

### SECTION III.
*Unhappy close of life.*

1. How shocking must thy summons be, O Death!
To him that is at ease in his possessions!
Who counting on long years of pleasure here,
Is quite unfurnish'd for the world to come!
In that dread moment, how the frantic soul
Raves round the walls of her clay tenement;
Runs to each avenue, and shrieks for help;
But shrieks in vain! How wishfully she looks
On all she's leaving, now no longer hers!
2. A little longer; yet a little longer;
O might she stay to wash away her stains;
And fit her for her passage! Mournful sight!
Her very eyes weep blood; and ev'ry groan

She heaves is big with horror. But the foe,
Like a staunch murd'rer, steady to his purpose,
Pursues her close, thro' ev'ry lane of life;
Nor misses once the track; but presses on,
Till, forc'd at last to the tremendous verge,
At once she sinks to everlasting ruin.   R. BLAIR.

## SECTION IV.
*Elegy to pity.*

1. HAIL, lovely pow'r! whose bosom heaves the sigh,
   When fancy paints the scene of deep distress;
Whose tears spontaneous crystallize the eye,
   When rigid fate denies the pow'r to bless.

2. Not all the sweets Arabia's gales convey
   From flow'ry meads, can with that sigh compare;
Not dew-drops glitt'ring in the morning ray,
   Seem near so beauteous as that falling tear.

3. Devoid of fear, the fawns around thee play;
   Emblem of peace, the dove before thee flies;
No blood-stain'd traces mark thy blameless way;
   Beneath thy feet no hapless insect dies.

4. Come, lovely nymph, and range the mead with me,
   To spring the partridge from the guileful foe;
From secret snares the struggling bird to free;
   And stop the hand uprais'd to give the blow.

5. And when the air with heat meridian glows,
   And nature droops beneath the conqu'ring gleam,
Let us, slow wand'ring where the current flows,
   Save sinking flies that float along the stream.

6. Or turn to nobler, greater tasks thy care,
   To me thy sympathetic gifts impart;
Teach me in friendship's griefs to bear a share,
   And justly boast the gen'rous feeling heart.

7. Teach me to sooth the helpless orphan's grief;
   With timely aid the widow's woes assuage;
To mis'ry's moving cries to yield relief;
   And be the sure resource of drooping age.

8. So when the genial spring of life shall fade,
   And sinking nature own the dread decay,
Some soul congenial then may lend its aid,
   And gild the close of life's eventful day.

## SECTION V.

*Verses supposed to be written by Alexander Selkirk, during his solitary abode in the Island of Juan Fernandez.*

1. I AM monarch of all I survey,
      My right there is none to dispute;
   From the centre all round to the sea,
      I am lord of the fowl and the brute.
   Oh solitude! where are the charms,
      That sages have seen in thy face?
   Better dwell in the midst of alarms,
      Than reign in this horrible place.

2. I am out of humanity's reach,
    I must finish my journey alone;
Never hear the sweet music of speech;
    I start at the sound of my own.
The beasts that roam over the plain,
    My form with indifference see:
They are so unacquainted with man,
    Their tameness is shocking to me.
3. Society, friendship, and love,
    Divinely bestow'd upon man,
Oh had I the wings of a dove,
    How soon would I taste you again!
My sorrows I then might assuage
    In the ways of religion and truth;
Might learn from the wisdom of age,
    And be cheer'd by the sallies of youth.
4. Religion! what treasure untold
    Resides in that heavenly word!
More precious than silver or gold,
    Or all that this earth can afford.
But the sound of the church-going bell
    These vallies and rocks never heard;
Ne'er sigh'd at the sound of a knell,
    Or smil'd when a sabbath appear'd.
5. Ye winds that have made me your sport,
    Convey to this desolate shore,
Some cordial endearing report
    Of a land I shall visit no more.
My friends, do they now and then send
    A wish or a thought after me?
O tell me I yet have a friend,
    Though a friend I am never to see.
6. How fleet is a glance of the mind!
    Compar'd with the speed of its flight,
The tempest itself lags behind,
    And the swift-wing'd arrows of light.
When I think of my own native land,
    In a moment I seem to be there;
But, alas! recollection at hand
    Soon hurries me back to despair.
7. But the sea-fowl is gone to her nest,
    The beast is laid down in his lair;
Even here is a season of rest,
    And I to my cabin repair.
There's mercy in every place;
    And mercy—encouraging thought!
Gives even affliction a grace,
    And reconciles man to his lot.

COWPER.

### SECTION VI.
*Gratitude.*

1. WHEN all thy mercies, O my God!
    My rising soul surveys,

Transported with the view, I'm lost
　　In wonder, love, and praise.
2. O how shall words, with equal warmth,
　　The gratitude declare,
That glows within my ravish'd heart?
　　But thou canst read it there.
3. Thy Providence my life sustain'd,
　　And all my wants redrest,
When in the silent womb I lay,
　　And hung upon the breast.
4. To all my weak complaints and cries,
　　Thy mercy lent an ear,
Ere yet my feeble thoughts had learn'd,
　　To form themselves in pray'r.
5. Unnumber'd comforts to my soul,
　　Thy tender care bestow'd,
Before my infant heart conceiv'd
　　From whom those comforts flow'd.
6. When, in the slipp'ry paths of youth,
　　With heedless steps, I ran,
Thine arm, unseen, convey'd me safe,
　　And led me up to man.
7. Through hidden dangers, toils, and deaths,
　　It gently clear'd my way;
And through the pleasing snares of vice,
　　More to be fear'd than they.
8. When worn with sickness, oft hast thou,
　　With health renew'd my face;
And, when in sins and sorrows sunk,
　　Reviv'd my soul with grace.
9. Thy bounteous hand, with worldly bliss,
　　Has made my cup run o'er;
And, in a kind and faithful friend,
　　Has doubled all my store.
10. Ten thousand thousand precious gifts,
　　My daily thanks employ;
Nor is the least a cheerful heart,
　　That tastes those gifts with joy.
11. Through ev'ry period of my life,
　　Thy goodness I'll pursue;
And, after death, in distant worlds,
　　The glorious theme renew.
12. When nature fails, and day and night,
　　Divide thy works no more,
My ever-grateful heart, O Lord!
　　Thy mercy shall adore.
13. Through all eternity, to thee,
　　A joyful song I'll raise,
For O! eternity's too short
　　To utter all thy praise.　　　　ADDISON.

## SECTION VII.

*A man perishing in the snow; from whence reflections are raised on the miseries of life.*

1. As thus the snows arise; and foul and fierce,
All winter drives along the darken'd air;
In his own loose-revolving field, the swain
Disaster'd stands; sees other hills ascend,
Of unknown joyless brow; and other scenes,
Of horrid prospect, shag the trackless plain;
Nor finds the river, nor the forest, hid
Beneath the formless wild; but wanders on,
From hill to dale, still more and more astray;
Impatient flouncing through the drifted heaps,
Stung with the thoughts of home; the thoughts of home
Rush on his nerves, and call their vigour forth
In many a vain attempt.

2.                        How sinks his soul!
What black despair, what horror fills his heart!
When, for the dusky spot, which fancy feign'd
His tufted cottage rising through the snow,
He meets the roughness of the middle waste,
Far from the track, and blest abode of man;
While round him night resistless closes fast,
And ev'ry tempest howling o'er his head,
Renders the savage wilderness more wild.

3. Then throng the busy shapes into his mind,
Of cover'd pits, unfathomably deep,
A dire descent, beyond the pow'r of frost!
Of faithless bogs; of precipices huge,
Smooth'd up with snow; and what is land, unknown,
What water, of the still unfrozen spring,
In the loose marsh or solitary lake,
Where the fresh fountain from the bottom boils.

4. These check his fearful steps; and down he sinks
Beneath the shelter of the shapeless drift,
Thinking o'er all the bitterness of death,
Mix'd with the tender anguish nature shoots
Through the wrung bosom of the dying man,
His wife, his children, and his friends unseen.

5. In vain for him th' officious wife prepares
The fire fair-blazing, and the vestment warm;
In vain his little children, peeping out
Into the mingled storm, demand their sire,
With tears of artless innocence. Alas!
Nor wife, nor children, more shall he behold;
Nor friends, nor sacred home. On every nerve
The deadly winter seizes; shuts up sense;
And, o'er his inmost vitals creeping cold,
Lays him along the snows a stiffen'd corse,
Stretch'd out and bleaching in the northern blast.

6. Ah, little think the gay licentious proud,
Whom pleasure, pow'r, and affluence surround;
They who their thoughtless hours in giddy mirth,
And wanton, often cruel riot, waste;

Ah little think they, while they dance along,
How many feel, this very moment, death,
And all the sad variety of pain!
7. How many sink in the devouring flood,
Or more devouring flame! How many bleed,
By shameful variance betwixt man and man!
How many pine in want, and dungeon glooms,
Shut from the common air, and common use
Of their own limbs! How many drink the cup
Of baleful grief, or eat the bitter bread
Of misery! Sore pierc'd by wintry winds,
How many shrink into the sordid hut
Of cheerless poverty! How many shake
With all the fiercer tortures of the mind,
Unbounded passion, madness, guilt, remorse!
8. How many, rack'd with honest passions, droop
In deep retir'd distress! How many stand
Around the death-bed of their dearest friends,
And point the parting anguish! Thought fond man
Of these, and all the thousand nameless ills,
That one incessant struggle render life,
One scene of toil, of suffering, and of fate,
Vice in his high career would stand appall'd,
And heedless rambling impulse learn to think;
The conscious heart of charity would warm,
And her wide wish benevolence dilate;
The social tear would rise, the social sigh;
And into clear perfection, gradual bliss,
Refining still, the social passions work. THOMSON.

## SECTION VIII.
### A morning hymn.

1. These are thy glorious works, parent of good,
Almighty, thine this universal frame,
Thus wond'rous fair; thyself how wond'rous then!
Unspeakable, who sitt'st above these heavens,
To us, invisible, or dimly seen
In these thy lower works; yet these declare
Thy goodness beyond thought, and pow'r divine.
2. Speak ye who best can tell, ye sons of light,
Angels; for ye behold him, and with songs
And choral symphonies, day without night,
Circle his throne rejoicing; ye, in heaven,
On earth, join all ye creatures to extol
Him first, Him last, Him midst, and without end.
Fairest of stars, last in the train of night,
If better thou belong not to the dawn,
Sure pledge of day, that crown'st the smiling morn
With thy bright circlet, praise him in thy sphere,
While day arises, that sweet hour of prime.
Thou sun, of this great world, both eye and soul,
Acknowledge him thy greater, sound his praise
In thy eternal course, both when thou climb'st,
And when high noon hast gain'd, and when thou fall'st.

3. Moon, that now meet'st the orient sun, now fly'st,
With the fix'd stars, fix'd in their orb that flies;
And ye five other wand'ring fires that move
In mystic dance, not without song, resound
His praise, who out of darkness call'd up light.
Air, and ye elements, the eldest birth
Of nature's womb, that in quaternion run
Perpetual circle, multiform, and mix
And nourish all things; let your ceaseless change
Vary to our great MAKER still new praise.

4. Ye mists and exhalations that now rise
From hill or steaming lake, dusky or gray,
Till the sun paint your fleecy skirts with gold,
In honour to the world's great AUTHOR rise!
Whether to deck with clouds th' uncolour'd sky,
Or wet the thirsty earth with falling show'rs,
Rising or falling still advance his praise.

5. His praise, ye winds, that from four quarters blow,
Breathe soft or loud; and wave your tops, ye pines,
With ev'ry plant, in sign of worship wave.
Fountains, and ye that warble as ye flow
Melodious murmurs, warbling tune his praise.
Join voices, all ye living souls; ye birds
That singing, up to heaven's gate ascend,
Bear on your wings and in your notes his praise.

6. Ye that in waters glide, and ye that walk
The earth, and stately tread, or lowly creep;
Witness if I be silent, morn or even,
To hill or valley, fountain, or fresh shade
Made vocal by my song, and taught his praise.
Hail, UNIVERSAL LORD! be bounteous still
To give us only good; and if the night
Has gather'd aught of evil, or conceal'd,
Disperse it, as now light dispels the dark.—MILTON.

---

## CHAPTER VI.

### PROMISCUOUS PIECES.

#### SECTION I.

*Ode to content.*

1. O THOU, the nymph with placid eye!
O seldom found, yet ever nigh!
Receive my temp'rate vow:
Not all the storms that shake the pole,
Can e'er disturb thy halcyon soul,
And smooth, unalter'd brow.

2. O come, in simplest vest array'd,
With all thy sober cheer display'd,
To bless my longing sight;
Thy mien compos'd, thy even pace,
Thy meek regard, thy matron grace,
And chaste subdu'd delight.

3. No more by varying passions beat,
O gently guide my pilgrim feet
To find thy hermit cell;
Where in some pure and equal sky,
Beneath thy soft indulgent eye,
The modest virtues dwell.
4. Simplicity in attic vest,
And Innocence, with candid breast,
And clear undaunted eye;
And Hope, who points to distant years,
Fair op'ning thro' this vale of tears
A vista to the sky.
5. There Health, thro' whose calm bosom glide,
The temp'rate joys in even tide,
That rarely ebb or flow;
And Patience there, thy sister meek,
Presents her mild, unvarying cheek,
To meet the offer'd blow.
6. Her influence taught the Phrygian sage
A tyrant master's wanton rage,
With settled smiles, to meet:
Inur'd to toil and bitter bread,
He bow'd his meek submitted head,
And kiss'd thy sainted feet.
7. But thou, O nymph, retir'd and coy!
In what brown hamlet dost thou joy
To tell thy tender tale?
The lowliest children of the ground,
Moss-rose and violet blossom round,
And lily of the vale.
8. O say what soft propitious hour
I best may choose to hail thy pow'r,
And court thy gentle sway?
When autumn, friendly to the muse,
Shall thy own modest tints diffuse,
And shed thy milder day?
9. When eve, her dewy star beneath,
Thy balmy spirit loves to breathe,
And ev'ry storm is laid?
If such an hour was e'er thy choice,
Oft let me hear thy soothing voice,
Low whisp'ring through the shade. BARBAULD.

## SECTION II.

### *The shepherd and the philosopher.*

1. REMOTE from cities liv'd a swain,
Unvex'd with all the cares of gain;
His head was silver'd o'er with age,
And long experience made him sage;
In summer's heat and winter's cold,
He fed his flock and penn'd the fold;
His hours in cheerful labour flew,
Nor envy nor ambition knew:

His wisdom and his honest fame
Through all the country rais'd his name.
2. A deep philosopher (whose rules
Of moral life were drawn from schools)
The shepherd's homely cottage sought,
And thus explor'd his reach of thought.
"Whence is thy learning? Hath thy toil
O'er books consum'd the midnight oil?
Hast thou old Greece and Rome survey'd,
And the vast sense of Plato weigh'd?
Hath Socrates thy soul refin'd,
And hast thou fathom'd Tully's mind?
Or, like the wise Ulysses, thrown,
By various fates, on realms unknown,
Hast thou through many cities stray'd,
Their customs, laws, and manners weigh'd?"
3. The shepherd modestly replied,
"I ne'er the paths of learning tried;
Nor have I roam'd in foreign parts,
To read mankind, their laws and arts;
For man is practis'd in disguise,
He cheats the most discerning eyes.
Who by that search shall wiser grow?
By that ourselves we never know.
The little knowledge I have gain'd,
Was all from simple nature drain'd;
Hence my life's maxims took their rise,
Hence grew my settled hate of vice.
4. The daily labours of the bee
Awake my soul to industry.
Who can observe the careful ant,
And not provide for future want?
My dog (the trustiest of his kind)
With gratitude inflames my mind:
I mark his true, his faithful way,
And in my service copy Tray.
In constancy and nuptial love,
I learn my duty from the dove.
The hen, who from the chilly air,
With pious wing, protects her care,
And ev'ry fowl that flies at large,
Instructs me in a parent's charge.
5. From nature too I take my rule,
To shun contempt and ridicule.
I never, with important air,
In conversation overbear.
Can grave and formal pass for wise,
When men the solemn owl despise?
My tongue within my lips I rein;
For who talks much must talk in vain.
We from the wordy torrent fly:
Who listens to the chatt'ring pye?
Nor would I, with felonious flight,
By stealth invade my neighbour's right:

Q

6. Rapacious animals we hate;
Kites, hawks, and wolves, deserve their fate.
Do not we just abhorrence find
Against the toad and serpent kind?
But envy, calumny, and spite,
Bear stronger venom in their bite.
Thus ev'ry object of creation
Can furnish hints to contemplation;
And, from the most minute and mean,
A virtuous mind can morals glean."
7. "Thy fame is just," the sage replies;
"Thy virtue proves thee truly wise.
Pride often guides the author's pen,
Books as affected are as men:
But he who studies nature's laws,
From certain truth his maxims draws;
And those, without our schools, suffice
To make men moral, good, and wise."——GAY.

### SECTION III.
*The road to happiness open to all men.*

1. OH happiness! our being's end and aim!
Good, pleasure, ease, content! whate'er thy name;
That something still which prompts th' eternal sigh,
For which we bear to live, or dare to die:
Which still so near us, yet beyond us lies,
O'erlook'd, seen double, by the fool and wise;
Plant of celestial seed, if dropt below,
Say, in what mortal soil thou deign'st to grow?
2. Fair op'ning to some court's propitious shrine,
Or deep with diamonds in the flaming mine?
Twin'd with the wreaths Parnassian laurels yield,
Or reap'd in iron harvests of the field?
Where grows? where grows it not? if vain our toil,
We ought to blame the culture, not the soil.
Fix'd to no spot is happiness sincere;
'Tis no where to be found, or ev'ry where;
'Tis never to be bought, but always free;
And, fled from monarchs, St. John! dwells with thee.
3. Ask of the learn'd the way. The learn'd are blind;
This bids to serve, and that to shun mankind:
Some place the bliss in action, some in ease;
Those call it pleasure, and contentment these:
Some sunk to beasts, find pleasure end in pain;
Some swell'd to gods, confess ev'n virtue vain;
Or indolent, to each extreme they fall,
To trust in ev'ry thing, or doubt of all.
4. Who thus define it, say they more or less
Than this, that happiness is happiness?
Take nature's path, and mad opinions leave;
All states can reach it, and all heads conceive;
Obvious her goods, in no extreme they dwell;
There needs but thinking right, and meaning well;
And mourn our various portions as we please,
Equal is common sense, and common ease.

Remember, man, "the universal cause
"Acts not by partial, but by gen'ral laws;"
And makes what happiness we justly call,
Subsist not in the good of one, but all.——POPE.

## SECTION IV.
### *The goodness of Providence.*

1. THE Lord my pasture shall prepare,
And feed me with a shepherd's care;
His presence shall my wants supply,
And guard me with a watchful eye;
My noon-day walks he shall attend,
And all my midnight hours defend.
2. When in the sultry glebe I faint,
Or on the thirsty mountains pant;
To fertile vales, and dewy meads,
My weary wand'ring steps he leads:
Where peaceful rivers, soft and slow,
Amid the verdant landscape flow.
3. Tho' in the paths of death I tread,
With gloomy horrors overspread,
My steadfast heart shall fear no ill;
For thou, O Lord, art with me still:
Thy friendly crook shall give me aid,
And guide me through the dreadful shade.
4. Tho' in a bare and rugged way,
Through devious lonely wilds I stray,
Thy bounty shall my pains beguile;
The barren wilderness shall smile,
With sudden greens and herbage crown'd,
And streams shall murmur all around.——ADDISON.

## SECTION V.
### *The Creator's works attest his greatness.*

1. THE spacious firmament on high,
With all the blue ethereal sky,
And spangled heav'ns, a shining frame,
Their great original proclaim:
Th' unwearied sun, from day to day,
Does his Creator's pow'r display,
And publishes to ev'ry land,
The work of an Almighty hand.
2. Soon as the ev'ning shades prevail,
The moon takes up the wond'rous tale,
And, nightly, to the list'ning earth,
Repeats the story of her birth;
Whilst all the stars that round her burn,
And all the planets in their turn,
Confirm the tidings as they roll,
And spread the truth from pole to pole.
3. What though, in solemn silence, all
Move round the dark terrestrial ball!
What tho' nor real voice nor sound,
Amid their radiant orbs be found!

In reason's ear they all rejoice,
And utter forth a glorious voice,
For ever singing as they shine,
"The hand that made us is Divine."——ADDISON.

## SECTION VI.
### *An address to the Deity.*

1. O THOU! whose balance does the mountains weigh;
Whose will the wild tumultuous seas obey;
Whose breath can turn those wat'ry worlds to flame,
That flame to tempest, and that tempest tame;
Earth's meanest son, all trembling, prostrate falls,
And on the boundless of thy goodness calls.
2. O! give the winds all past offence to sweep,
To scatter wide, or bury in the deep.
Thy pow'r, my weakness, may I ever see,
And wholly dedicate my soul to thee.
Reign o'er my will; my passions ebb and flow
At thy command, nor human motive know!
If anger boil, let anger be my praise,
And sin the graceful indignation raise.
My love be warm to succour the distress'd,
And lift the burden from the soul oppress'd.
3. O may my understanding ever read
This glorious volume which thy wisdom made!
May sea and land, and earth and heav'n, be join'd,
To bring th' eternal Author to my mind!
When oceans roar, or awful thunders roll,
May thoughts of thy dread vengeance shake my soul!
When earth's in bloom, or planets proudly shine,
Adore, my heart, the Majesty divine!
4. Grant I may ever at the morning ray,
Open with pray'r the consecrated day;
Tune thy great praise, and bid my soul arise,
And with the mounting sun ascend the skies;
As that advances, let my zeal improve,
And glow with ardour of consummate love;
Nor cease at eve, but with the setting sun
My endless worship shall be still begun.
5. And Oh! permit the gloom of solemn night,
To sacred thought may forcibly invite.
When this world's shut, and awful planets rise,
Call on our minds, and raise them to the skies;
Compose our souls with a less dazzling sight,
And show all nature in a milder light;
How ev'ry boist'rous thought in calm subsides!
How the smooth'd spirit into goodness glides!
6. Oh how divine! to tread the milky way,
To the bright palace of the Lord of Day;
His court admire, or for his favour sue,
Or leagues of friendship with his saints renew;
Pleas'd to look down and see the world asleep;
While I long vigils to its Founder keep!

Canst thou not shake the centre? Oh control,
Subdue by force, the rebel in my soul;
Thou, who canst still the raging of the flood,
Restrain the various tumults of my blood;
Teach me, with equal firmness, to sustain
Alluring pleasure, and assaulting pain.
7. O may I pant for thee in each desire!
And with strong faith foment the holy fire!
Stretch out my soul in hope, and grasp the prize,
Which in eternity's deep bosom lies!
At the great day of recompense behold,
Devoid of fear, the fatal book unfold!
Then wafted upward to the blissful seat,
From age to age my grateful song repeat;
My Light, my Life, my God, my Saviour see,
And rival angels in the praise of thee!——YOUNG.

## SECTION VII.

*The pursuit of happiness often ill-directed.*

1. THE midnight moon serenely smiles
   O'er nature's soft repose;
   No low'ring cloud obscures the sky,
   Nor ruffling tempest blows.
2. Now ev'ry passion sinks to rest,
   The throbbing heart lies still;
   And varying schemes of life no more
   Distract the lab'ring will.
3. In silence hush'd to reason's voice,
   Attends each mental pow'r:
   Come, dear Emilia, and enjoy
   Reflection's fav'rite hour.
4. Come; while the peaceful scene invites,
   Let's search this ample round;
   Where shall the lovely fleeting form
   Of happiness be found?
5. Does it amidst the frolic mirth
   Of gay assemblies dwell;
   Or hide beneath the solemn gloom,
   That shades the hermit's cell?
6. How oft the laughing brow of joy,
   A sick'ning heart conceals!
   And, through the cloister's deep recess,
   Invading sorrow steals.
7. In vain, through beauty, fortune, wit,
   The fugitive we trace;
   It dwells not in the faithless smile,
   That brightens Clodia's face.
8. Perhaps the joy to these deny'd,
   The heart in friendship finds:
   Ah! dear delusion, gay conceit
   Of visionary minds!
9. Howe'er our varying notions rove,
   Yet all agree in one,

  To place its being in some state,
   At distance from our own.
10. O blind to each indulgent aim,
  Of power supremely wise,
  Who fancy happiness in aught
   The hand of Heav'n denies!
11. Vain is alike the joy we seek,
  And vain what we possess,
  Unless harmonious reason tunes
   The passions into peace.
12. To temper'd wishes, just desires,
  Is happiness confin'd;
  And, deaf to folly's call, attends
   The music of the mind.——CARTER.

## SECTION VIII.

*The fire-side.*

1. DEAR Chloe, while the busy crowd,
 The vain, the wealthy, and the proud,
  In folly's maze advance;
 Tho' singularity and pride
 Be call'd our choice, we'll step aside,
  Nor join the giddy dance.
2. From the gay world, we'll oft retire
 To our own family and fire,
  Where love our hours employs;
 No noisy neighbour enters here,
 No intermeddling stranger near,
  To spoil our heart-felt joys.
3. If solid happiness we prize,
 Within our breast this jewel lies;
  And they are fools who roam:
 The world has nothing to bestow;
 From our own selves our joys must flow,
  And that dear hut, our home.
4. Of rest was Noah's dove bereft,
 When with impatient wing she left
  That safe retreat, the ark;
 Giving her vain excursion o'er,
 The disappointed bird once more
  Explor'd the sacred bark.
5. Tho' fools spurn Hymen's gentle pow'rs,
 We, who improve his golden hours,
  By sweet experience know,
 That marriage rightly understood,
 Gives to the tender and the good
  A paradise below.
6. Our babes shall richest comfort bring;
 If tutor'd right, they'll prove a spring
  Whence pleasures ever rise:
 We'll form their minds, with studious care,
 To all that's manly, good, and fair,
  And train them for the skies.

7. While they our wisest hours engage,
They'll joy our youth, support our age,
   And crown our hoary hairs:
They'll grow in virtue ev'ry day,
And thus our fondest loves repay,
   And recompense our cares.
8. No borrow'd joys! they're all our own,
While to the world we live unknown,
   Or by the world forgot:
Monarchs! we envy not your state;
We look with pity on the great,
   And bless our humbler lot.
9. Our portion is not large, indeed!
But then how little do we need!
   For nature's calls are few:
In this the art of living lies,
To want no more than may suffice,
   And make that little do.
10. We'll therefore relish, with content,
Whate'er kind Providence has sent,
   Nor aim beyond our pow'r;
For if our stock be very small,
'Tis prudence to enjoy it all,
   Nor lose the present hour.
11. To be resign'd, when ills betide,
Patient when favours are denied,
   And pleas'd with favours giv'n:
Dear Chloe, this is wisdom's part;
This is that incense of the heart,
   Whose fragrance smells to heav'n.
12. We'll ask no long protracted treat,
Since winter-life is seldom sweet;
   But when our feast is o'er,
Grateful from table we'll arise,
Nor grudge our sons, with envious eyes,
   The relics of our store.
13. Thus, hand in hand, thro' life we'll go
Its checker'd paths of joy and wo,
   With cautious steps, we'll tread;
Quit its vain scenes without a tear,
Without a trouble or a fear,
   And mingle with the dead.
14. While conscience, like a faithful friend,
Shall thro' the gloomy vale attend,
   And cheer our dying breath;
Shall, when all other comforts cease,
Like a kind angel whisper peace,
   And smooth the bed of death.——COTTON.

## SECTION IX.

*Providence vindicated in the present state of man.*

1. HEAV'N from all creatures hides the book of fate,
All but the page prescrib'd, their present state;

From brutes what men, from men what spirits know;
Or who could suffer being here below?
The lamb thy riot dooms to bleed to-day,
Had he thy reason, would he skip and play?
Pleas'd to the last, he crops the flow'ry food,
And licks the hand just rais'd to shed his blood.
2. Oh blindness to the future! kindly giv'n,
That each may fill the circle mark'd by Heav'n;
Who sees with equal eye, as God of all,
A hero perish, or a sparrow fall;
Atoms or systems into ruin hurl'd,
And now a bubble burst, and now a world.
3. Hope humbly then; with trembling pinions soar;
Wait the great teacher Death; and God adore.
What future bliss he gives not thee to know,
But gives that hope to be thy blessing now.
Hope springs eternal in the human breast:
Man never is, but always TO BE blest.
The soul, uneasy, and confin'd from home,
Rests and expatiates in a life to come.
4. Lo, the poor Indian! whose untutor'd mind
Sees God in clouds, or hears him in the wind;
His soul proud science never taught to stray
Far as the Solar Walk or Milky Way;
Yet simple nature to his hope has giv'n,
Behind the cloud-topt hill, a humbler heav'n;
Some safer world in depth of woods embrac'd,
Some happier island in the wat'ry waste;
Where slaves once more their native land behold,
No fiends torment, no Christians thirst for gold.
5. To BE, contents his natural desire;
He asks no angel's wing, no seraph's fire:
But thinks, admitted to that equal sky,
His faithful dog shall bear him company.
Go, wiser thou! and in thy scale of sense,
Weigh thy opinion against Providence;
Call imperfection what thou fanciest such;
Say here he gives too little, there too much.—
6. In pride, in reas'ning pride, our error lies;
All quit their sphere, and rush into the skies.
Pride still is aiming at the blest abodes;
Men would be angels, angels would be gods.
Aspiring to be gods, if angels fell,
Aspiring to be angels, men rebel:
And who but wishes to invert the laws
Of ORDER, sins against th' ETERNAL CAUSE.—POPE.

## SECTION X.
*Selfishness reproved.*

1. HAS God, thou fool! work'd solely for thy good,
Thy joy, thy pastime, thy attire, thy food?
Who for thy table feeds the wanton fawn,
For him as kindly spreads the flow'ry lawn.
Is it for thee the lark ascends and sings?
Joy tunes his voice, joy elevates his wings.

Is it for thee the linnet pours his throat?
Loves of his own, and raptures swell the note.
2. The bounding steed you pompously bestride,
Shares with his lord the pleasure and the pride.
Is thine alone the seed that strews the plain?
The birds of heav'n shall vindicate their grain.
Thine the full harvest of the golden year?
Part pays, and justly, the deserving steer.
The hog, that ploughs not, nor obeys thy call,
Lives on the labours of this lord of all.
3. Know, nature's children all divide her care;
The fur that warms a monarch, warm'd a bear.
While man exclaims, "See all things for my use."
"See man for mine!" replies a pamper'd goose.
And just as short of reason he must fall,
Who thinks all made for one, not one for all.
4. Grant that the pow'rful still the weak control;
Be man the wit and tyrant of the whole:
Nature that tyrant checks; he only knows,
And helps another creature's wants and woes.
Say, will the falcon, stooping from above,
Smit with her varying plumage, spare the dove?
Admires the jay, the insect's gilded wings?
Or hears the hawk when Philomela sings?
5. Man cares for all: to birds he gives his woods,
To beasts his pastures, and to fish his floods;
For some his int'rest prompts him to provide,
For more his pleasures, yet for more his pride.
All fed on one vain patron, and enjoy
Th' extensive blessing of his luxury.
6. That very life his learned hunger craves,
He saves from famine, from the savage saves:
Nay, feasts the animal he dooms his feast;
And, till he ends the being, makes it blest:
Which sees no more the stroke, nor feels the pain,
Than favour'd man by touch ethereal slain.
The creature had his feast of life before;
Thou too must perish, when thy feast is o'er!—POPE.

## SECTION XI.
*Human frailty.*

1. WEAK and irresolute is man;
   The purpose of to-day,
Woven with pains into his plan,
   To-morrow rends away.
2. The bow well bent, and smart the spring,
   Vice seems already slain;
But passion rudely snaps the string,
   And it revives again.
3. Some foe to his upright intent,
   Finds out his weaker part;
Virtue engages his assent,
   But pleasure wins his heart.
4. 'Tis here the folly of the wise,
   Through all his art we view;

And while his tongue the charge denies,
  His conscience owns it true.
5. Bound on a voyage of awful length,
  And dangers little known,
  A stranger to superior strength,
  Man vainly trusts his own.
6. But oars alone can ne'er prevail
  To reach the distant coast;
  The breath of heav'n must swell the sail,
  Or all the toil is lost.

## SECTION XII.
### Ode to peace.

1. COME, peace of mind, delightful guest!
  Return, and make thy downy nest
  Once more in this sad heart:
  Nor riches I, nor pow'r pursue,
  Nor hold forbidden joys in view;
  We therefore need not part.
2. Where wilt thou dwell, if not with me,
  From av'rice and ambition free,
  And pleasure's fatal wiles;
  For whom, alas! dost thou prepare
  The sweets that I was wont to share,
  The banquet of thy smiles?
3. The great, the gay, shall they partake
  The heav'n that thou alone canst make;
  And wilt thou quit the stream,
  That murmurs through the dewy mead,
  The grove and the sequester'd shade,
  To be a guest with them?
4. For thee I panted, thee I priz'd,
  For thee I gladly sacrific'd
  Whate'er I lov'd before;
  And shall I see thee start away,
  And helpless, hopeless, hear thee say—
  Farewell, we meet no more?——COWPER.

## SECTION XIII.
### Ode to adversity.

1. DAUGHTER of Heav'n, relentless power,
  Thou tamer of the human breast,
  Whose iron scourge, and tort'ring hour,
  The bad affright, afflict the best!
  Bound in thy adamantine chain,
  The proud are taught to taste of pain,
  And purple tyrants vainly groan
With pangs unfelt before, unpitied and alone.
2. When first thy sire to send on earth
  Virtue, his darling child, design'd,
  To thee he gave the heav'nly birth,
  And bade to form her infant mind.
  Stern rugged nurse! thy rigid lore
  With patience many a year she bore.
  What sorrow was, thou bad'st her know;
And from her own she learn'd to melt at others' wo.

3. Scar'd at thy frown terrific, fly
   Self-pleasing folly's idle brood,
   Wild laughter, noise, and thoughtless joy,
   And leave us leisure to be good.
   Light they disperse; and with them go
   The summer-friend, the flatt'ring foe.
By vain prosperity receiv'd,
To her they vow their truth, and are again believ'd.
4. Wisdom, in sable garb array'd,
   Immers'd in rapt'rous thought profound,
   And melancholy, silent maid,
   With leaden eye that loves the ground,
   Still on thy solemn steps attend;
   Warm charity, the gen'ral friend,
   With justice to herself severe,
And pity, dropping soft the sadly pleasing tear.
5. Oh, gently, on thy suppliant's head,
   Dread power, lay thy chast'ning hand!
   Not in thy gorgon terrors clad,
   Nor circled with the vengeful band,
   (As by the impious thou art seen,)
   With thund'ring voice, and threat'ning mien,
   With screaming horror's fun'ral cry,
Despair, and fell disease, and ghastly poverty.
6. Thy form benign, propitious, wear,
   Thy milder influence impart;
   Thy philosophic train be there,
   To soften, not to wound my heart.
   The gen'rous spark extinct revive;
   Teach me to love, and to forgive;
   Exact my own defects to scan;
What others are to feel; and know myself a man.—GRAY.

## SECTION XIV.

*The creation required to praise its Author.*

1. BEGIN, my soul, th' exalted lay!
   Let each enraptur'd thought obey,
      And praise th' Almighty's name:
   Lo! heaven and earth, and seas and skies,
   In one melodious concert rise,
      To swell th' inspiring theme.
2. Ye fields of light, celestial plains,
   Where gay transporting beauty reigns,
      Ye scenes divinely fair!
   Your Maker's wond'rous pow'r proclaim,
   Tell how he form'd your shining frame,
      And breath'd the fluid air.
3. Ye angels, catch the thrilling sound!
   While all th' adoring thrones around,
      His boundless mercy sing:
   Let ev'ry list'ning saint above
   Wake all the tuneful soul of love,
      And touch the sweetest string.

4. Join, ye loud spheres, the vocal choir;
   Thou dazzling orb of liquid fire,
      The mighty chorus aid:
   Soon as gray ev'ning gilds the plain,
   Thou, moon, protract the melting strain,
      And praise him in the shade.
5. Thou heav'n of heav'ns, his vast abode;
   Ye clouds, proclaim your forming God,
      Who call'd yon worlds from night:
   "Ye shades dispel!"—th' Eternal said;
   At once th' involving darkness fled,
      And nature sprung to light.
6. Whate'er a blooming world contains,
   That wings the air, that skims the plains,
      United praise bestow:
   Ye dragons, sound his awful name
   To heav'n aloud; and roar acclaim,
      Ye swelling deeps below.
7. Let ev'ry element rejoice;
   Ye thunders burst with awful voice,
      To HIM who bids you roll:
   His praise in softer notes declare,
   Each whispering breeze of yielding air,
      And breathe it to the soul.
8. To him, ye graceful cedars, bow;
   Ye tow'ring mountains, bending low,
      Your great Creator own;
   Tell, when affrighted nature shook,
   How Sinai kindled at his look,
      And trembled at his frown.
9. Ye flocks that haunt the humble vale,
   Ye insects flutt'ring on the gale,
      In mutual concourse rise;
   Crop the gay rose's vermeil bloom,
   And waft its spoils, a sweet perfume,
      In incense to the skies.
10. Wake all ye mounting tribes, and sing;
    Ye plumy warblers of the spring,
       Harmonious anthems raise
    To HIM who shap'd your finer mould,
    Who tipp'd your glitt'ring wings with gold,
       And tun'd your voice to praise.
11. Let man, by nobler passions sway'd,
    The feeling heart, the judging head,
       In heav'nly praise employ;
    Spread his tremendous name around,
    Till heav'n's broad arch rings back the sound,
       The gen'ral burst of joy.
12. Ye whom the charms of grandeur please,
    Nurs'd on the downy lap of ease,
       Fall prostrate at his throne:
    Ye princes, rulers, all adore;
    Praise him, ye kings, who makes your pow'r
       An image of his own.

13. Ye fair, by nature form'd to move,
O praise th' eternal SOURCE OF LOVE,
With youth's enliv'ning fire:
Let age take up the tuneful lay,
Sigh his bless'd name—then soar away,
And ask an angel's lyre.———OGILVIE.

## SECTION XV.
*The universal prayer.*

1. FATHER OF ALL! in ev'ry age,
In ev'ry clime, ador'd,
By saint, by savage, and by sage,
Jehovah, Jove, or Lord!
2. Thou GREAT FIRST CAUSE, least understood,
Who all my sense confin'd
To know but this, that Thou art good,
And that myself am blind;
3. Yet gave me, in this dark estate,
To see the good from ill;
And binding nature fast in fate,
Left free the human will.
4. What conscience dictates to be done,
Or warns me not to do,
This teach me more than hell to shun,
That more than heav'n pursue.
5. What blessings thy free bounty gives,
Let me not cast away;
For God is paid, when man receives;
'T' enjoy is to obey.
6. Yet not to earth's contracted span
Thy goodness let me bound,
Or think thee Lord alone of man,
When thousand worlds are round.
7. Let not this weak, unknowing hand
Presume thy bolts to throw;
And deal damnation round the land,
On each I judge thy foe.
8. If I am right, thy grace impart,
Still in the right to stay;
If I am wrong, O teach my heart
To find that better way!
9. Save me alike from foolish pride,
Or impious discontent,
At aught thy wisdom has denied,
Or aught thy goodness lent.
10. Teach me to feel another's wo;
To hide the fault I see;
That mercy I to others show,
That mercy show to me.
11. Mean tho' I am, not wholly so,
Since quicken'd by thy breath:
O lead me wheresoe'er I go,
Thro' this day's life or death!

R

12. This day, be bread and peace my lot:
　　All else beneath the sun,
　　Thou know'st if best bestow'd or not,
　　And let thy will be done.
13. To thee, whose temple is all space,
　　Whose altar, earth, sea, skies!
　　One chorus let all beings raise!
　　All nature's incense rise.——POPE.

## SECTION XVI.
### Conscience.

1. O TREACH'ROUS conscience! while she seems to sleep
On rose and myrtle, lull'd with syren song;
While she seems, nodding o'er her charge, to drop
On headlong appetite the slacken'd rein,
And give us up to license, unrecall'd,
Unmark'd;—see, from behind her secret stand,
The sly informer minutes ev'ry fault,
And her dread diary with horror fills.

2. Not the gross act alone employs her pen;
She reconnoitres fancy's airy band,
A watchful foe! the formidable spy,
List'ning, o'erhears the whispers of our camp;
Our dawning purposes of heart explores,
And steals our embryos of iniquity.

3. As all rapacious usurers conceal
Their doomsday-book from all-consuming heirs;
Thus, with indulgence most severe, she treats
Us spendthrifts of inestimable time;
Unnoted, notes each moment misapply'd;
In leaves more durable than leaves of brass,
Writes our whole history; which death shall read
In ev'ry pale delinquent's private ear;
And judgment publish; publish to more worlds
Than this; and endless age in groans resound.—YOUNG

## SECTION XVII.
### On an infant.

1. To the dark and silent tomb,
Soon I hasten'd from the womb:
Scarce the dawn of life began,
Ere I measur'd out my span.

2. I no smiling pleasures knew;
I no gay delights could view:
Joyless sojourner was I,
Only born to weep and die.—

3. Happy infant, early bless'd!
Rest, in peaceful slumber, rest;
Early rescu'd from the cares,
Which increase with growing years.

4. No delights are worth thy stay,
Smiling as they seem, and gay;
Short and sickly are they all,
Hardly tasted ere they pall.

5. All our gaiety is vain,
    All our laughter is but pain;
    Lasting only, and divine,
    Is an innocence like thine.

## SECTION XVIII.
### The cuckoo.

1. HAIL, beauteous stranger of the wood,
    Attendant on the spring!
   Now heav'n repairs thy rural seat,
    And woods thy welcome sing.
2. Soon as the daisy decks the green,
    Thy certain voice we hear:
   Hast thou a star to guide thy path,
    Or mark the rolling year?
3. Delightful visitant! with thee
    I hail the time of flow'rs,
   When heav'n is fill'd with music sweet,
    Of birds among the bow'rs.
4. The school-boy, wand'ring in the wood,
    To pull the flow'rs so gay,
   Starts, thy curious voice to hear,
    And imitates thy lay.
5. Soon as the pea puts on the bloom,
    Thou fly'st the vocal vale,
   An annual guest, in other lands,
    Another spring to hail.
6. Sweet bird! thy bow'r is ever green,
    Thy sky is ever clear;
   Thou hast no sorrow in thy song,
    No winter in thy year!
7. O could I fly, I'd fly with thee;
    We'd make, with social wing,
   Our annual visit o'er the globe,
    Companions of the spring.——LOGAN.

## SECTION XIX.
### Day. A pastoral in three parts.
#### MORNING.

1. IN the barn the tenant cock,
    Close to Partlet perch'd on high,
   Briskly crows, (the shepherd's clock!)
    Jocund that the morning's nigh.
2. Swiftly, from the mountain's brow,
    Shadows, nurs'd by night retire;
   And the peeping sun-beam, now
    Paints with gold the village spire.
3. Philomel forsakes the thorn,
    Plaintive where she prates at night;
   And the lark to meet the morn,
    Soars beyond the shepherd's sight.
4. From the low-roof'd cottage ridge,
    See the chatt'ring swallow spring;

Darting through the one-arch'd bridge,
  Quick she dips her dappled wing.
5. Now the pine-tree's waving top
  Gently greets the morning gale;
Kidlings, now, begin to crop
  Daisies, on the dewy dale.
6. From the balmy sweets, uncloy'd,
  (Restless till her task be done,)
Now the busy bee's employ'd,
  Sipping dew before the sun.
7. Trickling through the crevic'd rock,
  Where the limpid stream distils,
Sweet refreshment waits the flock,
  When 'tis sun-drove from the hills.
8. Colin's for the promis'd corn
  (Ere the harvest hopes are ripe)
Anxious;—whilst the huntsman's horn,
  Boldly sounding, drowns his pipe.
9. Sweet—O sweet, the warbling throng,
  On the white emblossom'd spray!
Nature's universal song
  Echoes to the rising day.

### NOON.

10. FERVID on the glitt'ring flood,
  Now the noontide radiance glows:
Drooping o'er its infant bud,
  Not a dew-drop's left the rose.
11. By the brook the shepherd dines,
  From the fierce meridian heat,
Shelter'd by the branching pines,
  Pendent o'er his grassy seat.
12. Now the flock forsakes the glade,
  Where uncheck'd the sun-beams fall,
Sure to find a pleasing shade
  By the ivy'd abbey wall.
13. Echo, in her airy round,
  O'er the river, rock, and hill,
Cannot catch a single sound,
  Save the clack of yonder mill.
14. Cattle court the zephyrs bland,
  Where the streamlet wanders cool;
Or with languid silence stand
  Midway in the marshy pool.
15. But from mountain, dell, or stream,
  Not a flutt'ring zephyr springs;
Fearful lest the noontide beam
  Scorch its soft, its silken wings.
16. Not a leaf has leave to stir,
  Nature's lull'd—serene—and still!
Quiet e'en the shepherd's cur,
  Sleeping on the heath-clad hill.
17. Languid is the landscape round,
  Till the fresh descending show'r,

Grateful to the thirsty ground,
Raises ev'ry fainting flow'r.
18. Now the hill—the hedge—are green,
Now the warblers' throats in tune;
Blithsome is the verdant scene,
Brighten'd by the beams of Noon!

EVENING.

19. O'ER the heath the heifer strays
Free—(the furrow'd task is done:)
Now the village windows blaze,
Burnish'd by the setting sun.
20. Now he sets behind the hill,
Sinking from a golden sky:
Can the pencil's mimic skill
Copy the refulgent dye?
21. Trudging as the ploughmen go,
(To the smoking hamlet bound,)
Giant-like their shadows grow
Lengthen'd o'er the level ground.
22. Where the rising forest spreads
Shelter for the lordly dome!
To their high-built airy beds,
See the rooks returning home!
23. As the lark, with vary'd tune,
Carols to the ev'ning loud;
Mark the mild resplendent moon,
Breaking through a parted cloud!
24. Now the hermit owlet peeps
From the barn or twisted brake;
And the blue mist slowly creeps,
Curling on the silver lake.
25. As the trout in speckled pride,
Playful from its bosom springs;
To the banks a ruffled tide
Verges in successive rings.
26. Tripping through the silken grass,
O'er the path-divided dale,
Mark the rose-complexion'd lass,
With her well-pois'd milking pail!
27. Linnets with unnumber'd notes,
And the cuckoo bird with two,
Tuning sweet their mellow throats,
Bid the setting sun adieu.——CUNNINGHAM.

## SECTION XX.
*The order of nature.*

1. SEE, thro' this air, this ocean, and this earth,
All matter quick, and bursting into birth.
Above, how high progressive life may go!
Around, how wide! how deep extend below:
Vast chain of being! which from God began,
Nature ethereal, human; angel, man;
Beast, bird, fish, insect, what no eye can see,
No glass can reach; from infinite to thee,

From thee to nothing.—On superior pow'rs
Were we to press, inferior might on ours;
Or in the full creation leave a void,
Where, one step broken, the great scale's destroy'd:
From nature's chain whatever link you strike,
Tenth or ten thousandth, breaks the chain alike.

2. And, if each system in gradation roll,
Alike essential to th' amazing whole,
The least confusion but in one, not all
That system only, but the whole must fall.
Let earth, unbalanc'd from her orbit fly,
Planets and suns run lawless thro' the sky;
Let ruling angels from their spheres be hurl'd,
Being on being wreck'd, and world on world;
Heav'n's whole foundations to their centre nod,
And nature tremble to the throne of God.
All this dread ORDER break—for whom? for thee?
Vile worm! Oh madness! pride! impiety!

3. What if the foot, ordain'd the dust to tread,
Or hand, to toil, aspir'd to be the head?
What if the head, the eye, or ear repin'd
To serve mere engines to the ruling mind?
Just as absurd for any part to claim
To be another, in this gen'ral frame:
Just as absurd, to mourn the tasks or pains,
The great directing MIND OF ALL ordains.

4. 'All are but parts of one stupendous whole,
Whose body nature is, and God the soul:
That, chang'd thro' all, and yet in all the same,
Great in the earth, as in th' ethereal frame;
Warms in the sun, refreshes in the breeze,
Glows in the stars, and blossoms in the trees;
Lives thro' all life, extends thro' all extent,
Spreads undivided, operates unspent;
Breathes in our soul, informs our mortal part,
As full, as perfect, in a hair as heart;
As full, as perfect, in vile man that mourns,
As the rapt seraph that adores and burns:
To him no high, no low, no great, no small;
He fills, he bounds, connects, and equals all.

5. Cease then, nor ORDER imperfection name:
Our proper bliss depends on what we blame.
Know thy own point: this kind, this due degree
Of blindness, weakness, Heav'n bestows on thee.
Submit.—In this or any other sphere,
Secure to be as blest as thou canst bear:
Safe in the hand of one disposing Pow'r,
Or in the natal, or the mortal hour.
All nature is but art, unknown to thee;
All chance, direction, which thou canst not see;
All discord, harmony not understood;
All partial evil, universal good;
And, spite of Pride, in erring Reason's spite,
One truth is clear,—WHATEVER IS, IS RIGHT.——POPE.

## SECTION XXI.

*Confidence in Divine protection.*

1. How are thy servants blest, O Lord!
    How sure is their defence!
  Eternal wisdom is their guide,
    Their help Omnipotence.
2. In foreign realms, and lands remote,
    Supported by thy care,
  Through burning climes I pass'd unhurt,
    And breath'd in tainted air.
3. Thy mercy sweeten'd ev'ry soil,
    Made ev'ry region please;
  The hoary Alpine hills it warm'd,
    And smooth'd the Tyrrhene seas.
4. Think, O my soul, devoutly think,
    How with affrighted eyes,
  Thou saw'st the wide extended deep
    In all its horrors rise!
5. Confusion dwelt in ev'ry face,
    And fear in ev'ry heart,
  When waves on waves, and gulfs in gulfs,
    O'ercame the pilot's art.
6. Yet then, from all my griefs, O Lord,
    Thy mercy set me free;
  While in the confidence of pray'r
    My soul took hold on thee.
7. For tho' in dreadful whirls we hung
    High on the broken wave,
  I knew thou wert not slow to hear,
    Nor impotent to save.
8. The storm was laid, the winds retir'd,
    Obedient to thy will;
  The sea that roar'd at thy command,
    At thy command was still.
9. In midst of dangers, fears, and deaths,
    Thy goodness I'll adore;
  And praise thee for thy mercies past,
    And humbly hope for more.
10. My life, if thou preserve my life,
    Thy sacrifice shall be;
  And death, if death must be my doom,
    Shall join my soul to thee.

## SECTION XXII.

*Hymn on a review of the seasons.*

1. THESE, as they change, Almighty Father! these
  Are but the varied God. The rolling year
  Is full of thee. Forth in the pleasing spring
  Thy beauty walks, Thy tenderness and love.
  Wide flush the fields; the soft'ning air is balm;
  Echo the mountains round; the forest smiles,
  And ev'ry sense, and ev'ry heart is joy.

2. Then comes Thy glory in the summer months,
With light and heat refulgent. Then Thy sun
Shoots full perfection thro' the swelling year;
And oft Thy voice in dreadful thunder speaks;
And oft at dawn, deep noon, or falling eve,
By brooks and groves, in hollow-whisp'ring gales.
3. Thy bounty shines in autumn unconfin'd,
And spreads a common feast for all that lives.
In winter, awful Thou! with clouds and storms
Around Thee thrown, tempest o'er tempest roll'd,
Majestic darkness! On the whirlwind's wing,
Riding sublime, Thou bidst the world adore;
And humblest nature with Thy northern blast.
4. Mysterious round! what skill, what force divine,
Deep felt, in these appear! a simple train,
Yet so delightful mix'd, with such kind art,
Such beauty and beneficence combin'd;
Shade, unperceiv'd, so soft'ning into shade,
And all so forming an harmonious whole,
That as they still succeed, they ravish still.
5. But wand'ring oft, with brute unconscious gaze,
Man marks not Thee, marks not the mighty hand,
That, ever busy, wheels the silent spheres;
Works in the secret deep; shoots, steaming, thence
The fair profusion that o'erspreads the spring;
Flings from the sun direct the flaming day;
Feeds ev'ry creature; hurls the tempest forth;
And, as on earth this grateful change revolves,
With transport touches all the springs of life.
6. Nature, attend! join ev'ry living soul,
Beneath the spacious temple of the sky:
In adoration join! and, ardent, raise
One general song!————
Ye, chief, for whom the whole creation smiles,
At once the head, the heart, and tongue of all,
Crown the great hymn!
7. For me, when I forget the darling theme,
Whether the blossom blows, the summer ray
Russets the plain; inspiring autumn gleams;
Or winter rises in the black'ning east;
Be my tongue mute, may fancy paint no more,
And, dead to joy, forget my heart to beat!
8. Should fate command me to the farthest verge
Of the green earth, to distant barb'rous climes,
Rivers unknown to song; where first the sun
Gilds Indian mountains, or his setting beam
Flames on th' Atlantic isles; 'tis nought to me;
Since God is ever present, ever felt,
In the void waste as in the city full;
And where HE vital breathes there must be joy.
9. When e'en at last the solemn hour shall come,
And wing my mystic flight to future worlds,
I cheerful will obey; there, with new pow'rs,
Will rising wonders sing: I cannot go

Where UNIVERSAL LOVE not smiles around,
Sustaining all yon orbs, and all their suns;
From seeming evil still educing good,
And better thence again, and better still,
In infinite progression. But I lose
Myself in HIM, in light ineffable!
Come then, expressive silence, muse his praise.

THOMSON.

## SECTION XXIII.

### On solitude.

1. O SOLITUDE, romantic maid!
Whether by nodding towers you tread,
Or haunt the desert's trackless gloom,
Or hover o'er the yawning tomb,
Or climb the Andes' clifted side,
Or by the Nile's coy source abide,
Or, starting from your half-year's sleep,
From Hecla view the thawing deep,
Or, at the purple dawn of day,
Tadmor's marble wastes survey;
You, recluse, again I woo,
And again your steps pursue.

2. Plum'd conceit himself surveying,
Folly with her shadow playing,
Purse-proud elbowing insolence,
Bloated empiric, puff'd pretence,
Noise that through a trumpet speaks,
Laughter in loud peals that breaks,
Intrusion, with a fopling's face,
(Ignorant of time and place,)
Sparks of fire dissension blowing,
Ductile, court-bred flattery bowing,
Restraint's stiff neck, grimace's leer,
Squint-ey'd censure's artful sneer,
Ambition's buskins, steep'd in blood,
Fly thy presence, Solitude!

3. Sage reflection, bent with years,
Conscious virtue, void of fears,
Muffled silence, wood-nymph shy,
Meditation's piercing eye,
Halcyon peace on moss reclin'd,
Retrospect that scans the mind,
Rapt earth-gazing revery,
Blushing artless modesty,
Health that snuffs the morning air,
Full-ey'd truth with bosom bare,
Inspiration, nature's child,
Seek the solitary wild.

4. When all nature's hush'd asleep,
Nor love, nor guilt, their vigils keep,
Soft you leave your cavern'd den,
And wander o'er the works of men;

But when Phosphor brings the dawn,
By her dappled coursers drawn,
Again you to the wild retreat,
And the early huntsman meet,
Where, as you pensive pass along,
You catch the distant shepherd's song;
Or brush from herbs the pearly dew,
Or the rising primrose view,
Devotion lends her heaven-plum'd wings,
You mount, and nature with you sings.
5. But when mid-day fervours glow,
To upland airy shades you go,
Where never sun-burnt woodman came,
Nor sportsman chas'd the timid game:
And there, beneath an oak reclin'd,
With drowsy waterfalls behind,
You sink to rest.
Till the tuneful bird of night,
From the neighb'ring poplar's height,
Wake you with her solemn strain,
And teach pleas'd echo to complain.
6. With you roses brighter bloom,
Sweeter every sweet perfume;
Purer every fountain flows,
Stronger every wilding grows.
Let those toil for gold who please;
Or, for fame renounce their ease.
What is fame? An empty bubble;
Gold? a shining, constant trouble.
Let them for their country bleed!
What was Sidney's, Raleigh's meed?
Man's not worth a moment's pain;
Base, ungrateful, fickle, vain.
7. Then let me, sequester'd fair,
To your sybil grot repair;
On yon hanging cliff it stands,
Scoop'd by nature's plastic hands,
Bosom'd in the gloomy shade
Of cypress not with age decay'd;
Where the owl still hooting sits,
Where the bat incessant flits;
There in loftier strains I'll sing
Whence the changing seasons spring;
Tell how storms deform the skies,
Whence the waves subside and rise,
Trace the comet's blazing tail,
Weigh the planets in a scale;
Bend, great God, before thy shrine;
The bourneless macrocosm's thine.
8. Since in each scheme of life I've fail'd,
And disappointment seems entail'd;
Since all on earth I valued most,
My guide, my stay, my friend is lost;

O Solitude, now give me rest,
And hush the tempest in my breast.
O gently deign to guide my feet
To your hermit-trodden seat;
Where I may live at last my own,
Where I at last may die unknown.
I spoke: she turn'd her magic ray;
And thus she said, or seem'd to say;

9. Youth, you're mistaken, if you think to find
In shades, a med'cine for a troubled mind:
Wan grief will haunt you wheresoe'er you go,
Sigh in the breeze, and in the streamlet flow.
There, pale inaction pines his life away;
And satiate mourns the quick return of day:
There, naked frenzy laughing wild with pain,
Or bares the blade, or plunges in the main:
There, superstition broods o'er all her fears,
And yells of demons in the zephyr hears.
But if a hermit you're resolv'd to dwell,
And bid to social life a last farewell;
'Tis impious.————

10. God never made an independent man;
'Twould jar the concord of his general plan.
See every part of that stupendous whole,
"Whose body nature is, and God the soul;"
To one great end the general good conspire,
From matter, brute, to man, to seraph, fire.
Should man through nature solitary roam,
His will his sovereign, every where his home,
What force would guard him from the lion's jaw?
What swiftness wing him from the panther's paw?
Or should fate lead him to some safer shore,
Where panthers never prowl, nor lions roar,
Where liberal nature all her charms bestows,
Suns shine, birds sing, flowers bloom, and water flows,
Fool, dost thou think he'd revel on the store,
Absolve the care of Heav'n, nor ask for more?
Tho' waters flow'd, flow'rs bloom'd, and Phœbus shone,
He'd sigh, he'd murmur, that he was alone.
For know, the Maker on the human breast
A sense of kindred, country, man, impress'd.

1. Though nature's works the ruling mind declare,
And well deserve inquiry's serious care,
The God (whate'er misanthropy may say,)
Shines, beams in man with most unclouded ray.
What boots it thee to fly from pole to pole?
Hang o'er the sun, and with the planets roll?
What boots through space's furthest bourns to roam?
If thou, O man, a stranger art at home.
Then know thyself, the human mind survey;
The use, the pleasure, will the toil repay.

2. Nor study only, practise what you know;
Your life, your knowledge, to mankind you owe.

With Plato's olive wreath the bays entwine;
Those who in study, should in practice shine.
Say, does the learned lord of Hagley's shade,
Charm man so much by mossy fountains laid,
As when arous'd he stems corruption's course,
And shakes the senate with a Tully's force?
When freedom gasp'd beneath a Cesar's feet,
Then public virtue might to shades retreat:
But where she breathes, the least may useful be,
And freedom, Britain, still belongs to thee.

13. Though man's ungrateful, or though fortune frown;
Is the reward of worth a song, or crown?
Nor yet unrecompens'd are virtue's pains;
Good Allen lives, and bounteous Brunswick reigns.
On each condition disappointments wait,
Enter the hut, and force the guarded gate.
Nor dare repine though early friendship bleed;
From love, the world, and all its cares, he's freed.
But know, adversity's the child of God:
Whom Heaven approves of most, must feel her rod.
When smooth old Ocean, and each storm's asleep,
Then ignorance may plough the watery deep:
But when the demons of the tempest rave,
Skill must conduct the vessel through the wave.

14. Sidney, what good man envies not thy blow?
Who would not wish Anytus* for a foe?
Intrepid virtue triumphs over fate:
The good can never be unfortunate;
And be this maxim graven in thy mind;
The height of virtue is, to serve mankind.
But when old age has silver'd o'er thy head,
When memory fails, and all thy vigour's fled,
Then mayst thou seek the stillness of retreat,
Then hear aloof the human tempest beat;
Then will I greet thee to my woodland cave,
Allay the pangs of age, and smooth thy grave.

GRAINGER.

* One of the accusers of Socrates.

FINIS.

Deacidified using the Bookkeeper process.
Neutralizing agent: Magnesium Oxide
Treatment Date: Oct. 2006

**PreservationTechnologies**
A WORLD LEADER IN PAPER PRESERVATION
111 Thomson Park Drive
Cranberry Township, PA 16066
(724) 779-2111

CPSIA information can be obtained
at www.ICGtesting.com
Printed in the USA
LVHW081646250223
740420LV00010B/810